THE OBLIGATED SELF

NEW JEWISH PHILOSOPHY AND THOUGHT
Zachary J. Braiterman

THE OBLIGATED SELF

Maternal Subjectivity and Jewish Thought

Mara H. Benjamin

INDIANA UNIVERSITY PRESS

This book is a publication of

Indiana University Press
Office of Scholarly Publishing
Herman B Wells Library 350
1320 East 10th Street
Bloomington, Indiana 47405 USA

iupress.indiana.edu

© 2018 by Mara H. Benjamin

The paper used in this publication meets
the minimum requirements of the
American National Standard for
Information Sciences—Permanence of
Paper for Printed Library Materials,
ANSI Z39.48-1992.

Manufactured in the United States of
America

Cataloging information is available from
the Library of Congress.

ISBN 978-0-253-03433-5 (cloth)

ISBN 978-0-253-03432-8 (paperback)

ISBN 978-0-253-03434-2 (ebook)

1 2 3 4 5 23 22 21 20 19 18

To my mother, Judith Benjamin,
And to the memory of my mother-in-law, Celia Kabakow ז״ל

*To Miryam Kabakov, with whom I share the gift of motherhood and a
life together,*

*And to my daughters
with boundless love*

Contents

Acknowledgments

AMONG THE MANY pleasures of finishing a book is the opportunity to acknowledge publicly the many individuals whose support is otherwise only privately visible, and, in addition, to acknowledge the institutions that sustain intellectual work. I am delighted to be able to thank my friends, colleagues, and family. Their presence in my life enabled me to write this book.

I undertook this project while I was a member of the Religion Department at St. Olaf College. During my years there, I was privileged to work alongside colleagues who brought me into a discourse that I initially met with trepidation and who helped me claim theology as a Jewish intellectual pursuit. Anantanand Rambachan, Jamie Schillinger, and David Booth in particular helped me find a home in the department. Teaching and talking with Patricia (Trish) Beckman nurtured me on a daily basis. I am grateful to have had caring and insightful students who made teaching a pleasure and with whom I shared pieces of this book.

At a moment when the humanities and intellectual life in general have come under assault in the highest echelons of American government, I am especially mindful of the critical role of public and private institutions in providing the material support that makes inquiry possible. The Hadassah-Brandeis Institute provided me with support in the early stages of this project in the form of two research awards and the Rosalie Katchen Travel Grant. The National Endowment for the Humanities enabled me to pursue work on this book with a summer stipend and a year-long fellowship. I am most grateful for the privilege of a sabbatical funded in part by St. Olaf College and the Virginia Dekker Groot Professional Development Grant. The Cashmere Subvention Grant, awarded by the Association for Jewish Studies Women's Caucus, helped defray some of the costs of publishing. During a sabbatical in 2014–15, the Jewish Theological Seminary of America provided a lovely private office, a world-class Judaica library, and many opportunities for intellectual companionship.

Colleagues at many institutions offered suggestions, ideas, their own work in progress, corrections, and new directions for this project. I am thankful for the opportunity to present my work to the Jewish Feminist Reading Group in New York in 2014, the Feminist Commentary on the Talmud working group during its summer gathering at the University of Pennsylvania in 2015, and to colleagues and students at Stanford University, the Graduate Theological Union, Vanderbilt University, and the University of Minnesota. For engaging in conversation about the project, reading drafts, and more, I thank Liz Shanks Alexander, Beth Berkowitz, Zachary Braiterman, Amy Eilberg, Arnie Eisen, Steven Fraade, Judith Hauptman, Michael Gottsegen, Jane Kanarek, Sarit Kattan Gribetz, Elie Kaunfer, Martin Kavka, Ken Koltun-Fromm, Marjorie Lehman, Jon Levenson, Jon Levisohn, Catherine Madsen, Bonnie Miller-McLemore, Leslie Morris, Louis Newman, Hannah Polin-Galay, Naomi Seidman, Claire Sufrin, Ethan Tucker, John Penniman, Jordan Rosenblum, Jason Rubenstein, Jonathan Schofer, Cristina Traina, and Wendy Zierler. Thanks as well to Ilene Green.

In addition to these friends and colleagues, I offer special gratitude to a handful of exceptional friends and conversation partners who gave me the encouragement I needed to undertake this experimental work and sustenance as I pursued it. Dianne Cohler-Esses first suggested to me the germ-cell of this book: the idea that the constant, unceasing demands of child-rearing comprise a set of obligations that are ontologically primary to the *mitzvot,* and even the model for them; I was privileged to continue a fruitful dialogue with her in our midrash hevruta. Through many evenings out and whispered discussions during shul, Riv-Ellen Prell encouraged me to take the leap into constructive work, cheered me on, and offered thoughtful critiques throughout the undertaking. Deena Aranoff and Charlotte Fonrobert were reliable sources of intellectual rigor and good humor over the years during which I worked on this book. Judith Plaskow became a treasured reader and friend and was both guide and delightful company in the underpopulated territory of Jewish feminist theology. My time spent working through key halakhic sources for this book with my devoted, patient teacher, Devorah Zlochower, was one of the great delights of my sabbatical. Finally, my endless outlines and notes would never have turned into finished prose without the raw talent, practical advice, and cheerful optimism of writing coach extraordinaire Gillian Steinberg.

Zachary Braiterman encouraged me to bring my manuscript to the New Jewish Philosophy and Thought series, and Dee Mortensen's enthusiasm for the project signaled the hospitable home for it that Indiana University Press has been. Paige Rasmussen, Rachel Rosolina, and Julie Davis at IUP were responsive and helpful at every stage. I would also like to thank the anonymous reviewers who read the work carefully and offered excellent advice.

This book about motherhood emerged thanks all of the people who participated in the work of raising my children and the creation of a community in which to do so. The idea of the "Third" (chap. 6) had its concrete embodiment in Maria Wright and Amal Ahmed, who fed my children literally and metaphorically. I thank also my children's many teachers at Children's Country Day School; Mendota Elementary School; Solomon Schechter Day School in Manhattan; and Heilicher Minneapolis Jewish Day School. Special thanks also to the members of the loving Minnesota "village" in which my children thrived, especially Shosh Dworsky, Jonathan and Arielle Ehrlich, Tamar Grimm, Barbie Levine, Judy Levitan, Mitch Multer, Sara Lynn Newberger, Ann Silver, and Rosanne Zaidenweber, and the Beth Jacob community as a whole.

As the following pages make clear, my family made this book possible in multiple senses. It is my great fortune to have the unconditional support of a loving family, including especially my parents, my extended family, and my in-laws: Judith and Mark Benjamin, Ken Collins, Ossie and Harry Hanauer, Ruth Lidsky ז״ל, Celia ז״ל and Bernie Kabakow, and Sara Kabakov and Greg Pitts. My wife, Miryam, and my daughters, R. and S., gave me the gift of motherhood, a family of my own, and so much else besides. Their love sustains me.

ראש חודש ניסן תשע״ח
March 2018

Introduction

T HE WEEKDAY MORNING ritual of *tefillin* practiced by religiously observant Jews stages the key narrative of the people of Israel. During prayer, small boxes containing words of scripture are wrapped with black leather straps to one arm and the crown of one's head. The daily act of quite literally placing the words of Torah on the body is understood as a fulfillment of the biblical command to study and remember words of Torah in the midst of daily life: "Bind [these words] as a sign on your hand and let them serve as a symbol between your eyes; inscribe them on the doorposts [*mezuzot*] of your house and on your gates" (Deut. 6:8). Binding the body in Torah affirms God's redemption of the Jewish people.

To be a Jew is not to be free from constraint; rather, it is regularly to experience the movement from ignoble bondage in Egypt (*'avdut*) to divine service (*'avodah*): "For unto Me the children of Israel are servants; they are My servants whom I brought forth out of the land of Egypt: I am YHVH your God" (Lev. 25:55).[1] By wrapping oneself in tefillin, the worshipper reenacts this narrative and assents to it.

The liturgical basis for placing the tefillin straps around the finger, from the prophet Hosea (2:19), attests that the yoke of divine service is borne in love: "And I will betroth thee unto Me for ever; yea, I will betroth thee unto Me in righteousness, and in justice, and in lovingkindness, and in compassion. I will betroth thee unto Me in faithfulness; and thou shalt know YHVH." Server and served are bound in love. By matching words of betrothal to the act of laying tefillin, the rabbis implicitly claim that the Torah and *mitzvot* were given as a lasting sign of divine commitment and devotion. The Jew who binds his arm responds to this gift by committing himself to a life of steadfast service.[2]

My gendered language is intentional. The commandment of tefillin was, for centuries, a commandment associated with and largely restricted to men;

the commandment to study, recite, and internalize Torah, at least since the late antique period, quintessentially symbolized an ideal for Jewish male religious practice.[3] In recent decades, some observant Jewish women, mostly in the liberal movements of Judaism, have taken on this practice, and, as a feminist, I laud the important changes that have led to greater expansion of the world of normative piety to include women. But for many centuries—and still in many segments of the Jewish community—only men's lives were structured by the privileged boundedness made manifest in tefillin.

Jewish women, like many other women throughout the centuries, have intimately known their own distinctive form of boundedness and attachment: the boundedness of living with, being responsible for, and attending to children. As with tefillin, this boundedness is marked on the body: carved on muscles taut from the weight of carrying children; etched on the face in lines of sleeplessness, worry, and delight; engraved in the visceral response to the cry and needs of one's child. Child-rearing is a commitment in which love flows between mothers and children, and is expressed in the responsibility that women take in caring for their children. But whereas the male Jewish self is told, in the imperative, to bind himself to the words of God, a living human being gives maternal selves this imperative countless times a day, inscribing them with the dynamic Torah of their child.[4] Men's subjection is aspirational and metaphysical; women's, genuine and concrete.

This book places maternal experience into constructive conversation with central themes in Jewish religious thought. In maternal experiences of boundedness, dynamic responsiveness, autonomy redirected or challenged, and contingent power, I excavate a long-overlooked quarry for religious thought. As is the case in many religious traditions, Jewish theology has tended to engage with these critical religious questions through the lens of male actors and male institutions. The concrete, urgent, loud, and usually inconvenient needs of young children—and the experiences of those who care for them—have been relegated to the margins of religious thought.

This neglect of the lived reality of child-rearing, and the profound existential and ethical questions that arise for those immersed in it, has impoverished Jewish thought. By placing maternal subjectivity at the center of inquiry, I demonstrate that child-rearing presents circumstances in which adults confront *in vivo* precisely those issues that are taken up in abstract ways in religious thought. Examined with an eye toward the theological, existential, and ethical questions that arise daily within it, maternal experience offers a resource for transforming Jewish thought.

To the extent I draw on metaphors from human experience to speak about the divine, my project is embedded in the theological discourse of modernity. From Ludwig Feuerbach to Sigmund Freud, modern theorists of religion have insisted that theology arises from human experience. God, in this tradition, has been named as merely a projection of human desires and anxieties. Freud in particular named this projection as specifically infantile: the personal God is simply the exalted image of a powerful, protective father figure.[5] Rather than seeking to evade the legacy of modernity, I hope to unearth a potentially subversive implication that runs counter to its secularizing thrust: to be a parent is to gain insight into what it means to be the God of the Hebrew Bible and the rabbinic imagination.

The dilemmas inherent in a fully imagined maternal subjectivity exist implicitly everywhere—if explicitly (almost) nowhere—in biblical texts and their rabbinic elaboration. Many, even most, of the textual sources on which I draw in this book—including biblical and rabbinic texts; narrative, legal, and liturgical sources; and modern Jewish philosophical and theological writings—do not explicitly speak about motherhood or mothers. I have found texts concerning the relationship between God and the people of Israel the richest for this project, because in it, instantly recognizable maternal quandaries surface again and again. My readings demonstrate how feminist readers may locate elements of women's experience, and thus of the human condition, in such texts, despite the patriarchal structures that shaped these sources and their reception.

In addition to ancient and late antique Jewish sources, I draw on twentieth-century Jewish religious philosophy while seeking to expand its scope. Many of the great central European Jewish thinkers of the previous century—Hermann Cohen, Franz Rosenzweig, Martin Buber, and Emmanuel Levinas—recast the anthropology of the "obligated self" they inherited from classical Judaism into relational terms. In the realm of interpersonal relationships and embodied daily life, they saw the potential to understand the nature of the divine, or at least the tools with which to investigate the human relationship to the divine. These thinkers reread obligation, seeing in it not the burden imposed by a commanding God on the Jewish people, but rather a status generated in the encounter between two subjects in everyday human relationships.

Like modern Jewish thinkers before me, I find relationships theologically productive. Interpersonal relationships serve as our primary entry point into the nature of obligation, love, and power. However, my best-known twentieth-century predecessors assumed adult male subjects, imagined relationships in highly stylized terms, and turned even "daily life" or "everydayness" into a philosophical abstraction. Life with children demands a more full-bodied reckoning with relationality. Engaging with the details of material life does not detract from but rather enhances our ability to engage the theological and ethical significance of the world we inhabit.

The themes that I explore in this book reflect intersections between common elements of daily maternal experience and distinctive facets of Jewish religious thought. But although this book uses a Jewish religious lexicon, I do not claim that Jewish ideas or modes of inquiry have a privileged role or superior interpretive power for investigating maternal experience. The project I have undertaken with regard to Jewish sources could be, and has been, undertaken through the lenses of other religious traditions.[6]

The "keyword" approach I use in this book anchors each chapter's treatment of a wide range of sources, ancient and modern, and a diverse set of approaches. The four chapters in part I each focus on a constitutive element of maternal experience that has resonance in Jewish religious discourse. Chapter 1 ("Obligation") begins by examining the powerful maternal sense of being tethered to a child or children by ties of responsibility, obligation, and affection. I argue that reflection on maternal freedom and boundedness offers a resource for rethinking the persistently fraught problems of obligation and commandment in modern Jewish thought.

Chapter 2 ("Love") considers the often overwhelming, debilitating, and transformative love of one's child in conversation with Jewish biblical and liturgical sources. I investigate biblical representations of divine affectivity, in which intimate relationships give rise to tenderness, frustration, and rage, as a corrective to common images of maternal love as pacific, selfless, and unconditional. Rabbinic and especially liturgical conceptions of love as practical devotion offer especially compelling resources for articulating a rich Jewish theological conception of maternal love.

Chapter 3 ("Power") maps the complexities of maternal power to engage and expand contemporary feminist discourse. Against the desire to expunge "power-over" from the feminist lexicon, I argue that maternal power, like divine power as depicted in Pentateuchal sources and their midrashic elaborations, cannot but involve some degree of domination. Yet maternal power and agency always necessarily contend with children's agency, and children too wield power. Just as God must contend with becoming "dependent" on the recognition of Israel, parents engaged in daily life with their children must negotiate, not merely exercise, power.

Chapter 4 ("Teaching") posits an ethic of maternal teaching that focuses on nonverbal and preverbal means of communicating knowledge, in its most expansive sense, to children. I juxtapose this ethic to the algorithm of the classical Jewish enterprise of teaching and learning, which figures the scholastic community in *contrast* to and in *tension* with the family. In this chapter, I retrieve elements from a rabbinic lexicon of teaching and learning while translating a patriarchal, elite community of discipleship into a feminist ethos of maternal teaching.

The chapters in part II examine the parent/child dyad and the other parties who intersect with the parent/child pair. Chapter 5 ("The Other") deploys the potent theological and existential concept of the "Other" to think about how one encounters one's child. In twentieth-century Jewish treatments of intersubjectivity, the Other, whether understood as God or the human subject, connotes the opaque figure to whom the self is always already obligated. But the acute questions of power, dependency, and obligation in parent/child relationships I address in the previous chapters challenge the sufficiency of this concept of the Other. I offer, instead, an approach to the child that includes both mysterious otherness and an assertion of affiliation, participation, and "sameness."

Chapter 6 ("The Third") argues for expanding the paradigm of parent and child to include intimate others—teachers, nannies, and caregiving kin—who care for children alongside the parent(s). I use key biblical and rabbinic texts to draw new constellations of caregiving and develop a theological framework within which multiplicity can be more fully recognized and affirmed.

Finally, in chapter 7 ("The Neighbor"), I expand the circle outward further to investigate the realm of ordinary social interaction for the work of child-rearing. I argue that parental love contains within it the possibility for a new lens on an ancient bedrock of social ethics: the commandment to love one's neighbor as oneself. The particularity of one's own child, in my formulation, serves the purpose of strengthening rather than undermining social ties with others.

"Parenting" is a term that masks what has been one of the most pronounced sites of gender difference in society. Men and women have been each expected, in the majority of cultures, to have *distinctive* tasks in the work of rearing their offspring. It is only recently that speakers of English have devised the single, gender-neutral term "parenting." This gerund suggests that men and women engage in a single broader task of rearing their young, and that the task itself is more significant than any differences between what mothers and fathers do (or what they are expected to do). If used without qualification, the contemporary, gender-neutral term "parent" risks whitewashing a reality that still bears a strongly gendered aspect. This reality includes the fact that women's lives still are radically affected, as men's are not, by the biological possibility of becoming pregnant through heterosexual sex; the cultural expectation of childbearing and child-rearing that shapes women's lives, whether or not they ever bear or raise children; and the fact that children, at least in their early years, are primarily cared for by women (mothers and others). Even though men increasingly serve as primary caregivers for their children, for many or perhaps most people, child-rearing remains differentiated along gendered lines, and caring for children is coded as female.

I have chosen neither wholly to subsume maternal subjectivity into a broader category of "parental experience" nor to use exclusively the term "mother" for caretaking parents of any gender.[7] I use both terms, "parent" and "mother," throughout what follows, as context demands. My hope is that the differential experience of raising and caring for children will diminish, and that parents of all genders will experience the profound reshaping of self that occurs through the course of daily life with young children.

* * *

My own experiences of motherhood have shaped my choice of topic for this project and the contours of its inquiry. At times in what follows, I bring some of these experiences onto the page throughout the chapters of this book, making visible a dimension of intellectual inquiry that is often concealed. Subjectivity, for me, acts simultaneously as a landscape to be explored and as a resource to be excavated. Even more, subjectivity is a question to be posed. The result of these multiple approaches is a mode of inquiry that gestures toward phenomenology: I investigate that which occurs or appears in the everyday experience of consciousness in the subjective, social realm, and I include, and at times begin from, my own subjective experience in the aim of unearthing knowledge that reaches beyond myself. Yet I do not claim this knowledge to be structural in consciousness or universal, as in the discipline of phenomenology. Instead, I regard my own experiences as shaped by specific social, historical, geographic, and other realities. Reflecting briefly on these experiences will, I hope, situate this project and its orientation for readers. This personal dimension of my intellectual inquiry does not primarily concern a sociological catalogue of my "identities"—though, without question, being white, North American, Ashkenazi Jewish, lesbian, educated, upper-middle-class, an academic, and so on has shaped my life horizons. Rather, I regard my social location as giving rise to a set of circumstances, longings, and experiences. Out of this recognition of my own particularity, I invite readers, whose lives and subjectivities inevitably differ from mine, to reflect on the parameters of their own maternal subjectivities.

My female partner gave birth to our older daughter, and I gave birth to our younger daughter. At the time our children were born, two women could not be recognized as a child's legal wards at birth in any state in the U.S.; the nonbiological parent had to formally adopt the child (a process called second-parent adoption) in order for her name to be listed as a recognized parent on government documents. (Some states still follow this protocol, and some states explicitly prohibit second-parent adoption for nonheterosexual couples.) In legal-bureaucratic terms, I adopted our older daughter and my partner adopted our younger daughter. Even though each of us had participated in both children's conception and gestation, we had to appear in family court to gain official recognition as a family.

A generation ago, legal recognition for two women as parents of their children was nearly unthinkable; a generation hence, my children will, I hope, be able to look back on the legal bureaucracy we navigated as an antiquated, perhaps bizarre, relic of a bygone era. But the haphazard, rapidly-changing legal world at the turn of the twenty-first century presented me with two quite different means of establishing the bonds of motherhood: court order and birthgiving, each of which I experienced.

I am grateful to have had both experiences. The two modes of becoming a parent set me on a course of thinking about the means by which adults become permanently obligated to care for specific children. With my older, nonbiological daughter, a formal ceremony marked my assumption of the rights, privileges, and responsibilities of parenthood. In this ceremony, I had to verbally assent to becoming my daughter's legal parent. With my second child, by contrast, I attained the legal status of "mother" to my daughter when I gave birth to her. There was no public, formal ceremony by which I voluntarily entered into a relationship with this child. The absence of ritual, or even any particular act of will, to accompany the beginning of my relationship with my biological child stood in marked contrast to the logistical effort, time, and money it took to establish legal recognition of relationship with my nonbiological daughter.

The difference between becoming a mother through legal-bureaucratic means and becoming a mother by virtue of giving birth raised, for me, an unexpected question: why *didn't* I have to take on the responsibility of being a mother to my biological daughter voluntarily, publicly, and of my own accord, as I had with my nonbiological daughter?

This question, as it turns out, opens up a set of questions that currently occupy attention in the study of religion generally and in Jewish thought particularly. In Jewish theological terms, the discussion might be regarded as revolving around how any individual—and how the people of Israel as a whole—enter into their unique covenant with God. In many streams of rabbinic thought, a Jew can never abrogate her status as a Jew and her obligations to God and Torah. Like parenthood, being a Jew is a status that, once established, can be dissolved only under extreme conditions (if at all). For born Jews, the covenant to which they are party precedes any single individual's life span or voluntary assent; Jews start out in some sense "always already obligated" to the covenant. Its obligations can only be transgressed, not voided. Moreover, moments of ritual significance (such as bar or bat mitzvah, in contemporary Judaism) mark a new level of responsibility for these obligations, but they do not enact a new covenant. By contrast, converts to Judaism undergo a formal process, including examination, assent, and ritual action; but once they enter into the covenant, their membership can be abrogated no more than that of the born Jew. In both cases—becoming part of the Jewish people and becoming a mother—two distinct models are available: entrance into the relationship is accomplished either biologically, without need (or even possibility) of assent, or as an act of intention, with the accompanying demonstration of will through ritual act.

In our era, the model of voluntary affirmation—what Seligman et al. have referred to as "sincerity"—has reigned as self-evidently superior to "ritual."[8] In nineteenth-century Reform Jewish communities, the assumption of the priority of sincerity led to the development of confirmation ceremonies; only a chosen identity, in other words, is a valid identity. The hegemony of "choice" finds expression even in Sara Ruddick's feminist claim that biological mothers who raise the children whom they deliver are "adoptive" in that they choose to care for, rather than abandon, the children they bear.[9] Agency, for moderns, is bound up with explicit, uncoerced choice.

But important recent developments in the study of religion have demonstrated the inadequacy of the dichotomy between agency and submission, autonomy and heteronomy. In the work of many recent scholars influenced by Michel Foucault and, more recently, Talal Asad, the notion of agency has become much more nuanced and contested. As my own experiences of motherhood over the years have demonstrated, the boundaries between "external" and "internal"— like the difference between the law of the other and the law of the self—are not so clear. Not only bearing a child, but also loving and caring for one, breaks down these formal categories. The child for whom one takes responsibility becomes part of oneself. When that happens, it is impossible to know whether the law comes from outside or from within.

* * *

Writing this book, I have oscillated between two disorienting, mutually opposing orientations toward Jewish texts. At times, I have felt that one of the most important elements of human experience, child-rearing, has been all but invisible to normative religious thought; a cavernous intellectual silence has reigned where centuries-long, voluble conversation ought to have been. But at other times, I have suspected the opposite: that the rabbis, and their later readers and reinterpreters, intuited that the primal heart of Torah and mitzvot could only be truly known through the relationships of care and obligation we experience daily. This intuition remains just below the surface, perhaps suppressed. But it lurks there nonetheless.

I have come to relate to these different, almost oppositional, intuitions dialectically. At the very core of Jewish tradition lies an ineradicable distortion—we may call it patriarchy, or elitism, or misogyny—*and* sparks of divinity that await discovery and ascent. For me, neither the critical nor the constructive approach can be relinquished. Neither has the final say. Both inclinations arise out of a deep sense of ownership toward the texts and traditions of the past: I "own" these texts, and they, in turn, have a claim on me.[10] The double stance toward Jewish religious thought each approach implies informs my thinking throughout this book.

The need for both stances is evident for a feminist encountering the rabbinic discussion of the very first mishnah in the first tractate of the Babylonian Talmud. In this famous mishnah, the time before which one must recite the evening *Shem'a*—the daily declaration in which one professes God's unity, singularity, and dominion—occurs "from the time when the *kohanim* [priests] go in to eat their *terumah* [produce consecrated for priestly consumption], until the end of the first watch—so says Rabbi Eliezer" (mBerakhot 1:1). In explaining that "three watches" demarcate the time within the night, Rabbi Eliezer veers from the remarkable to the quotidian:

> "Until the end of the first watch" ... What opinion does Rabbi Eliezer hold? ... that the night has three watches, but he wants to teach us that there are watches in heaven as well as on earth. For it has been taught: R. Eliezer says: The night has three watches, and at each watch the Holy One, blessed be He, sits and roars like a lion. For it is written: THE LORD DOES ROAR FROM ON HIGH, AND RAISE HIS VOICE FROM HIS HOLY HABITATION; ROARING HE DOTH ROAR BECAUSE OF HIS FOLD [Jer. 25:30]. And the sign of the thing is: In the first watch, the ass brays; in the second, the dogs bark; *in the third, the child sucks from the breast of his mother, and the woman talks with her husband* (bBerakhot 3a).[11]

Celestial time and divine time provide the clock on which the time of ritual obligation—the recitation of the Shema, the first obligation considered in the Mishnah—is calculated. But according to Rabbi Eliezer, ritual time is *itself* derivative. It takes on its meaning from domestic life: we humans reckon ritual time in terms of ordinary daily activity in which humans naturally engage. The scenes Rabbi Eliezer conjures, moreover, include not just any human activity, but the sounds of everyday *interpersonal* activities. A wife exchanges words with her spouse while her head still rests on the pillow. The hungry baby alerts her nursing mother to the coming of daytime. These ordinary moments, unlike the first two "watches" of the night, are defined by the audible interactions between two intimate human beings. Here, in the heart of rabbinic Judaism, the inner workings of the divine are to be known through the sounds of nursing babies. The ritual obligation of reciting the Shema, at least for Rabbi Eliezer, becomes the expression of the ontologically prior category of interpersonal attachments.[12]

This insight informs no less than the ritual obligation of tefillin. As I noted above, tefillin appear to be the rabbis' vehicle for promoting, in the adult male Jew, the consciousness of freedom-as-obligation that comes quite naturally to anyone substantially involved in the care for young dependent others. But a curious Talmudic passage helps us return to tefillin with new eyes, seeing in this ritual practice not only male privilege but also an indication that the rabbis themselves saw attachment as the *Ur*-meaning of their religious acts.[13]

The passage comments on a mishnah concerning the adornments allowable on Shabbat: "Boys may go out with knots, and royal children may go out with bells, and all people [may do likewise], but the sages spoke in present tense [i.e., of the usual practice]...." (mShabbat 6:9). The Gemara (bShabbat 66b) then aims to make sense of these "knots" or "ties": "What is meant by 'knots'? Avin bar Huna said in the name of Rav Ḥama son of Guria: A son who longs for his father: he takes a strap from his right shoe and ties it to his left [hand/arm]. Rav Naḥman bar Yitzḥak said: And your mnemonic [simanekha] is tefillin."

In rapid succession, we encounter an emotion (longing); a material object (the shoe strap); and a ritual obligation (tefillin). What is the link between them in this cryptic text?

The great medieval commentator Rashi hazards the following connection between the first two elements: "He [the boy] misses him [the father] and cannot be separated from him, and this [shoestrap] is a remedy."[14] The physical object soothes the child caught in the throes of missing his father. For Rashi, the intensity of the longing and the capacity for its remedy follow from the boy's primary attachment to his father.[15]

The act of placing a token of the parent on the child extends to adults as well. Rabbenu Ḥananel (Kairouwan, ca. 990–1050) writes, "There are some who say that when the son grows up and is mourning the father upon his death, he takes a shoestrap from his father's right shoe and ties it on his left [arm] and his heart is calmed."[16] Adults facing loss, like children grappling with a temporary separation, are consoled by reminders of the parent's love. The ritual object of tefillin builds on this primary attachment: the shoe strap, the physical reminder of the parent's love, is wrapped around the child's left hand. This combination of material and placement, not surprisingly, suggests to the rabbis the practice of wrapping leather on the arm and hand: "Rav Naḥman bar Yitzḥak said: And your mnemonic is tefillin."

Tefillin, in this case, do not serve as an emblem of male privilege but as tokens of attachment. They are the ultimate theological "transitional objects," by which individuals recall the sustenance of attachment and cope with the pain of loss. The "knots" [qesharim] of the mishnah, which recall the Shema's imperative ("you shall attach [u-qeshartem] them"), are knots of relationality; wrapping tefillin around one's arm becomes an act that signifies the vulnerability of longing and the reassurance of ongoing presence that attachment provides. God, too, becomes the primary caregiver for whom we long.[17] The ritual of tefillin, in this reading, simultaneously signifies and attempts to negotiate the breach.

Adults who care for young children bind themselves daily with ties of obligation and love, a template for the abstract theological and social attachments ritualized in tefillin. In reflecting on the experience of tying these knots from the position of maternal subjects, we rediscover the terrain, long disregarded by religious thought, in which primal truths are sown.

Notes

1. Throughout this book, I rely on the JPS translation of the Tanakh, with minor changes of my own. Many commentators rely on distinction between these two forms of "bondage" articulated in the Gemara: FOR THE CHILDREN OF ISRAEL ARE SLAVES TO ME [Lev. 25:55]—and not slaves to slaves" (bBaba Qamma 116b).

2. On love as behavioral devotion in Deuteronomy, see the classic article by William Moran, "Ancient near Eastern Background of the Love of God in Deuteronomy," *Catholic Biblical Quarterly* 25, no. 1 (1963). Of the voluminous work since then, see especially Bill T. Arnold, "The Love-Fear Antinomy in Deuteronomy 5–11," *Vetus Testamentum* 61 (2011); Jon D. Levenson, *The Love of God: Divine Gift, Human Gratitude, and Mutual Faithfulness in Judaism* (Princeton, NJ: Princeton University Press, 2015).

3. For a study of tefillin as magical amulets in the Second Temple period and beyond, see Yehudah Cohn, *Tangled up in Text: Tefillin and the Ancient World* (Providence, RI: Society of Biblical Literature, 2008). On tefillin and gender in late antiquity, see Elizabeth Shanks Alexander, *Gender and Timebound Commandments in Judaism* (New York: Cambridge University Press, 2013). In her work on medieval Jewish piety, Elisheva Baumgarten argues that "evidence indicates that in late antiquity and the early Middle Ages, most Jews did not keep the commandment of tefillin" in diaspora communities; see Baumgarten, *Practicing Piety in Medieval Ashkenaz: Men, Women, and Everyday Religious Observance* (Philadelphia: University of Pennsylvania Press, 2014), 141ff.

4. Cf. the notion of chosen subjection in descriptive religious ethics, as in Jonathan Wyn Schofer, "Self, Subject, and Chosen Subjection: Rabbinic Ethics and Comparative Possibilities," *Journal of Religious Ethics* 33, no. 2 (2005).

5. Sigmund Freud and James Strachey, *The Future of an Illusion* (New York: Norton, 1975), 56.

6. For example, see Bonnie J. Miller-McLemore, *Also a Mother: Work and Family as Theological Dilemma* (Nashville, TN: Abingdon Press, 1994).

7. Cf. Sara Ruddick, *Maternal Thinking: Toward a Politics of Peace* (Boston: Beacon Press, 1989), 44–45.

8. Adam Seligman et al., *Ritual and Its Consequences: An Essay on the Limits of Sincerity* (New York: Oxford University Press, 2008).

9. Ruddick, *Maternal Thinking*, 51.

10. This double move, as a staple of feminist scriptural hermeneutics, builds on Paul Ricoeur's famous "hermeneutics of suspicion" and "hermenueutics of retrieval."

11. Emphasis mine.

12. I am indebted here to Sarit Kattan Gribetz's meticulous discussion of the gendered and specifically maternal elements of this Talmudic passage in Sarit Kattan Gribetz, *Conceptions of Time and Rhythms of Daily Life in Rabbinic Literature, 200–600 C.E.* (PhD diss., Princeton University, 2013), 124–128.

13. I thank Rabbi Elie Kaunfer for pointing me to this Talmudic passage and discussing it with me.

14. Rashi bShabbat 66b, s.v. "longing."

15. Rashi explains this point in the continuation of his comment: "It is not done for females, since the father doesn't dote on them as much when they are young, such that they would miss him." In other words, a girl is not in need of this "remedy" since she and her father don't form a strong bond to begin with. Or, to gloss Rashi in keeping with my argument, attachment follows from daily caregiving, not the other way around.

16. Rabbenu Ḥananel on bShabbat 66b, s.v. "knots."

17. God, in the rabbinic imagination, is equally attached to "His" children. According to bBerakhot 6a, God also "lays tefillin," and the words in the divine *batim* (boxes) reciprocally declare God's love for the unique people of Israel: "Rav Naḥman bar Isaac asked Rab Ḥiyya bar 'Avin, What is written in the tefillin of the Lord of the Universe? He answered, AND WHO IS LIKE THY PEOPLE ISRAEL, A SINGULAR NATION ON EARTH? (I Chron. 17:21)."

PART I

CHAPTER 1

Obligation

To be a Jew, according to the classical textual tradition, is to be obligated. Acts of service to one's neighbor and to God devolve on the individual simply by virtue of being a Jew. This foundational assumption forms the substructure of the commandments enjoined to the people of Israel; few are the matters the realm of obligation does not touch. This privileging of deontology over virtue, of obligation over voluntarism, finds quintessential expression in the Talmudic dictum: "Greater is one who is commanded and does than he who is not commanded and does" (bQiddushin 31a).[1] Obligation has been a "fundamental word" that structures Jewish thought and behavior for centuries.[2]

The project of modernity, as it unfolded in late eighteenth-century central and western Europe, sought to dismantle this sort of obligation in both its religious and its existential forms. In classical liberalism, individual obligation extended only to the obeying of natural law and reason. Agency was formulated in opposition to constraint. In this light, inherited obligations appeared contrary, benighted.

Although the liberal critique of religion primarily targeted church authority, a number of Enlightenment thinkers used the ritual, historical, and communal obligations of Jewish life—and the rabbinic presumption of obligation as a condition of human existence—as a negative illustration in their arguments. The *mitzvot* appeared as a particularly egregious example of illegitimate compulsion; Judaism's commands "are of such a kind that even a political constitution can be concerned with them and impose them as coercive laws, because they pertain merely to external actions; and although before reason the Ten Commandments would already hold as ethical ones, even if they had not been given publicly, in that legislation they have not been given at all with the demand on one's *moral attitude* in obeying them (wherein Christianity later posited its main work), but have been directed absolutely only to the external observance."[3] In keeping with the preference for liberal rationalism, empiricism, and individual autonomy, Jews largely jettisoned the framework that had grounded their communal functions and religious life.[4]

In recent decades, Western thinkers have interrogated the presumptions of the modern critique of religion. The ideals of liberalism now suggest a fantasy in which individuals stand outside of language, body, and history, surveying the world and inherited truths from an Archimedean remove. The supposedly "universal" truths prized in dominant strains of Enlightenment thought, we now understand, can never be known outside of the particularities of specific existences in time and space. The rabbinic idiom of obligation may be unfamiliar, but postmodernity has attuned us to the inevitability of being conditioned by the world and responsive to it—that is, to the most basic meaning of obligation.

Obligation, as its root suggests, refers to what binds us to others and the world (*ob-*, toward; *ligare*, bind). Obligation constitutes us as subjects; "already from the first, and with every act of sensation, the world is 'there' as a field of phenomenality, as a world of claims imposing themselves with an ever-present and evident presence. These claims put one under a primary obligation," as Michael Fishbane writes.[5] The work of "coming to be" in a world demands attention and response; we are constituted by the contingent, dynamic networks of relationships in which we are embedded. We are tethered to linguistic, spatial, social, and temporal landscapes; we cannot escape them no matter how far we travel.

Maternity, particularly in the contemporary West, compels acute attention to the fact of being planted in and responsive to a world. Maternity presents a primal experience of being *subject to* rather than *master over*. Tied by knots of obligation and service to another person and to her world, the adult caregiver knows what it is to be tethered, materially and bodily. Maternity simultaneously induces and reveals this inner core of our existence as given. At the same time, it demands a dialectical understanding of the relationship between obligation and agency, for the imposed condition of obligation does not produce a singular response. Rather, it generates human creativity in its multiplicity.

Analysis of maternal experience yields insight into this condition of obligation in ways that are productive for Jewish thought in particular and for contemporary thought as a whole. Maternal obligation, in both its practical and its existential dimensions, offers contemporary Western people's most substantive experience with the meaning of obligation. Raising a child demands an episodic and complex subjection of self that confronts notions of individual freedom. This subjection, for Kant and others, was pejoratively called "heteronomy," that is, submission to "the law of another." Viewing maternal subjectivity as a simultaneous exercise in submission *and* an exercise of agency within a set of constraints offers a new lens on obligation in Jewish thought. A feminist analysis of maternal subjectivity demands critique of traditional Jewish understandings of obligation and, at the same time, suggests a starting point for reappropriating Judaism's religious discourse of obligation.

* * *

A theological anthropology of the individual as "bound" or "yoked" shaped Jewish thought and practice from the rabbinic period until the advent of modernity. In the rich repository of traditional Jewish legal and narrative texts, to be a Jewish self means to have entered a social world already encumbered with tasks, duties, and relationships. The mitzvot that devolve on the Jew constitute the outward expression of this more fundamental orientation.[6]

The rabbis detailed extensive and diverse obligations that Jews owe to parents, teachers, the community as a whole, one's fellow Jew, non-Jews, the (non-Jewish) government, and God. These obligations, taken together, establish a lexicon of practical action suited to different occasions, places, and occurrences, and to arbitrating the inevitable conflicts among these duties. The obligations debated and illustrated in normative Jewish texts were likely not executed in a way remotely resembling how they are presented in the classical literature; many of them by definition could not be.[7] Nonetheless, this literature is instructive for understanding the rabbinic imagination at work, sorting out complex webs of multiple relationships and exploring the interlocking, often competing, obligations those relationships create.

The rabbis employ a powerful metaphor to communicate this understanding of the Jewish self as tethered to Torah and mitzvot. In keeping with the theme of divine redemption as distinct from negative liberty, the normative self envisioned by rabbinic Judaism is imagined as a beast of burden, an ox on whom a yoke—the "yoke of God's dominion" ('ol malkhut shamayim) and the "yoke of the commandments" ('ol mitzvot)—is placed.[8] The great medieval commentator Rashi explains the metaphor in no uncertain terms: "The commandments were not given to Israel to fulfill them for their enjoyment, but were given to be a yoke around their necks."[9] This historical and collective acceptance of the yoke (qabbalat 'ol) is ritually reenacted through the daily recitation of the Shema and performed in the vast system of ritual, civil, and ethical commandments that create the texture of normative rabbinic piety.

This posture of obligation provides an inviting entry point for rethinking subjectivity and selfhood in the present moment. Contemporary scholars of religion have become increasingly interested in the project of self-formation through discipline, constraint, and subjection in pre- or nonmodern traditions.[10] These modes of thought represent a challenge to the presuppositions encoded in liberal thought.

However, in the case of rabbinic Judaism, any impulse toward retrieval cannot proceed far without questioning the very possibility of speaking about a "Jewish self," even within the framework of normative legal texts.[11] For the obligated self of rabbinic Judaism is normatively adult, male, able-bodied, and Jewish. Furthermore, obligation may be the default status for males and females in the classical tradition, but the "official" or normative commandments in Jewish religious life are unevenly distributed.[12] All adult Jews are commanded, as it were, but some Jews are more commanded than others. Whole classes of people, including females, are temporarily or congenitally exempt from the category of mitzvot referred to as "positive time-bound commandments," which have long held a particular status of importance and visibility among Jews.[13]

In her classic work *Standing Again at Sinai*, Judith Plaskow draws attention to the roots of this differential in the "origin story" of the mitzvot: "There can be no verse in Torah more disturbing to the feminist than Moses' warning to his people in Ex. 19:15, 'Be ready for the third day; do not go near a woman.' For here, at the very moment that the Jewish people stands at Sinai ready to receive the covenant ... Moses addresses the community only as men."[14] Sinai is a locus of command and, for readers attuned to gender, of exclusion.

If the metaphor of the yoked ox disregards this gender differentiation, other metaphors of rabbinic literature telegraph the maleness of Jewish selfhood explicitly. The mitzvot as visible tokens of the physical intimacy of God's love are, for instance, connected to the male body, as in the following midrash:[15]

> Beloved is Israel, for they are surrounded with commandments: tefillin on their heads and tefillin on their arms, *mezuzot* on their doorways and *tzitzit* on their clothes. Concerning them [these commandments], David said: SEVEN TIMES A DAY I HAVE PRAISED YOU FOR YOUR RIGHTEOUS COMMANDMENTS [Ps. 119:164]. When David entered the bathhouse and saw that he was naked, he said, "Woe is me, that I should am naked of commandments. [When] he saw his circumcision, he felt comforted and began to compose praise: TO THE CHOIR LEADER, ON THE EIGHTH DAY [i.e., the day of circumcision], A PSALM OF DAVID."[16]

The male Jew walks through the world garbed and even physically inscribed by the visible signs of divine election. Clothing and other external markers of Jewish identity might conceivably be worn by women (as they are for some religiously observant Jewish women today), but for the rabbis, clothes-as-mitzvot were decidedly male garb.[17] If there were any doubt, circumcision is used as the specifically and exclusively male physical sign of the mitzvot that, for the rabbis, cannot be erased.[18]

The values and assumptions the rabbis express underscore a historical, intellectual, and moral distance between their world and ours that is problematic as well as corrective. As Jonathan Schofer has argued, "late ancient rabbinic ethical instruction addressed a group defined by nation or ethnicity, gender, and elite community," largely excluding Gentile males, but also non-rabbinic Jewish men, and women of all social and ethnic subdivisions.[19] In drawing out the obligated self of rabbinic thought, we unintentionally catch unwanted presumptions in our net.

Nonetheless, a dialectical approach to rabbinic constructions of obligation enables us to apprehend maternity in a new light. Much as the rabbinic Jewish male finds both burden and reminder in his tallit and circumcision, mothers carrying their children are clothed in a kind of ritual garment and bodily sign of relationship. The juxtaposition of these postures of obligation becomes generative when we acknowledge both the parallels and the limits of the analogue: feminists cannot simply endorse the concept of heteronomy, so central to the rabbis' theological anthropology, in the context of maternal subjectivity. Heteronomous obligation—especially the obligation to bear and raise children—has, for centuries, underwritten women's subjugation.[20] Nonetheless, by placing these two forms of obligation into relationship with one another, we can move toward a feminist reengagement with rabbinic thought.

* * *

In the early days and months of first having a baby, the raw, immediate assault on my freedom—a freedom I had not even known I had previously enjoyed—struck me with overwhelming force. No sooner had this baby, this stranger, appeared than she held a claim on me. I was now responsible for addressing her needs and wishes, for seeking out the meaning of her unfamiliar body and its often cryptic language.

The obligation, the *ought*, was so powerful in those early days that it, more than delight, often took center stage in my psyche. Indeed, I longed for the simple fact of the love I felt for her to lighten the load. It did not. At times, wonder and gratitude did temper the overwhelming sense of burden. But more often, the obligation to take care of the young creature preoccupied me to the exclusion of other emotions. I felt the terror of my power, of my vast and direct responsibility for this baby's well-being. I was weighted down by the sheer inescapability of her.

My obligation was, on the most literal level, to locate myself in proximity to her and to do things for her, night and day. Her body demanded compliance. No longer was the usual calendar of day and night useful; a physically depleting cycle of half-wakefulness and short, interrupted portions of sleep became routine. The "witching hour," or hours, took the place of dinnertime. It no longer made sense to get myself ready for bed when I knew that just a short while later I would be up again. Again and again I found cold cups of tea scattered in every room, each time remembering what I had been doing when I had planned to sit down with a hot drink.

To leave the house, even for a short time, required gathering an enormous number of things I anticipated needing. Her accouterments weighed me down. Even more disorienting was the fact that baby *herself* became "stuff" to haul around. I apprehended her not only as a living, animate soul but also as material, as a package to be moved or carried or clothed, the epicenter of a vast apparatus of objects.[21]

I could no longer unthinkingly walk out the door with little but my own necessities, wearing my freedom lightly. I now noticed, savored, and sometimes maniacally sought out this temporary freedom when I left the baby with my partner or the babysitter. But ironically, although I longed for the unencumbered buoyancy of my previous freedom, that freedom was irretrievable: when I left the house alone, my giddiness mingled inextricably with a sense of escape. Even when I was by myself, I could no longer feel truly solitary. My temporary lightness was utterly unlike what I had experienced before having a child.

These shifts in my relationship to time, the material world, and my own autonomy comprised the becoming of an obligated self, a self radically bound up with someone else. In my child I recognized the one person from whom, I felt, I could not walk away. In rational moments, I recognized this to be untrue: parents of small children can and do free themselves from the obligations of daily care or other substantive involvement by *de facto* relinquishing the claim to parenthood. I knew that. Yet I found it unthinkable that I would refuse the role into which my new child had, by the fact of her existence, suddenly put me. She exerted a gravitational pull, and my role was now to orbit her.

To be an obligated self was to be subject to the law of another: the Law of the Baby. The law could not be fulfilled in abstract but only in active, embodied, material actions: soothing, feeding, cleaning, comforting, distracting, smiling, and wiping. It became the law of the crying toddler who sought out not just any, but specifically *our* (or *my*), comfort; the law of her seeking out our, or my, face for approval and interest.

The Law of the Baby was not the Law of Any Baby but rather the Law of This Baby. This Baby had to be woken up throughout the night to eat because she was born small. This Baby responded with great interest to one particular plush toy. This Baby's imperative was to hold her at a certain angle so she would fall asleep for a nap. The next day, the next week, This Baby no longer responded to that position or that toy.

Every child issues his or her own law: the baby who is colicky, the baby who is attached to tubes and needs his bandages changed to stay alive and healthy, the baby who needs to be walked around the room at a particular pace to fall asleep, the baby who cannot seem to latch on or who refuses a bottle, the baby who calms down at the sight of his older sibling, the baby who simply cannot nap in her stroller, the baby who cackles with joyous laughter at a particular sound.

These laws are no sooner issued than they are revoked and new laws are issued. The Law of This Baby in Particular is continually shifting, and so her law is continually eluded and rediscovered. Only care for the baby, day in and day out, attunes a parent to the subtleties of this shifting ground.

The force of the Law of Another was greater than anything I could have anticipated or to which I could have assented. I had never explicitly agreed to be subject to it, although as an adult who was *compos mentis*, clearly I had some idea what I was getting into: I had pursued having a child, needed medical intervention for my partner to conceive, and I had eagerly (and anxiously) anticipated motherhood. Nonetheless, I could not agree to the law before I was already subject to it. And once in place, I could only violate the law through inattention or frustration; I could not cast it off it. I transgressed the law as often as I fulfilled it, leaving my crying baby or comfort-seeking toddler to calm herself when I could not bring myself to respond. Nonetheless, it was clear to me that there was a law, and the law applied to me by virtue of being my child's parent.

* * *

This sense of overwhelming obligation—one that is widely shared among contemporary, middle-class women—is produced through the convergence of many elements of social life in the contemporary West.[22] "Children," as Jennifer Senior has written, "are the last binding obligation in a culture that asks for almost no other permanent commitments at all."[23] In broad strokes, this observation is certainly true. But the experience of obligation is not evenly distributed and cannot be construed as a universal or essential component of maternity. The experience of having children as a novel encounter with heteronomous obligation is one that occurs at the nexus of a set of specific social locations.

Obligation came to dominate the experience of maternity in the twentieth century, postindustrial West. Increasingly during the course of the last century, the family was defined as an emotional rather than as an economic unit. Whereas in agricultural and mercantile settings, children (especially sons) increased a family's capital and children in middle-class, children in industrial societies became "economically 'useless' while being emotionally 'priceless.'"[24] The rise in the reliability and availability of birth control, moreover, enabled adults to limit the number of children they had, contributing to a new economics of children. In having fewer children, parents "invested" time, money, and emotional labor on an increasingly smaller and thus more precious object. Increasingly reliable birth control, accessible abortion, and, later, assisted reproduction made it possible to "choose" to have children and thus eroded a landscape that had been formed by the expectation that heterosexual sex would inevitably lead to maternity.

Only with the possibility of a small number of children, or none at all, could this parental investment of time and money be so exorbitant and the burden of maternal obligation so acute. To speak today about having children is, at least for some people, to discuss "choosing" to have children; as Bowlby remarks, "the normalization of contraceptive practices brought notions of choice and plan to the fore."[25] The omnipresence of this language of choice makes the arresting force of obligation particularly paradoxical. In a moment of (at least partial) access to birth control, and in a postindustrial social world in which parenthood is a project, to choose parenthood is to choose both subjection and fulfillment. It is to willingly forfeit some element of "autonomy" and "freedom" for the sake of a different kind of fulfillment—one impossible to extricate from social expectation.[26]

In the context of these class- and social-historical developments, parenting became a self-conscious practice of cultivation. As Kathryn Lofton has argued, "No parent would claim to be comprehensive or ideal in their parenting. Yet all parents would now speak of parenting as an occupational force in their lives; to do otherwise is to commit a social heresy. Being a parent today is not a component of existence, but an ordering fact of existence, one which seems ... to press at the limits of sanity, wellness, time, budget, and ability."[27] The quasi-religious terminology in which parenting is discussed, and its binding force for adults today, forms the broader social context in which parenting itself comes to be the primary expression of obligation.

My own experience of maternal obligation was surely shaped by having been raised to aspire to the "freedom" to define myself as privileged white men do: without reference to obligation. Where previous generations of girls had been taught to regard motherhood as destiny and aspiration, my feminist mother emphasized meaningful and successful work—not to the exclusion of motherhood, but not subordinate to it, either. Having been reared without family members in abject need of my care, or a sense that other factors—racism, dire economic circumstances—might impinge on my aspirations, I was in my mid-thirties when I became a mother and had known for some time the freedom of "choosing my own path," as constructed within the constraints of my social class.

People who spend years as adults already operating on the presumption (or perhaps illusion) of their own autonomy—that they can and should legislate their "own law" for themselves—are likely to be particularly surprised and troubled when confronted with the demands on the self that a small child imposes. I was perfectly primed to experience an infant's raw, urgent, constant need as heteronomy *par excellence*, and to experience submission to the Law of Another as the most arresting and disorienting element of new parenthood. But this experience of maternity as a novel and disruptive form of obligation devolves differently along social lines in the postindustrial West. Parents with high degrees of social and thus often geographic mobility carry the main burdens of child-rearing without the familial contributions of time and effort that alleviate the overwhelming sense of personal burden. If bourgeois families are defined in part by the "nuclearism" that precludes substantive ties with other relatives, working-class and immigrant communities, by contrast, often distribute the burdens of care more widely, conscripting relatives and others to actively shoulder the burden of care.[28]

The phenomenological experience of maternal obligation is, like all human experience, conditioned by the contingencies of history and social location. Consideration of these contingencies thus informs how we must explore the contours of maternal obligation. Becoming aware of the cultural, class, and racial specificity of certain idealized, hypostatized concepts of motherhood can facilitate a broader conversation in which divergent conditions of maternal obligation can be engaged. The central and western European Jewish experience of emancipation, to which I now turn, illustrates one way that broader power systems shape religious thinkers' conceptions of intimate interpersonal relationships.

* * *

As Jews entered the crucible of modernity, they increasingly faced social and political conditions within which rabbinic concepts of obligation could not be sustained. Enlightenment thinkers, and the emergent European nation-states that aspired to Enlightenment ideals, condemned the heteronomous obligation that had long organized Jewish communal practice and individual piety. Enlightenment thinkers rebelled against "obligation" in the expansive sense of being bound to the world and to others. The new civil sphere would now expect demonstrations of Jewish loyalty and the relinquishment of competing communal loci of obligatory action, from ritual (such as the many practices that demarcated Jewish religious identity) to competing social and civil obligations (such as educational systems that reinforced Jewish languages and social formations) and political obligations (the *kahal* that had the power to sanction transgression).[29] The mitzvot, especially those that were the most "visible," increasingly offered proof of Jews' inadmissibility for emancipation and integration into the liberal, quasi-secular, nation-state.[30]

Most Jews in modernizing European societies—the Netherlands, France, the German states—enthusiastically supported religious reform, eagerly throwing off forms of obligation that hindered their participation in the wider civil society, and, when permitted, embracing new configurations of Jewish identity. Most Jews redefined their identity in voluntaristic, faith-based terms that downplayed and recast the heteronomous nature of Jewish obligation.[31]

But the condition of obligation did not simply disappear from Jewish thought. Rather, modernity necessitated a narrower sphere in which obligation might be legitimately construed. Most Jewish thinkers, while not entirely jettisoning the mitzvot, dramatically transformed their meaning and reference point. In the modern Jewish imagination, obligation would be confined to the intimate, inter-subjective realm.[32] The sphere of obligation was to be primarily realized within dyadic encounters between an individual and the "neighbor."

Jewish thinkers in the twentieth century responded to the challenge of a shifted intellectual, political, and social landscape by rendering obligation not as the status imposed by a commanding God on the Jewish people, but rather as the result of encounters between two subjects in everyday human relationships. The intersubjective dyad became an oasis, a realm untouched by the liberal critique of religion and its role in the public sphere. Instead of justifying the mitzvot, the performance of which became increasingly problematic in the modern nation-state, these thinkers conceived of humans as existentially, but not practically, obligated to the other.

Hermann Cohen, the first figure critical to this transformation, argued in *Religion of Reason Out of the Sources of Judaism* (1918) that the experience of sympathy evoked in a dyadic encounter with the other constituted the heart of religion itself. A person's encounter with the other—in particular, the vulnerable, oppressed other—shifts a person's understanding of herself. Individuals become true selves by becoming responsible for a particular other.[33]

Towering figures in twentieth-century Jewish thought built on Cohen's model of dyadic encounter by jettisoning its technical philosophical language and building a more vibrant concept of God and the other. One of Cohen's most important interpreters, Franz Rosenzweig, argued that movement toward the neighbor resulted from the soul's response to divine imperative, "Love me!"[34] In his best-known work, *The Star of Redemption* (1921), Rosenzweig portrayed the dyadic encounter between human and God as triggering a transformation for the human partner, in which the autonomous "self" becomes the relational "soul." Relationality, for Rosenzweig, concerned responsiveness to the other, and this responsiveness constituted the core of the mitzvot.[35] Rosenzweig himself appears to have been ambivalent about embracing traditional Jewish practice and the mitzvot; nonetheless, his most extensive treatment of relationship argued that obligation was the inevitable result of the individual's response to the (divine) other.

Emmanuel Levinas represents both the promise and the lingering prob-lems of this interpersonal construal of obligation. In *Totality and Infinity* (1961), Levinas acknowledges his debt to Rosenzweig, arguing that the face-to-face encounter with the other is constitutive of the self as an ethical subject—a subject responsible for others. But for Levinas, contact with the other remains "terres-trial," that is, devoid of a "vertical" (theological) component. This formulation secularizes Rosenzweig's theological model, but obligation nonetheless remains central.[36] Ethical subjecthood is generated through the *command* of the face of the other. For Levinas, the encounter is asymmetrical; the other simultaneously demands from and imposes on the self, thereby calling it into being. Indeed, Levinas refers to the Other as one's "master": he "reveals himself in his lordship" and holds the self hostage.[37] Here, then, is twentieth-century Jewish "obligation" distilled: it is the non-optional character of the human other's demand, to which the self is already responsive; it is an obligation that predates assent or refusal.

This restriction of obligation to the intersubjective sphere testifies both to theological creativity and, simultaneously, to the impoverishment of the scope of obligation in the modern period. The emergence of the modern liberal nation-state seemingly required the disruption if not dismantling of Jewish obligation's traditional ritual, civil, social, political, and economic reference points. What remained was the dyadic encounter with another individual, a realm protected from the social and political critiques that continued to vex practitioners of the mitzvot.

In an intellectual and political environment hostile to traditional Jewish life, Jewish religious philosophers landed on an ingenious strategy for retaining but transforming the significance of obligation. The cost of this approach, however, was a fully realized concept of the individual to whom the self is obligated. Most influential Jewish thinkers conceived of the intersubjective encounter, and therefore of the individuals who participate in it, in decidedly abstract terms. The "other" they envisioned has no specific social location or set of needs.[38] It is difficult, on the basis of these thinkers' writings, to imagine how such meetings occur in the course of ordinary life, and how duration of relationship, social proximity, and differences of power might affect them.[39] An insistent tendency toward abstraction enabled these thinkers to argue for the universality of dyadic encounter and obligation.

A turn to concrete manifestations of obligation, by contrast, reveals the possibilities and limits of the relocation of obligation to this privatized sphere of engagement. Adults' embodied, daily experiences of obligation vis-à-vis their children offer a path forward. Taking maternal experience as a starting point, obligation can become an alternative to both the privatized notion of obligation and the tendency toward abstraction we find in so much twentieth-century modern Jewish thought. And contrary to the construction of agency merely in terms of liberal, rational choice, a feminist examination of maternal subjectivity suggests that agency dialectically informs obligation and vice versa.

The theological implications of this pursuit are admittedly startling: if the rabbinic notion of obligation comes into felt experience most viscerally in caring for young children, then God is not an overlord but a vulnerable, dependent being who needs virtually constant attention. This concept inverts the biblical metaphorical economy, in which God is parent, not infant, and the rabbinic sources that speak of God as king and as father, not as subject or son.[40] But since these are metaphors, one in which God is imagined as a baby invites us to name the condition of being obligated to God as being compelled and beguiled, shackled and infatuated, all at once. The care for an infant perfectly captures the pairing of command and love at the heart of rabbinic thought. If God is not only loving parent but demanding baby, we may find within ourselves the resolve to meet the demand.

* * *

By its nature, a parent's obligation is to a *particular* child or set of children, each of whom has specific needs and desires. Some children's needs and desires are common to all young children: the need to be fed, clothed, carried, and comforted. These needs place a set of demands on all caregivers, parental or otherwise. But children vary enormously in temperament, ability, and interests. A parent's experience of obligation toward his or her child thus cannot be conceived only in terms of a universal set of demands that can be formulated only in abstract terms.[41] In the maternal context, obligation already contains within it the particularities of one's child and the specific circumstances in which both parent and child live.

Caring for a child requires constant engagement in a larger world in which both parent and child, along with many other individuals, participate. We engage in social, political, linguistic, and other structures not of our own making, which appear in a web of embedded familial relations. The modern liberal construction of child-rearing as a "private sphere" activity is belied by the concrete manifestations of civil society in this intimate form of relationship. As Sara Ruddick has argued, "Although a birthgiving woman and an infant are intensely coupled, they cannot survive alone.... Birthgiving presupposes an expanding network of affectionate, sturdy dependencies.... Any man or woman's mothering depends on partners, friends, and helpers. These mothering associates, like the mothers they work with, dependent on courts, economic policies, work schedules, medical practices, schools, and other institutions."[42] A privatized understanding of obligation cannot adequately account for the role of the many individuals and systems that shape the unfolding of particular experiences of obligation.

A feminist account of obligation that begins with maternal subjectivity demands a recognition of constraint as well as choice. In "choosing" to rear a child, I assent to an obligation that goes beyond my ability to assent. As Roger Burggraeve puts it, parents "can decide to conceive 'a' child, but they can never decide to conceive of 'this' child, the real child as it appears. This unique child escapes their power of decision. Even if they conceive 'a' child, they receive 'this' child. And it is precisely for 'this' child that they are responsible."[43] This formulation presumes biological parenthood, access to birth control, and the cultural possibility of "choosing" to have a child. But the same observation can be made with regard also to adoptive parenthood: one can choose to adopt a child, but never can know who *this* child is, or might become, at the moment of making a commitment to rear her. My obligation to my child in particular cannot be "chosen," if choice implies mastery over my will, my circumstances, and the uncontrollable and unknowable.[44] Maternal obligation challenges the model of choice as rational and unconstrained that has long dominated liberal political thought, the legacy of which still informs modern Jewish thought.[45]

But this liberal model of "choice" is not the only option; agency—understood as the exercise of action within constraints—shapes the world of anyone who seeks a child to raise.[46] This insight is articulated in the classical rabbinic conception of a "yoked" or bound subject. As the legal theorist Robert Cover has argued, "the Sinaitic myth [gave] rise to counter myths and accounts which stress human autonomy," almost in dialectical fashion.[47] The rabbis imagined agency within a framework that assumed obligation. A famous midrash (bShabbat 88a; bAvodah Zarah 2b) expresses precisely this dialectical movement between freedom, or agency, and the boundedness of the conditions of existence:

> AND THEY STOOD AT THE FOOT OF [lit. "under"] THE MOUNTAIN [Exodus 19:17]: Rabbi Avdimi the son of Hama the son of Hasa said, "This teaches that the Holy One, Blessed be He, held the mountain over them like a barrel and said, 'If you accept the Torah, it is good. And if not, here shall be your graves.'" Rav Aha bar Yaakov said, "From here there is a great claim against the Torah!" Rav said, "Even so, they accepted it in the days of Ahashverosh, as it is written, THEY UPHELD AND ACCEPTED [Esther 9:27]: they upheld what they already accepted.

The radical claims of the first part of this midrash are clear: the people of Israel's acceptance of Torah at Mt. Sinai is accomplished by threat of force. Rav Aha bar Yaakov objects: the validity of Torah itself is undermined if it was accepted only through coercion. Responding to this challenge, Rav states that in the days of Ahashverosh—a much later, exilic, time—they "accepted [again] what they had already accepted." Rav's answer does not rescue the moment of Sinai from the "claim" against it; the original moment of Sinai, he implicitly concedes, is a "non-choice." The Israelites, at Sinai, could hardly be said to "accept" Torah. Only later can agency find a place: the "choice" that was in fact coerced is transformed when Israel chooses to affirm its earlier coercion as its desire.[48] But this "coercion" of Israel at Sinai, in which the people stand under divine threat, also emphasizes obligation as a name for being always already in, bonded to, and responsive to a world.[49] In an essay called "The Temptation of Temptation," Levinas comments: "The teaching, which the Torah is, cannot come to the human being as a result of a choice. That which must be received in order to make freedom of choice possible cannot have been chosen, unless after the fact. In the beginning was violence. But we may be dealing here with a consent other than the one given after inspection ... wouldn't Revelation be precisely a reminder of this consent prior to freedom and non-freedom? ... The freedom taught by the Jewish text starts in a non-freedom which, far from being slavery or childhood, is a beyond-freedom."[50] "Torah" is not to be understood as the limited, particular bequest given to a limited, particular people, but rather as a stand-in for the sensible substructure of the universe.[51] Torah, like gravity, allows free movement on the planet. Humans are creatures who come to existence in a world of constraint, as constrained beings. We are responsive to others and to a world we did not choose.

This aspect of our existence can be veiled from us; we can be oblivious to the fact of being tied to the world until various experiences open our eyes to it. To live with and be responsible for a newborn, a baby, a toddler, is to suddenly wake up to one's un-freedom. It means having the concrete experience, dozens of times each day, of being beholden to another. This un-freedom feels at times like slavery (*'avdut*) and at times like service (*'avodah*). But this condition, so acutely, viscerally, and materially experienced in caring for a young child, reveals a basic, but easily occluded, fact of existence. Maternity lifts, sometimes rips, the veil from our eyes, opening us to recognizing our conditionality.

And yet, as the midrash conveys, we cannot simply submit, if the act of compliance is to retain its ethical force. If we are threatened into submission to this world of obligation, the system is morally and psychologically unsustainable; gravity becomes domination. Agency is crucial to human flourishing, even if it consists only in affirming the conditionality of our existence and thus upholding what we were forced to accept. The midrash insists on human agency as ethically necessary in affirming the conditions of our existence.

We always stand "under the mountain," positioned only to respond to the conditionality of our being and of the others who constitute our being in the world. Our freedom consists not in casting off all that binds us, but rather in recognizing that our boundedness and our agency are each parts of greater whole.

Notes

1. Also bBaba Qamma 87a. On this dictum, see David Benatar, "Obligation, Motivation, and Reward: An Analysis of a Talmudic Principle," *Journal of Law and Religion* 17, no. 1/2 (2002).

2. "Fundamental word": see Robert Cover, "Obligation: A Jewish Jurisprudence of the Social Order," *Journal of Law and Religion* 5, no. 1 (1987). As Cover argues, this basic orientation

of Jewish legal discourse sets it apart from its Western analogue, which is oriented toward a discourse of rights, and in particular, theories of natural rights. Cf. Isaiah Berlin, *Two Concepts of Liberty: An Inaugural Lecture Delivered before the University of Oxford on 31 October 1958* (Oxford: Clarendon Press, 1958).

3. Immanuel Kant, *Religion within the Bounds of Bare Reason* (Indianapolis: Hackett, 2009), 139–140. See also Spinoza's extensive treatment of what he sees as the illegitimacy of extending the stipulations in the "original Mosaic constitution" to a Jewish community without a state (Benedictus de Spinoza, *Theological-Political Treatise*, trans. Samuel Shirley, 2nd ed. [Indianapolis: Hackett, 2001]).

4. A vast literature has been devoted to tracing Jewish responses to liberal rationalism; for synthetic approaches to the relationship between these critiques and the changing status of ritual obligation in the modern period, see among others Arnold M. Eisen, *Rethinking Modern Judaism: Ritual, Commandment, Community* (Chicago: University of Chicago Press, 1998); Leora Faye Batnitzky, *How Judaism Became a Religion: An Introduction to Modern Jewish Thought* (Princeton, NJ: Princeton University Press, 2011).

5. Michael A. Fishbane, *Sacred Attunement: A Jewish Theology* (Chicago: University of Chicago Press, 2008), 192. In John Caputo's terms, "Obligations belong to the most elemental condition of what the young Heidegger called the situation of 'factical life,' the condition of our 'facticity.' As soon as we come to be, we find ourselves enmeshed in obligations" (John D. Caputo, *Against Ethics: Contributions to a Poetics of Obligation with Constant Reference to Deconstruction* [Bloomington: Indiana University Press, 1993], 7).

6. Despite the ample sources, interest in constructing a descriptive ethical picture of selfhood or theological anthropology in rabbinic Judaism has been limited. Exceptions include Efraim Elimelech Urbach, *The Sages, Their Concepts and Beliefs* (Jerusalem: Magnes Press, Hebrew University, 1975); E. Stiegman, "Rabbinic Anthropology," in *Aufstieg und Niedergang der römischen Welt*, ed. Wonfgang Haase (Berlin: Walter de Gruyter, 1979); Sacha Stern, *Jewish Identity in Early Rabbinic Writings* (Leiden: Brill, 1994). Jonathan Schofer has examined rabbinic descriptive ethics in comparative perspective; see Jonathan Wyn Schofer, *The Making of a Sage: A Study in Rabbinic Ethics* (Madison: University of Wisconsin Press, 2004); *Confronting Vulnerability: The Body and the Divine in Rabbinic Ethics* (Chicago: University of Chicago Press, 2010). On deontological and competing discourses in tannaitic literature, see Tzvi Novick, *What Is Good, and What God Demands: Normative Structures in Tannaitic Literature* (Boston: Brill, 2010).

7. On the diminutive status of rabbinic political and juridical power, respectively, see especially Seth Schwartz, *Imperialism and Jewish Society, 200 B.C.E. To 640 C.E* (Princeton: Princeton University Press, 2001); Beth A. Berkowitz, *Execution and Invention: Death Penalty Discourse in Early Rabbinic and Christian Cultures* (New York: Oxford University Press, 2006). See also Naftali S. Cohn, *The Memory of the Temple and the Making of the Rabbis* (Philadelphia: University of Pennsylvania Press, 2013). The interlocking legal and narrative dimensions of this Jewish discourse of obligation have been the object of lyrical reflection in early twentieth-century belletristic texts such as Hayyim Nahman Bialik, "Halachah and Aggadah," in *Revealment and Concealment: Five Essays* (Jerusalem: Ibis, 2000); Franz Rosenzweig, "The Builders," in *On Jewish Learning*, ed. Nahum Glatzer (New York: Schocken Books, 1965). See also the influential contribution to legal theory on this topic: Robert Cover, "Nomos and Narrative," *Harvard Law Review* 97, no. 4 (1983).

8. On metaphors that convey the sage pursuing Torah as the apex of Jewish selfhood, see especially Schofer, *The Making of a Sage*, 92–105.

9. Rashi s.v. *mitzvot lo lehanot nitnu* ("commandments were not given for enjoyment"), bRosh Hashana 28a.

10. Talal Asad, *Genealogies of Religion: Discipline and Reasons of Power in Christianity and Islam* (Baltimore: Johns Hopkins University Press, 1993); Peter Brown, *The Body and Society: Men, Women, and Sexual Renunciation in Early Christianity*, 20th anniversary ed. (New York: Columbia University Press, 2008); Jonathan Wyn Schofer, "Self, Subject, and Chosen Subjection: Rabbinic Ethics and Comparative Possibilities," *Journal of Religious Ethics* 33, no. 2 (2005). Adam Seligman et al., *Ritual and Its Consequences: An Essay on the Limits of Sincerity* (New York: Oxford University Press, 2008); C. M. Furey, "Body, Society, and Subjectivity in Religious Studies," *Journal of the American Academy of Religion* 80, no. 1 (2012).

11. Gender has been the subject of increasing attention as a central category in reevaluating what Schofer has called "chosen subjection." See Saba Mahmood, *Politics of Piety: The Islamic Revival and the Feminist Subject* (Princeton: Princeton University Press, 2005); Elizabeth Bucar, "Dianomy: Understanding Religious Women's Moral Agency as Creative Conformity," *Journal of the American Academy of Religion* 78, no. 3 (2010); R. Marie Griffith, *God's Daughters: Evangelical Women and the Power of Submission* (Berkeley: University of California Press, 1997); Mary Keller, *The Hammer and the Flute: Women, Power, and Spirit Possession* (Baltimore: Johns Hopkins University Press, 2002). On the role of social-historical and anthropological evidence in contesting normative categories such as those I am considering in Jewish practice, see especially Elisheva Baumgarten, *Practicing Piety in Medieval Ashkenaz: Men, Women, and Everyday Religious Observance* (Philadelphia: University of Pennsylvania Press, 2014); Susan Starr Sered, *Women as Ritual Experts: The Religious Lives of Elderly Jewish Women in Jerusalem* (New York: Oxford University Press, 1992).

12. Emphasis here must be placed on the "official tradition," as opposed to sources that attest to how people actually lived their lives and understood themselves. The rabbis had limited power to effect their norms. Anthropologists and historians have, by contrast, revealed a wide variety of customs and traditions that have coexisted parallel to the traditions of the elites. See, for example, Baumgarten, *Practicing Piety*. Note also that women are obligated in almost every negative commandment and virtually all positive, non-time-triggered commandments.

13. Of the many treatments of this issue, see especially Rachel Biale, *Women and Jewish Law: An Exploration of Women's Issues in Halakhic Sources* (New York: Schocken Books, 1984); Elizabeth Shanks Alexander, *Gender and Timebound Commandments in Judaism* (New York: Cambridge University Press, 2013); Natan Margalit, "Priestly Men and Invisible Women: Male Appropriation of the Feminine and the Exemption of Women from Positive Time-Bound Commandments," *AJS Review* 28, no. 2 (2004); Judith Hauptman, *Rereading the Rabbis: A Woman's Voice* (Boulder: Westview Press, 1998), 222–231.

14. Judith Plaskow, *Standing Again at Sinai: Judaism from a Feminist Perspective* (San Francisco: HarperCollins, 1991), 25. This verse is, to be sure, but one of many in which the Israelite partner in the covenantal is imagined to be specifically male, though cf. the explicitly inclusivist language of the Deuteronomic history, for example, Deut. 31:12 and Joshua 8:35.

15. For his insightful analysis of this text and the language of mitzvot as intimate and physical, I am indebted to Novick, *What Is Good*, 103. See also discussion of this passage and thematically similar texts in Yehudah Cohn, *Tangled up in Text: Tefillin and the Ancient World* (Providence: Society of Biblical Literature, 2008), 158–159.

16. Different versions of this text are found in bMenahot 43b; Midrash Tehillim (ed. Buber, 2:13); tBerakhot 6:25. I have quoted (and translated) the version in Sifre Deuteronomy 36 (Eliezer Finkelstein, *Sifre 'Al Sefer Devarim* [New York: Jewish Theological Seminary, 2001], 67–68). This passage is analyzed in Novick, *What Is Good*, 103; Baumgarten, *Practicing Piety*, 141.

17. *Berit milah* (the covenant of circumcision) highlights the fact that women are only "weakly" part of or brought into the covenant. This issue invites the larger question that is the simultaneously critical and absurd question: Are women Jews?, a question that orients Shaye J. D. Cohen, *Why Aren't Jewish Women Circumcised?: Gender and Covenant in Judaism* (Berkeley: University of California Press, 2005). For an important Talmudic discussion of *tevilah* (immersion) for conversion and women's entry into the covenant at Sinai, see bYevamot 46a and especially Rashi s.v. *be'avoteinu shemalu* and *'imahot*, bYevamot 46a.

18. In the late Second Temple period, a procedure known as epispasm could hide or reverse the appearance of having been circumcision. The rabbis, presumably in response to Jewish men's elective epispasm, instituted a method of practicing circumcision that would preclude this possibility as halakhically acceptable. See ibid.; Lawrence A. Hoffman, *Covenant of Blood: Circumcision and Gender in Rabbinic Judaism* (Chicago: University of Chicago Press, 1996).

19. Schofer, *Confronting Vulnerability*, 179.

20. Such is the argument that grounds Adrienne Rich, *Of Woman Born: Motherhood as Experience and Institution*, 10th anniversary ed. (New York: Norton, 1986 [1976]).

21. The ethical implications of the observation that "to live as a parent is to live burdened, carrying" in Jewish thought are briefly but interestingly explored in Laurie Zoloth, "Traveling with Children: Mothering and the Ethics of the Ordinary World" *Tikkun*, July-August 1995.

22. On the role of the "religion of parenting" as a key to unlocking the intertwined social, legal, juridical, political, and economic aspects of the contemporary age for child-rearing, see Kathryn Lofton, "Religion and the Authority in American Parenting," *Journal of the American Academy of Religion* 84, no. 1 (2016), 23.

23. Jennifer Senior, *All Joy and No Fun: The Paradox of Modern Parenthood* (New York: Harper Collins, 2014), 44.

24. Steven Mintz, *Huck's Raft: A History of American Childhood* (Cambridge, MA: Belknap Press, 2004); Viviana A. Zelizer, *Pricing the Priceless Child: The Changing Social Value of Children* (Princeton: Princeton University Press, 1994).

25. Rachel Bowlby, *A Child of One's Own: Parental Stories* (Oxford: Oxford University Press, 2013), 75. Bowlby's work, which is focused on literary treatments of parenthood and choice, is affirmed by social historians of America (e.g., Elaine Tyler May, *America and the Pill: A History of Promise, Peril, and Liberation* [New York: Basic Books, 2010] and *Barren in the Promised Land: Childless Americans and the Pursuit of Happiness* [New York: BasicBooks, 1995].)

26. I am not speaking here about the usually unwilling forfeiture of economic or labor security. Economic decline is a routine result of becoming a mother. But this effect is not inevitable; it is the direct result of social and economic policies. The economic aspect of the gender-differentiated effects of becoming a parent is called the "motherhood penalty;" the corollary effect for men has also been called the "fatherhood bonus," as in Michelle Budig, "The Fatherhood Bonus & the Motherhood Penalty: Parenthood and the Gender Gap in Pay," *Third Way*, 2014, last updated September 2, 2014, accessed November 8, 2017, http://www.thirdway.org/report/the-fatherhood-bonus-and-the-motherhood-penalty-parenthood-and-the-gender-gap-in-pay.

27. Lofton, "Religion and the Authority," 23 and passim.

28. The "nuclear" structure of the bourgeois family is, of course, belied most of all by the presence of paid "allomothers," such as nannies, whose labor is essential to the economic and, often, emotional functioning of the familial parents. Carol Stack and Linda M. Burton have explored how non-maternal relatives become more directly implicated in webs of obligation that they didn't themselves choose when they are "conscripted" (or, as they put it, "kinscripted") to engage in childrearing in working-class African-American communities;

see Carol B. Stack and Linda M. Burton, "Kinscripts: Reflections on Family, Generation, and Culture," in *Mothering: Ideology, Experience, Agency*, ed. Evelyn Nakano Glenn, Grace Chang, and Linda Rennie Forcey (New York: Routledge, 1994). Other important studies of race and motherhood include Patricia Hill Collins, "Shifting the Center: Race, Class, and Feminist Theorizing About Motherhood," in *Representations of Motherhood*, ed. Donna Bassin, Margaret Honey, and Meryle Mahrer Kaplan (New Haven: Yale University Press, 1994); Ruth Feldstein, *Motherhood in Black and White: Race and Sex in American Liberalism, 1930–1965* (Ithaca, NY: Cornell University Press, 2000); Evelyn Nakano Glenn, "Social Constructions of Mothering: A Thematic Overview," in *Mothering: Ideology, Experience, and Agency*, ed. Evelyn Nakano Glenn, Grace Chang, and Linda Rennie Forcey (New York: Routledge, 1994); Annette Lareau, *Unequal Childhoods: Class, Race, and Family Life* (Berkeley: University of California Press, 2003); Annelise Orleck, *Storming Caesars Palace: How Black Mothers Fought Their Own War on Poverty* (Boston: Beacon Press, 2005). Naomi Seidman's recent study of the effect of embourgeoisment on premodern Jewish familial arrangements in Ashkenaz is of special relevance for my argument; see Seidman, *The Marriage Plot: Or, How Jews Fell in Love with Love, and with Literature* (Stanford: Stanford University Press, 2016).

29. Modern liberal thought places the rational autonomous adult male self at its core and constructs an economic and social system that serves him. As many feminist critics have pointed out, that model cannot comprehend either the dependent child or the adult whose life is consumed by the need to attend to this child, either temporarily or for as long as she lives, depending on the child's needs. The classic study of liberal political thought and women, on which many others have since built, remains Susan Moller Okin, *Women in Western Political Thought* (Princeton: Princeton University Press, 1979); see also Okin's subsequent study, which focused especially on the family in liberal thought: *Justice, Gender, and the Family* (New York: Basic Books, 1989).

30. Eisen, *Rethinking Modern Judaism*.

31. Moses Mendelssohn, an outlier in this regard, argued Jews were fit participants in the liberal nation-state due to Judaism's non-dogmatic nature. Because the mitzvot regulated behavior, not thought, adherence to Judaism did not interfere with participation in the civil state (Moses Mendelssohn, *Jerusalem, or, on Religious Power and Judaism*, trans. Allan Arkush [Hanover: University Press of New England, 1983]). His argument, however, was exceptional and not persuasive in a climate increasingly skeptical of the harmony between traditional forms of Jewish piety and civil participation. As Paula Hyman noted, in the eyes of non-Jewish rulers and policy-makers, the end game of emancipation and acculturation was complete assimilation. Jews, by contrast, sought to maintain their identity while also acculturating (see Paula Hyman, *Gender and Assimilation in Modern Jewish History: The Roles and Representation of Women* [Seattle: University of Washington Press, 1995]).

32. Here I bracket consideration of highly segregated, aspirationally nonporous communities like Kiryas Yoel. On such communities as a function of liberal modernity, see Batnitzky, *How Judaism Became a Religion*.

33. See the complicated process by which this occurs especially in ch. 8 ("The discovery of man as fellowman") in Hermann Cohen, *Religion of Reason out of the Sources of Judaism*, trans. Simon Kaplan (Atlanta: Scholars Press, 1995).

34. Franz Rosenzweig, *The Star of Redemption*, trans. Barbara E. Galli (Madison, Wisconsin: University of Wisconsin Press, 2005). See my discussion of this issue in Mara H. Benjamin, *Rosenzweig's Bible: Reinventing Scripture for Jewish Modernity* (New York: Cambridge University Press, 2009), ch. 1.

35. In *The Star of Redemption*, this single foundational commandment (*Gebot*) is that from which the commandments (*Gesetz*) spring and toward which they aspire.

36. For Levinas, the human other, not God, commands. Nonetheless, the "command" is also is a site in which the transcendent may also appear (Samuel Moyn, *Origins of the Other: Emmanuel Levinas between Revelation and Ethics* [Ithaca, NY: Cornell University Press, 2005], 240).

37. Emmanuel Levinas, *Totality and Infinity: An Essay on Exteriority*, trans. Alphonso Lingis (Pittsburgh: Duquesne University Press, 1969), 101.

38. Hermann Cohen should be thought of as exceptional here, as he argued that the religiously generative encounter involved the encounter with the person suffering the "social sin" of poverty.

39. I have not included Martin Buber here, although his concept of dyadic encounter is crucial to twentieth-century Jewish philosophy. His thought does not include obligation; he is, indeed, quite antinomian. However, he was a critical interlocutor for Rosenzweig (Rivka Horwitz, *Buber's Way to "I and Thou:" The Development of Martin Buber's Thought and His "Religion as Presence" Lectures* [New York: Jewish Publication Society, 1988]).

40. The appearance of God as infant is a familiar image in Christian religious literature.

41. That we think of children as having individual temperaments to which parents should acclimate themselves is itself a construct of our time and culture; see here, for example, David F. Lancy, *The Anthropology of Childhood: Cherubs, Chattel, Changelings*, 2nd ed. (New York: Cambridge University Press, 2014).

42. Sara Ruddick, *Maternal Thinking: Toward a Politics of Peace* (Boston: Beacon Press, 1989), 211.

43. Roger Burggraeve, "The Ethical Voice of the Child: Plea for a Chiastic Responsibility in the Footsteps of Levinas," in *Children's Voices: Children's Perspectives in Ethics, Theology and Religious Education*, ed. Annemie Dillen and Didier Pollefeyt (Leuven: Peeters, 2010), 275.

44. Rachel Bowlby extends this point by considering the multiple (at least two) actors necessary for having a child: "The model of (rational) choice, of an individual 'right to choose' in matters of childbearing, has had huge political importance but it has also the disadvantage of simplification when tied up with the real complexities of decisions to do with having or not having children ... We speak of a choice in relation to having children as if it always involved, for any one person, a single mind" (Bowlby, *A Child of One's Own*, 85–86).

45. On Buber and Rosenzweig's struggle, see esp. ch. 7 in Arnold M. Eisen, *Rethinking Modern Judaism: Ritual, Commandment, Community* (Chicago: University of Chicago Press, 1998).

46. The same is true for a person who relinquishes a child.

47. Cover, "Obligation," 66. Cover here contrasts the Sinaitic notion and modern legal assumptions of contemporary American law regarding the rational, liberal subject, and argues that each system produced its countervailing concept. We see this tension even in a figure like Kant, whose name we associate with the liberal opposition between autonomy and heteronomy, yet who understands the autonomous individual nonetheless, paradoxically, in terms of "binding oneself" to the moral law. See Immanuel Kant, Allen W. Wood, and J. B. Schneewind, *Groundwork for the Metaphysics of Morals, Rethinking the Western Tradition* (New Haven: Yale University Press, 2002).

48. See Amram Tropper, "A Tale of Two Sinais: On the Reception of the Torah According to Bavli Shabbat 88a," in *From There to Here (מהתם להכא): Rabbinic Traditions between Palestine and Babylonia*, ed. R. Nikolsky and Tal Ilan (Leiden: Brill, 2014).

49. On "bonded" as a possible meaning of "commandment," Fishbane has argued, "the vector moves from the universal whole to specific concrescences of existence ... Such a

responsive and dutiful 'joining' of heaven and earth with spiritual awareness is the core of Jewish religious praxis, of *mitzvah*, understood here fundamentally as *tzavta* (or the 'bonding' of human consciousness with Divinity)" (Fishbane, *Sacred Attunement: A Jewish Theology*, 124). I thank Jason Rubenstein for sharing his insights on this point with me.

50. Emmanuel Levinas, *Nine Talmudic Readings* (Bloomington: Indiana University Press, 1994), 37, 40. For traditional commentators on this sugya, see the discussion in Lawrence Kaplan, "Israel under the Mountain: Emmanuel Levinas on Freedom and Constraint in the Revelation of the Torah," *Modern Judaism* 18, no. 1 (1998).

51. Levinas, *Nine Talmudic Readings*, 41. The Maharal of Prague (Judah Loew, c. 1525–1609) makes a similar argument, saying, "the entire universe is dependent upon the Torah, and if the Torah did not exist, the universe would revert to chaos" (*Tiferet Yisrael* ch. 32).

CHAPTER 2

Love

The primal, visceral quality so frequently associated with maternal love has been elusive for me. I marveled at my children when I first beheld them, but the disorienting, terrifying awe gripping me did not align with my expectations of what I would feel. I expected to experience an instantaneously visceral pull toward my new infants and, when I didn't, I was distressed by the mismatch between the fantasy of maternal love and its strange reality.

In the initial weeks and months of caring for my first child, I noticed that moments of seemingly primal protectiveness came and went; the intensity of my attachment to my daughter waxed with proximity and physical contact and waned without it. Over time, some of her gestures, noises, or expressions consistently melted me; others were reliably frustrating. But as soon as I'd acclimated to her little quirks, the little person who hollered from her crib the next morning had seemingly changed, ineffably and subtly, into a slightly different creature. The curiosity, astonishment, wonder, and terror of being responsible for another human being's life did not disappear; indeed, my own sense of vulnerability grew with the baby to whom I was ever more recognizable and whom I increasingly sought out. All of this seemed quite far from the pacific constancy of motherlove I had naively anticipated.

By contrast, the love and responsibility I came to know seemed remarkably reminiscent of religious forms of praxis with which I was familiar. In Jewish theology and practice, love is active and behavioral: God loves a particular people, Israel, with special intensity, and the covenant God makes with Israel mediates this love and obligates both parties. Love, furthermore, can be commanded, and this commanded love is performative. A daily praxis of service constitutes the proper response to divine love.

Juxtaposing embodied, maternal experiences of love and biblical expressions of divine love, as I do in this chapter, illuminates both the human and the divine. God's "firstborn," Israel, occasions intense disappointment, rage, pride, vulnerability, and anguish, just as children provoke in their human mothers. But the maternal position also parallels that of the people of Israel in the covenantal relationship, for the visceral imperative to care for one's children is accompanied by a visceral imperative to love them. "Thou shalt love YHVH your God"—or, as Rosenzweig glossed it, God's command, "Love me!"—is also the cry of the infant.[1] Both sides of the covenanted relationship between God and Israel, as envisioned in scripture and rabbinic tradition, reveal aspects of maternal love, and maternal experiences, in turn, give material reality to the nature of divine love.

Love's Bonds

The connection, so common in daily life for parents, between profound love and profound disappointment, frustration, and rage, has long confounded religious philosophers in contemplating God. Divine wrath, like maternal ambivalence, seems a contradiction in terms. But the emotional intensity of maternal care-giving reveals the seamless continuity between God's affection and fury as portrayed in the Hebrew Bible.

In journals kept when her sons were small, Adrienne Rich wrote of a "murderous alternation between bitter resentment and raw-edged nerves, and blissful gratification and tenderness," of a despair and the suppressed rage that give way, at other times, to being "melted with the sense of their helpless, charming, and quite irresistible beauty, ... their staunchness and decency and unselfconsciousness."[2] Emotional whiplash, a function of intimate, daily contact, can surprise new parents with its intensity. Yet experiences in which repetitive, time-consuming, emotionally and sensorially taxing work of caring for children beget love soon become familiar to any adult responsible for his or her child's material needs and daily well-being. Love emerges within the contradictions of caring for a child. It lies in the gap between the struggle to get an exhausted, cranky child down for a nap and longing to tiptoe in to gaze on or smell him as he sleeps.

The bond of obligation, as explored in the previous chapter, brings with it a degree of "bondage," and mothers experience these volatile oscillations precisely because of that bondage. Inescapability gives the tether its tautness, its potency for every imaginable emotional register. A mother who yearns for her child's warm skin at other times recoils from being clung to or touched; a mother who shouts or spanks may immediately be consumed with regret or self-castigation; a mother seeking to shelter her helpless fledging finds instead a fully realized other whose volition and capacities are abruptly unfamiliar.[3]

An honest reckoning with the prismatic variety of experience engendered by obligation and love helps us understand the Pentateuchal God's passion for the vulnerable, dependent other to whom he is indissoluably bound.[4] The God of the Pentateuch is a character for whom love is wound up with vexation and fury: no sooner does he show tenderness for Israel than he explodes in rage; his patient care can quickly devolve into a punishing outburst when he finds his people insufficiently mindful of him. God's love is expressed in declarations and acts of protection and favor, but it is also manifested in the disappointment and indignation that result from Israel failing to make good on God's beneficence. These oscillations are evident to Israel in inexplicable graciousness and nearly indiscriminate plague, an alternation that expresses the moral ambiguity of the universe and the ambiguity of the people of Israel's experience of God.[5]

To claim that this vast affective spectrum in the theological realm is continuous with, even necessitated by, maternal love unnerves readers. As early as the second century, Marcion of Sinope (ca. 85–160 CE) claimed that the wrathful god of the "Old Testament," revered by the Jews, was a tribal "alien god" bent on severe justice. By contrast, the universal and beneficent god revealed in the writings of Paul was, Marcion argued, a different god. The Marcionite position, while officially expunged from Orthodoxy in the early church, extended its long reach into twentieth-century Protestant theology. It was given its most important modern revival when the towering German Protestant theologian Adolf von Harnack published his 1921 tome on Marcion, a work that fueled Protestant anti-Judaism.[6]

The attempt to expunge God's "wrath" or "jealousy" from an authentic account of the divine extends even into contemporary feminist theologies, giving Marcionism new life. God's capricious violence, as depicted in the Hebrew Bible, becomes isomorphic with his maleness.[7] The antidote to patriarchal domination, it is argued, is maternal pacifism.[8] But ultimately, this feminist creation of a wholly pacific God repackages the anti-Jewish theological challenge in gendered form.[9]

A a useable understanding of love cannot separate divine love from the specific nature of God's concern. God's grand gestures of caretaking are equally—perhaps even proportionately—indexed to his vicious outbursts of frustration. Both stem from the nature of the covenant and God's role in initiating it. God "conceives" and "births" a people to love, a people who will, by definition, also drive him crazy. The oscillations between these extremes are terrifying, disorienting, destabilizing for all involved—child and mother, Israel and God. Yet they are produced by the intense care that defines the relationship.

Separating love from wrath, as Marcionites ancient and modern have attempted, obscures this existential responsibility's effect on the core of the self, activating it on all affective levels. God, as portrayed by the biblical authors, cannot disengage from Israel, as much as he might want to; such is the nature of covenant. God has "bonded" with Israel and thus experiences moments of bondage as a result. This bond, unbreakable once forged, comes from a wellspring at the heart of God's being. When Israel abandons or dismisses God's gift, God's sorrow, rage, and resignation are inevitable. All of these emotions testify to the nature of covenant, which finds its earthly expression everywhere in maternal experience.

The feminist attempt to wrestle honestly with maternal experience paves the way for a more fruitful theology. The shared origin of fierce love and fierce wrath, the pleasures and anguish of intimate attachment, become comprehensible when we see them as functions of the permanent obligation that defines parenthood.

Performative Love

Maternal experience of caregiving as love illuminates God's love for Israel and Israel's response in the performance of mitzvot. Maternity offers, in this way, a corrective in a culture that defines love strictly as an involuntary emotion, as irrational and therefore radically uncontrollable.[10] While Jewish sources recognize that love includes this mysterious, uncontrollable, and unwilled dimension, they also suggest that rigorous, active practice can cultivate love.

The Torah repeatedly enjoins Israel "to love" various objects: God, the neighbor, the stranger. This commanded love is manifested in observable behavior.[11] To "love God"—especially in Deuteronomy, a text that emphasizes this idea—has a primarily practical, behavioral meaning; the command instructs the listener "to be loyal to him, to walk in his ways, to heed his mitzvot, to do them," and so on: all activities that (unlike emotion) can be commanded.[12] The command "to render love to" the neighbor and the stranger is best glossed as "'cherish,' which implies taking care, providing for a beloved object."[13] Even the adverbial form of love—in which one is described as undertaking an action "with love" (be'ahava)—does not indicate the presence of a particular emotion so much as unreserved willingness, uncoerced volition, evident in specific actions and in the alacrity with which one performs them, as Yochanan Muffs argued.[14]

Rabbinic theological anthropologies build on the Torah's behavioral orientation: acts of service are the means by which we express our love for others. The rabbis, as Jon Levenson argues, strongly tether their understanding of commanded deeds to the affective experience of love from which such deeds spring.[15] Their attention to behavioral dimensions challenges contemporary readings of love as, at its most basic, inward and affective.

Parental caregiving manifests this performative aspect of love. Most of the time, affective state is not the key factor that drives parents to attend to their children or prevents them from doing so. Primal, visceral love of one's child, as powerful as it can be, does not always (or perhaps even usually) tell a parent what to *do* vis-à-vis one's child any more than does one's equally primal frustration or rage. As in Sara Ruddick's discussion of one's preservative love characteristic of maternal thinking, the right question is not "'What did you feel?' but rather 'What did you do?'"[16] This reorientation counters romanticized, sentimentalized notions of maternal love, according to which "intuition" rather than reflection guides maternal practice. Proper human action in daily life cannot rest or fall on enthusiasm, zeal, or intensity of feeling; certainly one cannot rely on these feelings to keep a dependent creature alive. Parents execute their daily acts of diaper-changing, cleaning, and feeding their young children as an expression of their love, but child-rearing demands that acts of service continue even when parents don't want to attend to their children and when they don't feel affectionate toward them.

Likewise, the people of Israel are to perform mitzvot out of, and as the expression of, their love of God.[17] The validity of the performance does not depend on whether an individual is gripped, moment to moment, by a sense of gratitude or love of God. Instead, performance becomes a means by which action can be regulated.[18]

For the rabbis, however, mitzvot do not merely *express* love, desire, or will; they also *cultivate* proper disposition. Performing God's will, in the rabbinic imagination, leads to increased intimacy with and desire for God. This seamless vector from obligated actions to affective disposition finds its quintessential expression in the daily liturgy:

> With abundant love have you loved us, YHVH our God; with great and exceeding compassion have you cared for us. Our father, our king, for the sake of our ancestors who trusted in you, as you taught them the statutes of life, so by grace teach us. Our father, merciful father, have mercy on us by making our hearts understand, discern, learn, study, teach, keep and fulfill all the words of your Torah in love. Enlighten our eyes in your Torah and make our hearts cleave to your commandments. Unite our hearts to love and to revere your name.... You have chosen us from among all peoples and tongues; you have granted us access to your great name, to praise you and declare your unity out of love. Blessed are you, God, who chooses his people Israel with love.[19]

This prayer, called *Ahavah Rabbah* ("great love"), immediately precedes the prayer's declaration of divine sovereignty and the acceptance of the commandments (the Shema).[20] The order of the prayers makes an implicit argument: the pray-er needs a reminder of God's great love *before* she can fully accept God's sovereignty and the yoke of the commandments.

However, at the same time, performing the commandments leads to the ability to respond in love.[21] As Reuven Kimelman argues, "The Torah and the commandments serve the dual function of expressing divine love and of providing the means for its reciprocation"; rather than merely suggesting that "compliance with the commandments expresses love for God, the blessing maintains that compliance with the commandments *engenders* such love."[22] The implication, simultaneously prescriptive and aspirational, portrays the mitzvot as a program for generating positive desire.

This paradigm for the relationship between performative action and inward disposition, a staple of rabbinic anthropology, finds explicit expression in a well-known midrash. Exodus 24:7 states, "[Moses] took the book of the covenant, and read in the hearing of the people; and they said: 'All that YHVH has spoken, we will do and hearken.'" The plain sense of the text suggests that Moses read the contents aloud so that the people would know to what they had committed themselves. The midrash inverts this meaning; the order of the final words, *na'aseh venishma* ("we will do and we will understand"), suggests to the midrashic reader that Israelites leapt to agree to the covenant *before* knowing what was involved in keeping its statues: "At the moment when the Jewish people said first 'We will do' and then 'We will understand,' a heavenly voice went out and said to them, Who revealed to my children this secret, employed by the angels, as it is written, PRAISE GOD, O GOD'S ANGELS, MIGHTY IN STRENGTH, WHO DO GOD'S WILL AND UNDERSTAND GOD'S WORD" [Psalms 103:20].[23] The midrash suggests that bodily performance is a means to disciplining the heart. By naming this logics as an "angelic secret," the text acknowledges that the logic is counterintuitive; nonetheless it asserts that herein lies the devotion of Israel.[24]

Maternal activity testifies to the role of performance in generating disposition. To spend many hours caring for one's child involves activity and participation, not standing and observing from afar. Intimate, repeated caregiving actions enable us to notice the creases and folds in chubby limbs; an inventive method of scooting across the floor; the sudden, arresting appearance of a new gesture—hand on hip, arched eyebrow; the squeal of delight and fear when a dog walks by; the need to move constantly; the slowing of breath as a child releases into sleep. Time and care transform a generic person into a unique person; to "discern, learn, teach, appreciate, do, and fulfill" the commandments of Torah transform Torah into a treasured gift.

In motherwork, however, the commander and the object of commandment are not God, but an infant or young child. The results of commanded action are more complicated, and less predictable, than the rabbinic ideal—or, for that matter, any ideal—would suggest. The relationship between what we might term "inward experience" and the realm of action is often indirect and opaque, as honest appraisal of maternal subjectivity reveals. For some people, the daily, material, emotionally variable work of being responsible for another person provides the soil in which maternal love can grow, and the repetitive cycle of daily care can promote intimate attunement, pleasure, and appreciation. The attachment one feels may be thought of as "cleaving" (Deut. 13:5).

But work of attending to the other, particularly in the embodied, material acts that characterize the care of young children, can and do lead in the opposite direction as well. As in Marilyn French's novel-cum-manifesto, *The Women's Room*, the care for small children can just as easily be summed up as "shit and string beans." Rather than positing boredom, exhaustion, or resentment, as the opposite of desire and affection, I believe they are the natural companion of the positively-marked emotions.[25]

Maternal love is contingent. The presence of certain conditions promotes the desire (and ability) to care for one's child. This once-radical notion has been demonstrated, in recent decades, from all corners of the intellectual world. Second-wave feminist thinkers like Betty Friedan, Shulamith Firestone, and others argued that motherhood under patriarchy could not but produce resentment and ambivalence.[26] (If motherhood were noncompulsory, and but one possibility among many that woman might choose, motherhood, these theorists argued, might become a site of desire; if women's cultural, economical, and social options did not dictate motherhood as fate, authentic maternal love could emerge.[27]) Anthropologists and historians such as Nancy Scheper-Hughes and John Boswell investigated the contingency of maternal love in conditions of poverty and social stigma, deconstructing basic assumptions about the transhistoricity and transcultural stability of maternal love.[28] Evolutionary biologists like Sarah Blaffer Hrdy have argued that maternal love is contingent by investigating the factors that predispose adults to want to take care of children, arguing that an inborn capacity to love is activated by the activity of caregiving.[29] "Maternal instinct" and "maternal love" have, through these investigations, ceased to function as stable, timeless concepts.[30]

This contingency of maternal love must also account for the child him- or herself. Some children are simply easier to love than others; some children are easier for their particular parent or parents to love. Parents need sustenance in order for the obligatory relationship with their children to generate love for them, and children have an indirect role in giving this sustenance. Children's delightful bodies nurture parental love and affection; Cristina Traina has argued that sensual delight has a positive role in enabling parental obligation to become animated by love:

> Simple delight in another will not carry love through the moments when she [the beloved] is not so delightful, when her attractiveness dims, when someone whose good should and must be sought is not inviting to begin with, when one must love someone who cannot love back. But neither can we endure a steady diet of self-sacrifice and self-subordination for long without the regenerating energy that the reciprocity and affirmation of eros provide for us. This is certainly the case in parenting. Quick navel raspberries during diaper changes fuel many less pleasant, more drawn-out dimensions of caring: evenings with a stiff, enraged, colicky baby, or even the diaper changes themselves on occasion![31]

Moreover, a host of other structural factors must be in place for caregiving parents: material resources, emotional support, desire to mother, time to oneself. Only then do quotidian, material acts of service to one's child have the potential to promote affective experiences of desire and affection.

Rabbinic texts, as I have argued, operate with the assumption that obligated activity, even without proper motivation, promotes a desired disposition, as in a rabbinic that, loosely translated, holds that "doing things for the wrong reason leads to doing them for the right reason."[32] The rabbis understood the phenomenology of love and obligation that many mothers experience daily. But rabbinic theological anthropology does not acknowledge the broader systems without which love cannot emerge from obligation. The acknowledgment of the contingency of maternal love on factors "external" to the mother herself—including even the very activity of caregiving—offers a challenge and an opportunity for thinking about the religious meaning of commanded love.

Contingent love has typically been treated as inferior in religious thought and ethics both Christian and Jewish. Christian theological ethicists speak of this in terms of the superiority of disinterested, spontaneous, and unmotivated love (*agape*) over love that is responsive to specific qualities of the beloved (*eros*).[33] Agape, in Anders Nygren's classic definition, is "spontaneous and unmotivated" by the desire for the love-object or any deficiency in the lover; it is "indifferent" to the inherent value of the love-object but creates value in that object.[34] A rabbinic maxim expresses a similar preference for love that is "independent" of transitory qualities: "Any love that is dependent on something, when that thing perishes, the love perishes. But [a love] that is not dependent on something does not ever perish. What is a love that is dependent on something? The love of Amnon and Tamar. And a love that is not dependent on something? The love of David and Jonathan" (Pirke Avot 5:16). The rabbinic version of the hierarchy, invoking scriptural narratives rather than qualities, suggests that selfless devotion to another person is superior to erotic or sexual desire.

Maternal love includes both love "not dependent on anything," on the one hand, and love that is "contingent," on the other. It is agapeistic, in that a mother gives, often unstintingly, to her child not because she "chose" him, and not because of any particular qualities he has, but because he is hers. And once a child becomes "one's own," love of and responsibility to a child lead parents to levels of devotion they could never have imagined.

But this agapeistic quality of love, when equated with an emotional desire and pleasure in self-sacrifice, occludes a complex emotional terrain mothers traverse daily.[35] The self that strives to love her child unstintingly is a self that also experiences pride, disappointment, satisfaction, and bewilderment in her child's response to that love. Christine Gudorf, reflecting on the dynamic, responsive quality of her love for her children, writes, "With our own children we realized very clearly that though much of the early giving seemed to be solely ours, this was not disinterested, because the children were considered extensions of us, such that our efforts for them rebounded to our credit. Failure to provide for them would have discredited us. And we had expectations that the giving would become more mutual."[36] These expectations are simply built into the nature of parental love, in which fleeting moments of selflessness compose only a part of a relationship that evolves over years. Yet theological tradition, it seems, can only comprehend these dimensions of maternal love within the framework "eros."

To name maternal love as having "erotic" qualities makes us squeamish, since colloquially, eros is sexual.[37] But a number of feminist theologians in recent years have articulated an expansive meaning of the erotic that includes, and is even grounded in, God. Wendy Farley, Carter Heyward, Catherine Keller, Rita Nakashima Brock, Sally McFague, and many others have sought to rethink "the relation between carnal and spiritual, passive and active, ascending and descending, creaturely and divine love" by locating the source of eros, and erotic love, in God, also called "Divine Eros" or "the Beloved."[38] The qualities of erotic love that characterize divine concern for Israel—exclusive attention; the desire for relationship (which requires agency on the part of the beloved); the concern for the body—speak equally to caregiving parents' love of their children.[39]

But whereas many feminist theologians of eros emphasize mutuality, divine eros is much more similar to maternal love than it is to love between equals. While mutuality is a desideratum in relationships between lovers (at least for most feminists), inequality between the parties is definitional to mother/child and divine/human relationships. In both cases, the more powerful party must restrain his or her erotic desire for the less powerful party. In both cases, the lesser party cannot flourish without the asymmetry in the relationship.[40] Necessary structural inequities between parent and child, which I explore in the next chapter, limit the extent to which mutuality can usefully orient maternal love.

For Nygren and others, longing, expectation, and desire have occupied the terrain of self-interested, contingent, erotic love. God, it is claimed, lacks nothing. But biblical and rabbinic sources do not support these philosophical formulations. In the Bible, God's gracious love is not disinterested in outcome. God, like human beings, seeks out a recipient—Israel—that will acknowledge, accept, and value the gift. In Jewish liturgy, God speaks as a father to a son: "I give you good instruction, do not forsake my teaching" (Proverbs 4:2).[41] God is the parent who longs for Israel to make good on God's gracious gift. By cherishing Torah and, through its actions, serving as an exemplum to the nations of the world, Israel fulfills God's hope; when Israel forsakes Torah, God sometimes retaliates in response to the perceived rejection.

Maternal love, like divine love, is "erotic" insofar as it is responsive to particular children's specific needs and unique selfhood. Unlike agape, which is "disinterested" and given without regard to the "quality, beauty, and worth" of the object of love, parents' love for their children is supremely *interested*. The love that is nurtured in caring for a one's child is alert and attuned to that specific self, to a unique body and temperament. To note that maternal love is "interested" is not to imply that it is conditional but rather to appreciate its dynamism. Parents cannot know in advance which of a child's qualities are transitory and which are enduring, but they nonetheless watch and participate in the whole of a child's changing, embodied existence.[42] God's love for his people is maternal love amplified: dynamic, volatile, and keenly attentive.

Notes

1. Franz Rosenzweig, *The Star of Redemption*, trans. Barbara E. Galli (Madison: University of Wisconsin Press, 2005), 190–192.

2. Adrienne Rich, *Of Woman Born: Motherhood as Experience and Institution*, 10th anniversary ed. (New York: Norton, 1986 [1976]), 21–22.

3. Explorations of the theological implications of maternal violence are few. Madsen takes up a specifically gendered reading of divine violence in "Notes on God's Violence," *Cross Currents* 51, no. 2 (2001). See also a model for taking up the issue of violence—especially maternal violence—in Jewish ethics using the (rabbinic) construct of the *yetzer ha-ra*: Laurie Zoloth, "Into the Woods: Killer Mothers, Feminist Ethics, and the Problem of Evil," in *Women and Gender in Jewish Philosophy*, ed. Hava Tirosh-Samuelson (Bloomington: Indiana University Press, 2004).

4. Here and throughout, I use the male pronoun when speaking of male-gendered portraits of God in biblical and rabbinic texts.

5. For an exploration of impersonal metaphors for this moral ambiguity, see Judith Plaskow, "Wrestling with God and Evil," in *Chapters of the Heart: Jewish Women Sharing the Torah of Our Lives*, ed. Sue Elwell and Nancy Fuchs Kreimer (Eugene, OR: Wipf and Stock Publishers, 2013).

6. Adolf von Harnack, *Marcion: The Gospel of the Alien God* [Marcion: Das Evangelium vom fremden Gott, eine Monographie zur Geschichte der Grundlegung der katholischen Kirche] (Durham, NC: Labyrinth Press, 1990).

7. See especially the influential work of Carol P. Christ, "Why Women Need the Goddess," in *Womanspirit Rising: A Feminist Reader in Religion*, ed. Carol P. Christ and Judith Plaskow, Harper Forum Books (San Francisco: Harper & Row, 1979). See also the recent dialogue between feminist theologians in Judith Plaskow and Carol Christ, *Goddess and God in the World: Conversations in Embodied Theology* (Minneapolis, MN: Augsburg Fortress, 2016).

8. Madsen, "God's Violence."

9. Katharina von Kellenbach, *Anti-Judaism in Feminist Religious Writings* (Atlanta: Scholars Press, 1994).

10. This perception of feelings, while invoked as common sense among nonscholars, has been challenged in recent decades in philosophy, cognitive science, psychology, and evolutionary biology; see, for example, Jack Katz, *How Emotions Work* (Chicago: University

of Chicago Press, 2001); Allison M. Jaggar, "Love and Knowledge: Emotion in Feminist Epistemology," *Inquiry* 32, no. 2 (1989); Thomas Lewis, Fari Amini, and Richard Lannon, *A General Theory of Love* (New York: Random House, 2000).

11. Among the best recent discussions of this issue is Jon D. Levenson, *The Love of God: Divine Gift, Human Gratitude, and Mutual Faithfulness in Judaism* (Princeton, NJ: Princeton University Press, 2015).

12. William Moran, "Ancient Near Eastern Background of the Love of God in Deuteronomy," *Catholic Biblical Quarterly* 25, no. 1 (1963). On the meaning of "love" in the context of the suzerainty treaties on which the covenant between God and Israel is modeled, see Jon D. Levenson, *The Love of God* and *Sinai and Zion: An Entry into the Jewish Bible* (Minneapolis, MN: Winston Press, 1985). Other important discussions of the "political" and "emotional" dimensions of covenantal love in Deuteronomy (and the question of whether such a distinction obtains for the text itself) include Susan Ackerman, "The Personal Is Political—Covenantal and Affectionate Love ('Aheb,' Ahaba) in the Hebrew Bible," *Vetus Testamentum* 52, no. 4 (2002); Bill T. Arnold, "The Love-Fear Antinomy in Deuteronomy 5–11," *Vetus Testamentum* 61, no. 4 (2011).

13. The dative formulation underscores love as something *rendered to* another person through actions. On the dative construct of these commands to love (*'ahav l-*), see Abraham Malamat, "You Shall Love Your Neighbor as Yourself: A Case of Misinterpretation," in *Die hebräische Bibel und ihre zweifache Nachgeschichte: Festschrift Für Rolf Rendtorff zum 65. Geburtstag*, ed. Erhard Blum, Chrsitian Macholz, and Ekkehard Stegemann (Neukirchen-Vluyn: Neukirchener, 1990); Paul Mendes-Flohr, *Love, Accusative and Dative: Reflections on Leviticus 19:18* (Syracuse, NY: Syracuse University Press, 2007). On "cherish" as a translation, see Mary Douglas, *Leviticus as Literature* (New York: Oxford University Press, 1999), 42–43.

14. Yochanan Muffs, *Love and Joy: Law, Language, and Religion in Ancient Israel* (New York: Jewish Theological Seminary of America, 1992).

15. Levenson, *The Love of God.*

16. Sara Ruddick, *Maternal Thinking: Toward a Politics of Peace* (Boston: Beacon Press, 1989), 70.

17. As Heschel notes, Rabbi Ishmael's school believed that love was an unruly emotion in need of discipline; in R. Ishmael's words, "Love can engender a frenzy that will lead one from the straight path"; therefore "to love God and to cleave to him mean to perform worthy deeds, to walk in his ways" (Abraham Joshua Heschel, *Heavenly Torah: As Refracted through the Generations*, trans. Gordon Tucker [New York: Continuum, 2005], 200, 194.). See also Ishay Rosen-Zvi, *Demonic Desires: Yetzer Hara and the Problem of Evil in Late Antiquity* (Philadelphia: University of Pennsylvania Press, 2011).

18. Ruddick, *Maternal Thinking*, 70.

19. This formulation reflects the morning, rather than the evening, version of this prayer. See bBerakhot 11b-12a for discussion of the order of the liturgy, in which *'ahavah rabbah* is recited before the Shema.

20. Trans. Reuven Kimelman, "The Shema' Liturgy: From Covenant Ceremony to Coronation," *Kenishta: Studies of the Synagogue World* 1 (2001): 40–41.

21. Kimelman, "The Shema' Liturgy," 50.

22. Kimelman, "The Shema' Liturgy," 50–51. My ital. See also Levenson, *The Love of God*, 31–32.

23. bShabbat 88a and elsewhere. A number of medieval commentators understand the verse in its more obvious sense: "Moses read out the contents so that the people would know what they had committed themselves to. Only by knowing the contents would they be prevented from violating the commandments inadvertently" (Seforno, ad loc. Ex. 24:7).

24. The attention to performance in religious studies has blossomed in recent decades, building on Foucault and others. For example, see Talal Asad, *Genealogies of Religion: Discipline and Reasons of Power in Christianity and Islam* (Baltimore, MD: Johns Hopkins

University Press, 1993); Adam Seligman et al., *Ritual and Its Consequences: An Essay on the Limits of Sincerity* (New York: Oxford University Press, 2008); Saba Mahmood, *Politics of Piety: The Islamic Revival and the Feminist Subject* (Princeton, NJ: Princeton University Press, 2005).

25. Marilyn French, *The Women's Room* (New York: Summit Books, 1977). In the novel, French holds patriarchy accountable for the main character's isolation, alienation, and oppression in motherhood. The implied solution is liberation from motherhood. This solution, however, cannot help us reckon with the fact that even "freely-chosen," empowered experiences of child-rearing nonetheless involve repetitive, and often unpleasant, tasks which caregivers often find burdensome.

26. Shulamith Firestone, *The Dialectic of Sex: The Case for Feminist Revolution* (New York: Morrow, 1970); Betty Friedan, *The Feminine Mystique* (New York: Norton, 1963). Among second-wave feminists, many white theorists argued that resentment, pent-up fury, and disempowerment arose from motherhood as fate. The solution was, for some, the rejection of motherhood entirely; for others, it was the liberation of women only from the imposition of motherhood. Many black feminists argued, by contrast, that the power to choose motherhood and to nurture their own children had been robbed from black women in the United States, and therefore sought to legitimize the desire for noncoerced, non-surrogate motherhood (Patricia Hill Collins, "Shifting the Center: Race, Class, and Feminist Theorizing About Motherhood," in *Representations of Motherhood*, ed. Donna Bassin, Margaret Honey, and Meryle Mahrer Kaplan [New Haven, CT: Yale University Press, 1994]).

27. Rich, *Of Woman Born*.

28. Nancy Scheper-Hughes, *Death without Weeping: The Violence of Everyday Life in Brazil* (Berkeley: University of California Press, 1992); John Boswell, *The Kindness of Strangers: The Abandonment of Children in Western Europe from Late Antiquity to the Renaissance* (New York: Pantheon Books, 1988). The most influential study in this vein was Philippe Ariès, *Centuries of Childhood: A Social History of Family Life*, trans. Robert Baldick (New York: Vintage Books, 1962). Many of his conclusions were challenged and overturned by later historical studies, but his work was foundational in that it argued that childhood itself has a history.

29. "If [the mother] allows it to happen, close contact with this baby does indeed transform her mindset and produces in her a need to be close to her baby, a need to smell her baby that, for some women (true in my case), borders on addiction. Whether or not this constitutes a gift given—and reciprocated—or bondage depends on what else a mother wants to be doing and who is there to help." Many mechanisms of a biological "conspiracy"—oxytocin, babies' fatness, etc.—are involved to make babies "infant[s] worth caring for" (Sarah Blaffer Hrdy, *Mother Nature: A History of Mothers, Infants, and Natural Selection* [New York: Pantheon Books, 1999], 536ff.; Lewis, Amini, and Lannon, *A General Theory of Love*.).

30. Elisabeth Badinter, *Mother Love, Myth and Reality: Motherhood in Modern History* (New York: Macmillan, 1981).

31. Cristina L. H. Traina, *Erotic Attunement: Parenthood and the Ethics of Sensuality between Unequals* (Chicago: University of Chicago Press, 2011), 211. For other writers on the erotic appeal of children, see Dorothy Dinnerstein, *The Mermaid and the Minotaur: Sexual Arrangements and Human Malaise* (New York: Harper & Row, 1976); Noelle Oxenhandler, *The Eros of Parenthood: Explorations in Light and Dark* (New York: St. Martin's Press, 2001).

32. *Mitoch shelo lishma ba lishma*: literally, "out of not-for-its-own-sake comes for-its-own-sake" (bPesachim 50b).

33. Feminist critique of the concept of selfhood nourished by Nygren's framework goes to the heart of feminist theology and ethics, starting as early as Valerie Saiving Goldstein, "The Human Situation: A Feminine View," *The Journal of Religion* 40, no. 2 (1960). Explicit feminist

engagement with and critique of Nygren and others' basic assumptions about the relative merits of different kinds of love is voluminous. A few key sources include Barbara Hilkert Andolsen, "Agape in Feminist Ethics," in *Feminist Theological Ethics: A Reader*, ed. Lois K. Daly and Margaret A. Farley (Louisville, KY: Westminster John Knox Press, 1994); Susan Frank Parsons, *Feminism and Christian Ethics*, New Studies in Christian Ethics (Cambridge: Cambridge University Press, 1996); Darlene Fozard Weaver, *Self Love and Christian Ethics* (New York: Cambridge University Press, 2002); Lisa Sowle Cahill, *Sex, Gender, and Christian Ethics* (New York: Cambridge University Press, 1996).

34. Anders Nygren, *Agape and Eros*, trans. Philip Watson (Philadelphia: Westminster Press, 1953).

35. Some of these tendencies—and the feminist rejection of them—are especially pronounced in Christian theological-ethical discourse. See Pope John Paul II's characterization of Mary's love for her son as "'self-offering,' 'limitless,' and 'tireless'" love, and therefore paradigmatic of maternal love as a whole (Irene Oh, "Motherhood in Christianity and Islam: Critiques, Realities, and Possibilities," *Journal of Religious Ethics* 38, no. 4 (2010): 639). The self-sacrificial element of maternal love here and elsewhere embodies a feminized ideal of *imitatio christi*. As Traina argues, "contemporary American culture['s] … moral, juridical vision of parenthood is taken directly from Nygren's agape" (Traina, *Erotic Attunement*, 191). Hence feminist Christian theologians often argue for correctives precisely on this point, for example: "'[M]othering' involves a lot more than loving. There is much in my experience of mothering that is more informative about the nature of resentment, or boredom, or the panic of being trapped, than about love … it is not the experience of *mothering* per se that offers a model for agape but only the mother-love which in my case undergirds the practice and explodes with intensity and clarity only sporadically in the midst of so much else" (Sally Purvis, "Mothers, Neighbors, and Strangers: Another Look at Agape," *Journal of Feminist Studies in Religion* 7, no. 1 (1991): 25).

36. Christine E. Gudorf, "Parenting, Mutual Love, and Sacrifice," in *Women's Consciousness and Women's Conscience: A Reader in Feminist Ethics*, ed. Barbara Hilkert Andolsen, Christine E. Gudorf and Mary D. Pellauer (San Francisco: Harper & Row, 1985), 181.

37. Oxenhandler, *The Eros of Parenthood*; Traina, *Erotic Attunement*.

38. Virginia Burrus and Catherine Keller, *Toward a Theology of Eros: Transfiguring Passion at the Limits of Discipline* (New York: Fordham University Press, 2006), xv.

39. See Traina, *Erotic Attunement*, 196–197.

40. As Bonnie Miller-McLemore has argued, "Children owe parents a great deal, what Jewish tradition describes as honor and respect. But they do not owe parents what parents have given them; they could not give such a thing if they tried, nor would most parents desire this" (Bonnie J. Miller-McLemore, "Feminism, Children, and Mothering: Three Books and Three Children Later," *Journal of Childhood and Religion* 2, no. 1 (2011): 23–24).

41. The statement in Proverbs is not attributed to God. But in Jewish liturgy, this verse is used to accompany the return of the Torah scroll to the ark, and worshippers implicitly perform a shift in attribution.

42. As Soskice notes, what Iris Murdoch called attentive love is paradoxical in that it involves attention to the particularity of the individual before us. Young children, who are at each moment in the process of becoming who they are, require an especially "attentive gaze," for it is a "gaze on a changing reality" (Janet Martin Soskice, *The Kindness of God: Metaphor, Gender, and Religious Language* [New York: Oxford University Press, 2007], 32).

CHAPTER 3

Power

In the previous chapter, I argued that love, in its maternal and divine expressions, is continuous with rage, frustration, and disappointment. When love is understood in terms of profound concern and acts of care, then a greater spectrum of genuine emotional registers becomes more comprehensible. This more expansive affective range within intimate relationships characterizes both the relationship between God and Israel and the everyday oscillations familiar to parents of small children.

In this chapter, I examine the analogous manifestations of power in the relationships between mothers and children and between God and Israel. Both relationships are simultaneously intimate and structurally asymmetrical. In explicating the position of parents in relationship to their children, I investigate the theological implications of aspects of power that parents must negotiate simultaneously. At any moment, a parent holds "power over" her child or children; seeks to empower her child; contends with her child's resistance to her power; and is subject to her child's own power and those of other adults and broader social structures. Accounting for the complex, sometimes paradoxical, manifestations of power between parents and children—and between God and Israel—requires reengaging feminist theories of power.

Divine Power, Maternal Power

Divine power in its most explicit biblical expression can be wrenching to behold:

> YHVH saw how great was the human being's wickedness on earth, and how every plan devised by his mind was nothing but evil all the time. And YHVH regretted that he had made man on earth, and his heart was saddened. YHVH said, "I will blot out from the earth the men whom I created—men together with beasts, creeping things, and birds of the sky; for I regret that I made them" [Gen. 6:5–7]. . . .

Then YHVH sent a plague upon the people, for what they did with the calf that Aaron made [Ex. 32:35]....

YHVH said to Moses, "Say to the Israelite people, 'You are a stiffnecked people. If I were to go in your midst for one moment, I would destroy you. Now, then, leave off your finery, and I will consider what to do to you.'" [Ex. 33:5]....

How long will this people spurn me, and how long will they have no faith in me despite all the signs that I have performed in their midst? I will strike them with pestilence and disown them.... [Num. 14:11].

God enacts his displeasure on the people who are subject to him—sometimes rashly, sometimes reflectively—with a capacity for destruction that far exceeds that of Israel.

In asserting God's absolute goodness and justice, and in making those attributes crucial to the moral vision of the Bible, centuries of theologians have set themselves up to face a serious quandary when encountering such passages: either read God's violence as the mere "collateral damage" of a just god or find convenient refuge in a tacit Marcionism. These choices result in a containment of God's power to bring plague and destruction, rather than a reckoning with this power as part of divine nature. Many recent constructive feminist theologians have also avoided or rejected God's overt expressions of power.[1] Few substantive theological engagements with God's parental and especially maternal power, including its less attractive aspects, exist.[2]

A more fully realized understanding of parental power offers rewards to Jewish theologians, and feminist theologians in particular. To date, erotic or companionate relationships have offered feminist theologians a model for how the relationship between God and individuals, or God and Israel, may be envisioned. Egalitarian distributions of power between two adults have helped theologians rework earlier metaphors that accepted power imbalance as part of heterosexual partnership. As important as this work has been, I argue in this chapter that parent/child relationships offer feminist theologians something we cannot accept in companionate relationships: a structural asymmetry in power that is both necessary and beneficial for both parties. Examining the imbalance of power between adults and children in the context of childrearing helps feminists grapple with structural asymmetries that apply both to human experience and to the human relationship with God.

The parallels between divine power and maternal power are manifest not only in the asymmetrical power relation between the two parties but also in the response of the less powerful party to the violence sometimes inflicted on them. What theologians call God's "justice"—and what parents call punishment or consequence—is, from the point of view of those on its receiving end, often experienced as excessive or simply capricious:

Far be it from you to do such a thing, to bring death upon the innocent as well as the guilty, so that innocent and guilty fare alike. Far be it from you!

[Gen. 18:25]... *When the people heard this harsh word, they went into mourning, and none put on his finery* [Ex. 33:4].... *The whole community broke into loud cries, and the people wept that night* [Num. 14:1].... *Look about and see: Is there any agony like mine, Which was dealt out to me when YHVH afflicted me on his day of wrath?* [Lam. 1:12].

Just like the people of Israel, children often perceive the expression of their parents' disapproval as unjust or cruel, whether it be in the denial of something desired, the withholding of approval, yelling, humiliation, or a swift spank.

Readers of Torah are predisposed to identify with Israel, with its laments and protestations against what the divine parent rationalizes as just punishment. By contrast, to inhabit the complicated territory of actual (rather than projected) parental experience is to partake in the audacious work of imagining the challenges God faces, many of which are clearly recounted in Torah. To be a parent is, in some sense, to *be* a child's "God." Reading God and Israel in terms of the mother/child relationship and vice versa helps us address the sometimes catastrophic effects of our power over our children and the vulnerability that accompanies that power.

In order to make claims about the theological and ethical challenges these dynamics present, I concentrate on certain common features of these relationships, largely leaving aside specific social structures that affect power distribution in parent/child relationships. For instance, immigrant parents relying on their children as interpreters may experience an uncomfortable inversion of the "natural order" of power and authority. Physically disabled adults who cannot exercise some forms of bodily power may formulate the role of physical power in childrearing quite differently than I do here. And parents rearing children with severe developmental or physical needs and who cannot expect that their children to become self-sufficient adults may depart from my conclusions at certain points.[3]

In addition, I do not index my discussion to issues of class, race, or other intersectional elements of social location beyond gender. Race and class, perhaps the two most important indices of privilege or marginalization in contemporary America, shape individual realities and are rightly understood as critical to understanding how power is manifested, undermined, and resisted in quotidian life.[4] Parents in poverty face structural powerlessness that wealthy, upper-middle-class, and middle-class parents do not.[5] Even the most economically privileged parents of African American children has good reason to fear that their children will be subject to disproportionate injustice and violence relative to parents of white children in the United States.[6] I attend throughout this chapter to some of the ways my claims require specific attention to social location, laying groundwork for further exploration from different vantage points.

My focus here concerns a different plane of power. I foreground what occurs between parents, especially mothers, and children in order to navigate under-explored theological and ethical terrain. Unevenly distributed social and political power operates *concurrently* with power dynamics embedded in parent and child relations. Parents who are subject to disenfranchisement and diminution of power nonetheless constantly exercise power in relationship to their children: in employing strategies to ensure a child's compliance with a directive, in presenting and setting limits on possibilities, by enabling a child to discover his own capabilities or prevent him from doing so, by channeling, opposing, or redirecting a child's will. And children, no matter how constrained, exercise power as well.

Contending with Bodily Power

In parenting, adults inhabit the superordinate, rather than the subordinate, position in an asymmetrical relationship. This power takes many forms, from the fact of greater strength and relative height to more subtle deployments of one's body and the power of psychological influence communicated by bodily means.

Able-bodied adults access a physical power that they can wield over small children. The ordinary, nonviolent aspects of greater physical power are experientially central to parental experience. We typically focus on violent or "aberrant" expressions of parents' greater physical power, such as mothers who murder or abuse their children. Less frequently do we inquire into common forms of physical power parents exercise over their children, but the ubiquity of these moderate expressions of bodily power over one's child invite examination.

Parents deploy their physical advantages over their children all the time: in the supermarket; at bedtime; when trying to get to an appointment on time; in saying goodbye to a sad or angry toddler who clutches at one's legs. The parent can walk out the door, put the Froot Loops out of reach, strap a screaming child into a stroller. The child cannot do the same to the parent. Both parties rely on this structural asymmetry, which reassures children that their most violent or greedy wishes will not break the structure that contains them.[7]

Parents, by contrast, have no such knowledge: they must rely on themselves and social context to modulate their power, whether in moments of extreme rage or in the ordinary negotiations of getting to and from the laundromat with a preschooler. The everyday, socially acceptable uses of physical advantage may cross over into the realm of violence. Ta-Nehisi Coates recalls slipping out of his parents' sight at a playground in Baltimore at age six, and the role of parental violence in learning the meaning of being a black male in America: "When they found me, Dad did what every parent I knew would have done—he reached for his belt. I remember watching him in a kind of daze, awed at the distance between punishment and offense. Later, I would hear it in Dad's voice—'Either I can beat him, or the police.' Maybe that saved me. Maybe it didn't. All I know is, the violence rose from the fear like smoke from a fire, and I cannot say whether that violence, even administered in fear and love, sounded the alarm or choked us at the exit."[8] Coates's father understood his own use of physical force against his son to be necessary for the sake of preserving his young child in the world. Upon reaching adulthood, that son rejected administering this violence to his own child. Although the outcomes were different for Coates and his father, both parents made deliberative decisions involving calculation, strategy, and hope. These decisions shed light on the complicated subjectivity of the more powerful party—especially when this subjectivity includes being structurally disempowered.

The responsibility inherent in occupying a position of relative strength can be both comforting and terrifying, especially for those unaccustomed to having it. Motherhood may be the one sphere in which a woman inhabits a superordinate position of power in interpersonal encounters. Knowledge of this power is a *sine qua non* of parental experience: "Even the most powerless woman knows that she is physically powerful, stronger than her young children. This, along with undeniable psychological power, gives her the resources to control her children's behavior and influence their perceptions. If a mother didn't have this control, her life would be unbearable."[9] The knowledge of this greater strength is a mother's bulwark against the "war of all against all" that might otherwise unfold. But the knowledge of one's capacity to deploy one's strength can just as easily frighten caregiving parents with its capacity to overwhelm their restraint.[10]

In this sense, maternal violence is the more overt and extreme exercise of a latent potential. Few parents actually annihilate their children, but even the most loving and pacific parents immersed in the daily tasks of life with their young children sometimes wish to annihilate them: to smother a screaming infant, to shake a noncompliant child. In these common, if disturbing, experiences for parents, the asymmetry is clear: when adults teach children not to bite or hit, they do so in conformity with a social convention; when parents restrain themselves from doing so, they do so knowing that they have the capacity to inflict serious harm or cause death.[11]

Power operates not only on the evident level of physical strength but also in the subtle organization of parental authority that is constantly asserted, resisted, and renegotiated. In many cases, it is difficult to disentangle physical power from other uses of the body that are intertwined with what we might call psychological power, such as the refusal to acknowledge a child or the use of a tone of voice that conveys threat, encouragement, interest, or disdain. In this sense, the power operative in intimate negotiations between parents and children bring to mind those Foucault has documented in the complex work of the modern prison, medicine, and other important loci of "power/knowledge."[12] The mere acts of meeting a child's gaze or refusing to do so are techniques of the body that rely on and reinforce a parent's authority.

But by the same token, physical power is not one-sided. To continue with Foucault's logic, the "less powerful" party in any encounter can contest the power of the "more powerful" party. The daily work of raising a child makes clear that even very young children use their bodies to assert their will. Much of the time parents experience this power as resistance: children stiffen or let their bodies go limp; they refuse to move; they cry, scream, or shout in protest. Young children's physical power is not as reliably effective as adults' in terms of sheer force, and their power does not always effect the desired outcome. But, as anyone who has tolerated his child's tantrum in a public place can attest, children can very successfully resist, evade, and (later) reason with their parents—all strategies for asserting their authority.[13]

Children exert their power not only in resistance to their parents' desires, but also as resourceful creative agents themselves: they employ the "disadvantage" of smallness into the ability to hide. They take objects adults recognize for one purpose and transform them into another: a ring of keys becomes a mesmerizing noisemaker; a cleaning cloth becomes a cape; a tree branch becomes a wand, an imaginary dog's leash, or a sword. Such assertions of creative force and children's capacity to remake their material worlds can be delightful; they can be confounding, as well, when they frustrate adult plans.

The common-sense notion that parents "hold more power" than their children is therefore a partial truth. While there are certainly many seemingly obvious ways in which parents have greater capacities and more resources to impose their desires on their children than do their children on them, parental power has considerably more nuance. It is not simply the raw imposition of will—after all, this form of power, for parents, is rarely employed explicitly. Parental power works within a set of constraints that already shape the will of both parent and child. Parental will is constrained by circumstances, including the circumstance of having and loving a child. It is, finally, constrained by the power that children exert as well.

Domination, Collaboration, Empowerment: Dimensions of Parental and Divine Power

The intrinsically contradictory nature of parental power lies in parents' occupation of two conflicting roles with regard to their children. First, parents must navigate and modulate their own bodily expressions of their power, often in response to extravagant resistance on the part of their children. At those moments, parents confront their children as *opposing* powers whom they may want or need to control.

But at the same time, parents generally recognize (intuitively or reflectively) that children need to learn how to cultivate, manage, and channel their *own* power, and that, as parents, they must aid that process. In this sense, parents exert a very different kind of power: that which facilitates or impedes the work children do to become conscious agents. This element of parental caregiving distinguishes it most sharply from other kinds of caregiving and thus from other kinds of power. This double stance, both components of which inherently belong to contemporary parental practice, complicates some of the most basic assumptions that govern feminist engagements with power, including both general philosophical treatments of power and, specifically, theological extensions of those discussions.

Many feminist theorists are critical of theoretical models in which power is defined as the ability to compel another person to do what he or she wishes despite resistance.[14] However, such a conception is foundational to twentieth-century social theory, from Max Weber to Foucault. This paradigm holds that power is exercised in situations of conflicting wills. Struggle is the theater in which we come to know what power is, and its force is measured by the capacity to coerce.[15]

This view of power, recognized by feminist theorists as linked to the subjugation of women, colonized peoples, and the environment, has been the object of social and theological critique. Diverse feminist theologians argued that models of power as domination are not limited to interpersonal relationships; they characterize how the God of the Bible and theology has too often been conceived. The claim that divine power legitimates and mirrors male rule became a fixture of feminist intervention, following Mary Daly's famous axiom, "If God in 'his' heaven is a father ruling 'his' people, then it is in the nature of things and according to divine plan and the order of the universe that society be male dominated."[16] In the wake of analyses that built on Daly's argument, a generation of feminist theologians exposed the links between gender and the models of power that, they argued, organized both traditional society and theology.

This analysis of patriarchal power brought attention to the deleterious effects of hierarchical power for women and other subjugated groups and marked the effort to redefine power as part of a feminist theological project. In contrast to patriarchal models that conceive of power as domination, feminist theorists offered alternative models of power as capacity and ability, sometimes referred to as "power-with," "power-from-within," or "power-to," rather than "power-over." Such proposals reimagined the possibilities inherent in relationships of asymmetrical power by speaking of power as that which facilitates transformation through empowering others. But the problems posed by *inherently* unequal relationships were largely overlooked. Instead, appeals to collaboration and mutuality became central, as if the only relationships worth addressing were those between social equals. A conversation coalesced in which the focal point became greater egalitarianism and mutuality in interpersonal relationships.

Many feminist theologians drew on Audre Lorde's essay, "The Erotic as Power" to link this vision of mutuality to a sexual/sensual expression of pleasure, on the one hand, and the social-political work of "sharing deeply any pursuit with another person" on the other.[17] The energy of collaboration, Lorde argued, represents a form of power that opposes the powerlessness embodied in "resignation, despair, self-effacement, depression, denial."[18] As Kathleen Sands observed, the claim that "erotic satisfaction provides a vision and a motive force by which to build the world women desire" became self-evident and Lorde's essay "virtually canonical."[19]

Christian and Jewish feminists drew on Lorde's essay to explore alternative expressions of power in mutuality. Christian feminists resuscitated eros as a theological category and reclaimed mutuality for theology. Beverly Wildung Harrison's orienting claim for this literature that "mutual love ... is love in its deepest radicality" guided theologians to focus on adult sexual relationships, where mutuality was most needed.[20] Jewish feminist theologians likewise built on Lorde's understanding of eros as creative energy. Like their Christian feminist counterparts, they sought to counter the constraints of patriarchal appropriations of sexuality, putting forth a vision in which "right relations in the moral universe moderns inhabit are characterized by reciprocity, mutuality, tenderness, and equal power."[21]

In these discussions, asymmetrical relationships figure as a deviation from the desired norm of mutuality and equality.[22] The feminist ideal of mutuality between human lovers, in turn, anchors a reimagining of the relationship between people and God. But in the swift move from erotic mutuality to a reconstructed theology informed by egalitarianism, interpersonal relationships in which mutuality is *not* an appropriate goal have been largely overlooked.[23] In some human relationships of deep care and affection—especially those between parents and children—asymmetry in power is not only fact but also necessity.

This greater power, and even the capacity to wield "power over" one's child, cannot be extirpated from the work of parenting itself, a point that some feminist theorists of maternity have failed to acknowledge. In arguing that "the power of a mothering person to empower others, to foster transformative growth, is a different sort of power from that of a stronger sword or a dominant will," we see this temptation to expunge all elements of coercion from maternal power.[24] But an honest conception of maternal power must wrestle with power understood both as something asserted in conflict and resistance *and* as the capacity to facilitate or prevent another person's discovery of her own capabilities. For children, these two forms of power may be intertwined: children resist parental control and in so doing discover their own strengths and capabilities. For parents, the felt contradiction between these two modes of power may be quite stark. Yet neither can be completely expunged from the work of parenting.

Feminist attempts to extirpate power-over from adult interpersonal relationships require supplementation if we are to formulate usable feminist analyses of parenting. Feminist work on power in mutuality provides *indirect* guidance, however, for the project of theorizing relationships of differential power. In Lorde's model of power, for instance, power is realized most fully in the joy of collaboration, or in relationships that have the potential for true mutuality, such as egalitarian, companionate partnership. This ideal can orient parents in their hopes for what their children will experience or realize as adults. In addition, feminist ideals of mutuality can help parents articulate their delight in moments of true collaboration with their children. Such moments may include the pride of accomplishment a parent may feel when a child masters a difficult skill in which the parent had a role as a teacher (a pride that often is shared with the child herself), be it a good latch during nursing or in a game of peek-a-boo, when parent and child are in sync. These experiences of collaboration play an important role in sustaining a parent's commitment to and enjoyment of his children.[25]

But for most parents who are truly "in the trenches" of caring for their children, moments of collaboration are nestled within many more conflictual or at best neutral interactions. The possibility of recognizing and enjoying collaborative moments depends in part on the temperaments of both parties and on a parent having sufficient time and attention to allow a child to co-determine activity together. But caregiving parents are also enforcers of responsibilities that children would often rather ignore. Most days are necessarily composed of the clashing of wills, not only of their alignment. Even if a parent can turn bedtime into a playful moment rather than a power struggle, the playful collaboration nonetheless takes place within a broader framework in which parents ultimately set and enforce boundaries. The ability to approach boundary-setting collaboratively rather than with authoritarian control depends on having sufficient reserves of patience, energy, and support, which many parents go without. At many moments, neither parents nor their children have the wherewithal, the time, the skills, or the imagination to collaborate.

Recognizing the obstacles that impede collaboration and the intrinsic pressures that often prevent the harmonious alignment of wills helps us avoid fetishizing collaboration. The imperative to avoid this temptation is especially necessary when considering maternity. For even feminist theology and care ethics tend to claim joyful experiences of collaboration between mother and child as the norm.[26] The danger of creating a sentimental, unrealistic portrayal of parental power in which we recognize only the positive valences of collaboration and mutuality and grant them privileged ontological status, does a disservice to the task of theorizing from actual experience. The recalibration I propose includes mutuality and collaboration but does not raise them to normative status.

The electric thrill of true collaboration is as elusive in our encounter with God as in our encounter with our children. Even in Song of Songs, the great scriptural testament to mutual desire the rabbis read as an allegory for the relationship between God and Israel, mutuality is tenuous and ephemeral; moments of attunement exist within a framework in which, most of the time, one party fails to make contact with the other.[27] The beloved Shulamite is not ready for, and is even resistant to, the lover when he knocks on the door (Song 5:2–6). The larger setting of patriarchal control prevents and disrupts the lovers' ability to meet each other literally and figuratively (Song 3:1–4, 5:7). Israel is not ready to meet God; God seeks out Israel to no avail. Rare indeed are the encounters in which perfect symmetry occur. Between God and Israel and between mother and child, synchronicity is hard to come by. And unlike an egalitarian arrangement between lovers, collaboration in these cases cannot escape the lopsided balance of power between the two parties.

However, the privileged place of empowerment in feminist theories of power does offers an instructive addition to the project of mapping parental power. Most parents today believe that they must help their children recognize and develop their own capacities: children need help in order to develop the myriad practical and emotional skills that will enable them to manage life by themselves, and parents promote their children's growth through active assistance and tactical restraint. This work depends on parents' ability to assess their children's capabilities. Some estimations are relatively easy to make: parents usually know that their toddlers can't tie shoelaces and that children's social skills do not emerge fully formed. But the capacities and limits of one's child, on which any possibility of "empowerment" rests, are far from self-evident, even to the closest of observers. It is often not clear whether a child would benefit from being pushed beyond her comfort zone or from developing greater comfort in a specific skill. Parents push and fail to push their children in the wrong ways all the time, discovering their errors only after the fact and demanding of their children capacities that arise from their own needs. Discovery of what a child can or can't do comes about indirectly, through exigency and miscalculation. Inevitably, parents miss the mark. The inescapability of failure lends parenting a dimension of tragedy.[28]

Parental failures become occasions for both positive growth and for calamity.[29] Parents cannot escape risk, conflict, failure, limitation, and loss that accompany their sojourn through childrearing. To apply feminist models of power-as-empowerment to parenting requires grappling with the loss inherent in the work of empowering one's child. Among the most trenchant cultural understandings we hold about child-rearing is that "successful" parenting is, in the end, self-effacing: it is the paradoxical project of pouring vast reserves of time and attention into someone whose *telos* is to live, or to be able to live, without the parents themselves. Each small achievement of independence, therefore, points toward the death of the parent.[30] Some parents rejoice at each step their children take toward independence, at which time a child can respond to her parents out of desire rather than need (or can just leave them alone). But for many parents, the experience of having "succeeded" in parenting is tinged with poignancy, as they recognize they are no longer needed as they once were.

The theological analogue of this parental work breaks down when we return to biblical texts. The prophets hope for the day when Israel will fully inhabit her covenanted, but subservient, position vis-à-vis God. God does not want Israel to attain self-sufficiency. Independence is not the goal.

But recognition of the ambivalent feelings associated with the maturation of one's dependent other informs midrashic texts. Images of God as a bereft parent characterize the rabbinic understanding of God's inability directly to influence his people: "From the time He leaves the Temple, God finds himself hopelessly trapped in the pathos of human existence, and precisely in the most mortal shapes of that existence: in grief, failure, frailty, senectitude, the presentiment of death."[31] In Lamentations Rabbah, God "likens himself to a man who built a wedding-chamber for his only son, only to have the son die inside the chamber."[32] When God weeps for Israel's suffering at the destruction of the Temple, he experiences the pain of the caretaking parent, even if his suffering, in the rabbinic imagination, is self-inflicted. When God laughs in the famous story of the oven of 'Akhnai (bBaba Metzia 59a-b), it is with explicit reference to his sons besting him. That these images of a God consistently use a male economy—God the father, Israel the son—should not obscure for us the rabbis' dramatization of God's loss and triumph.[33] God reacts as a parent whose love intensifies the pain of being unable to protect her child, and whose delight in the child's successes can be only partially claimed for herself.

Parents, Children, and Existential Power

Beyond the material and physical assertions of will by both adults and children lies a vast territory of non-agentic power. In addition to power-over (domination) and power-with (collaboration) in parent/child relationships, both parties have profound capacity for exerting existential power, that is, the power to shape another person's consciousness. The capacity for children to mark their parents, and not only parents to shape their children, highlights the role of vulnerability in speaking about both directions of power across the asymmetrical relationship.

Contemporary Western parents understand themselves to exercise a profound power to touch children's most primal level of being. This seemingly abstract concept of existential power manifests practically in daily interactions between parents and children, especially in young children, whom we recognize as particularly vulnerable and porous.[34] We see infants turn to their parents' gaze for affirmation of their own existence and the worth of their activity; we recognize how a parent's response to a child's injury shapes the child's experience of his own pain. Recognition of the profound existential power a parent wields often becomes the cudgel with which to berate parents, especially mothers, or to educate them into the mores of middle-class parental ideals. I highlight existential power, by contrast, to call attention to the inevitability of parental failure in this realm as well. Parents are enmeshed in complex webs of responsibility as part of their own subjecthood, and are drawn into the world as whole selves and not only as parents. Inevitably, many encounters, even with the people parents love most in the world, are not "I-Thou" but rather "I-It," such as when a child in vain seeks out his parent's gaze.

Children's vulnerability confers on parents a complicated, ambiguous, and sometimes tragic power, since they and their children often live in situations that are unjust, and thus parents perforce mediate a world of oppression and conflict to their children. The marks of parents' daily experiences of power on their children include interactions in which a child witnesses disempowerment: a parent arrives at the checkout line without enough cash or food stamps to pay for the groceries, she is mocked by a homophobic slur, he becomes distressed when lost in a new city. The parent who feels the sting of humiliation at the hands of others may respond not in beatific calm but with fury or despair, and from this a child learns as well. These episodes of humiliation or disempowerment, and the parent's response to them, shape a child's understanding of the parent's power (and, consequently, his own).[35]

Parents are not in control of the traces they leave on their children, nor of the formative structures they help develop in them. The nonagentic dimension of this power underscores the need for a broader framework within which finite actors act in the world. This recognition, in other words, underscores the appropriateness of a theological vocabulary in which we can articulate the moral ambiguity and the surplus of meaning produced by our activity.

Likewise, children also command an ambiguous, nonagentic power to profoundly reshape their parents' interior and external environments. Parents find themselves subject to a love that they could not have imagined, which renders them newly vulnerable: they are now tied by bonds of love to a creature they did not choose, whom indeed they could not have chosen, but who now claims them. In principle, this experience of vulnerability is part of any loving relationship. But the parent's power and responsibility for a child lends this vulnerability its particular vitality and agony. To hold direct responsibility for the well-being of a child's body, and to be entrusted with a critical role in caring for that child's being is to be uniquely, existentially wrapped up and deeply implicated in him.

Some theorists, like John Wall, have concluded that recognition of children's vulnerability should help us understand vulnerability as basic aspect of the human condition, a point that a number of feminists and disability theorists have also argued.[36] But rather than moving directly from children's vulnerability to the human condition, we must consider the specific kinds of vulnerability *parents* of children experience face simply by being responsible for and loving their children.[37] This vulnerability has a theological analogue that helps us articulate the contingent and complex nature of parental power.

Power and Vulnerability: Theological Implications

A heightened awareness of the creation and exploitation of vulnerability through oppressive social structures renders the quest to speak about power *as* vulnerability, or power *in* vulnerability, fraught. This is especially true among feminist theologians; many feminists, womanists, and theologians from other marginalized communities have been troubled by the harrowing theological abuse of women and the disempowered that has come with reading vulnerability as positive.[38] As Sarah Coakley has noted, "Precisely as male theology has wallowed in a new adulation of 'vulnerability' and 'receptivity' (perhaps aiming—consciously or unconsciously—to incorporate a repressed 'femininity' into its dogmatic system), feminist theology has emerged to make its rightful protest. Such a strategy, it has urged, merely reinstates, in legitimated doctrinal form, the sexual, physical, and emotional abuse that feminism seeks to expose. An abused God merely legitimates abuse."[39] Only the privileged need a theology of vulnerability.

To address this concern, Coakley and other feminist theologians have argued that the inversion of power represents, paradoxically, a more potent and redemptive power.[40] A Christian lexicon speaks of the self-emptying or *kenosis* of Christ, the potency of which derives from God becoming vulnerable in flesh. The mystery of this particular contradiction opens it as a possibility for feminist retrieval. This line of argument, of course, is not an innovation of feminist theology; Niebuhr and other twentieth-century Christian theologians have recast the "abasement" in traditional Christological understandings of the incarnate logos into the language of vulnerability.[41]

But vulnerability can indicate a different, and theologically generative, notion beyond abasement. Vulnerability can indicate the radical porousness of the self. Human beings, adults as well as children, are not integrated and complete wholes; we are shot through with inscriptions of the world beyond ourselves. Human selves are formed in response to elements beyond our control, and thus "the deeper meaning of vulnerability has to do, not with lack of agency, but with openness and relationality to the world."[42] To attend to vulnerability is therefore to attend to the ways in which we are fundamentally embodied, social creatures who not only *create* the worlds we inhabit but *are created by* them; as Wall argues, "being-in-the-world is from the very beginning both passively constructed by others and societies and actively constructed by a self."[43] The recognition of existential vulnerability, far from rendering social stratification and oppression inevitable, merely names those as violations. Unjust systems of oppression betray the fundamental fact of human vulnerability and its capacity to unlock the wellsprings of compassion.

The porousness that is most evident in the young does not stop when childhood ends. Although decisive patterns of thought and being are rooted in childhood experience, adults have the capacity to be formed and transformed by their experiences as well. Learning to be in relationship to one's child, for many people, can be a crucible in which new elements of selfhood often emerge, and the balance of elements within oneself is recalibrated by being deeply affected by one's child. With the power of responsibility comes vulnerability.

Porousness is not only the province of human beings. God as well is subject to being rendered vulnerable, not only rendering others so. As I have argued above, relationships between parents and children often, perhaps usually, include becoming dependent. The theological import of this phenomenon lies in the articulation of this dynamic as part of a divine reality to which the Torah and the prophets attest and which we find named quite explicitly in midrash: the commanding God is rendered vulnerable by his dependence on the very recognition of Israel as God: "AND YOU ARE MY WITNESSES, SAYS THE LORD, AND I AM GOD" (Is. 43:12). Rabbi Shim'on bar Yoḥai taught: "If you are my witnesses, says the Lord, I am God. And if you are not my witnesses, I am, as it were, not God."[44]

This midrash points to the multivalent meanings of power in the process of recognition. The paradoxical element captured so eloquently in the midrash can be explained in psychoanalytic and philosophical terms; as Jessica Benjamin, drawing on Hegel's understanding of the master and slave, has argued, "The need of the self for the other is paradoxical, because the self is trying to establish himself as an absolute, an independent entity, yet he must recognize the other as like himself in order to be recognized by him."[45] Early readers of the biblical text, like modern thinkers, recognize this dynamic's application to the relationship between God and Israel. The need for recognition renders the "master" dependent.

Dynamics of power and vulnerability are readily apparent in many biblical narratives and prophetic texts. The eminently necessary feminist engagement with the problems of the marriage metaphor, most famously in Hosea but in other sources as well, points to the history of legitimization of domestic violence this metaphor has been understood to support.[46] But what has sometimes been less clear in feminist appraisals is the degree to which God is portrayed as vulnerable to hurt and betrayal because of his commitment to Israel, his inability to be without them. Israel, in bringing some element of God into the world, holds the power to make God suffer.

God's vulnerability to the suffering of Israel is a theme throughout the prophets: "In all their affliction, he was afflicted" (Is. 63:9). The midrash on this verse underscores the radical implication that God experiences Israel's affliction not merely as a sympathetic witness but in the suffering of an almost bodily injury. "Rabbi Yannai said, Just as with twins, if one feels a pain in his head, the other feels the same. The Holy One Blessed Be He said, as it were, I AM WITH HIM IN HIS PAIN [Ps. 91:15]."[47] Abraham Joshua Heschel, who insisted on reckoning with God's "emotional" involvement with and vulnerability to the deeds of Israel, called this pathos. The prophets attribute God's responsiveness not to a lack of power, but to God's involvement with and care for creation: "in pathos, God is thought of as the supreme Master of heaven and earth, Who is emotionally affected by the conduct of man."[48]

Modern Jewish theologians have found it difficult to resist the specter of Maimonidean apophasis when speaking about divine vulnerability. Heschel argued that God's vulnerability is a form of self-limitation, or self-restraint, in which God both enters into relationship with the people of Israel and yet is not, in his essence, limited by this relationship. For Heschel, "The meaning of covenant is, at bottom, not that God needs man, but that *God has chosen to need man*."[49] Heschel's careful, and not entirely successful, balancing act between the Maimondiean critique of divine pathos—even when that pathos is widely attested in the most obvious reading of scripture—and the assertion of divine transcendence is evident in his assertion that "as a subject of pathos, God Himself is not pathos."[50]

The attempt to disentangle the Bible's affective portrait of God from the philosophical commitment to apophasis, however, is less relevant than the differential in potency between humans and God. God's actions are not constrained; ours are. The Torah shows us a God at whose word the world comes into being and at whose command thousands perish. By contrast, our powers of creativity and destruction are no less real, but they have an analogously sizable effect only in aggregate. As individuals, we are constrained by the limits of our mortality, our perspective, and our influence. God's "word is eternal" (Ps. 119:89); God "neither slumbers nor sleeps" (Ps. 121:4). "He" is immortal; we are subject to death and decay. We need sleep and food merely to exist. To be mortal is by definition to wield only a limited, contingent power.

In having and raising children, the effects of this constrained power are magnified. The contingencies the individual faces become even more material and practical when she becomes a parent, starting with the most basic questions of when a child or children will come into her life, and, later, what their needs will be. We become acutely aware of responding to responsibilities that shape our lives and are beyond our control: health and sickness, good fortune and bad, privilege and oppression. At the heart of parenting is the fact of constraint. This constraint is distributed unevenly, to be sure: it is exacerbated by poverty and discrimination and can be mitigated by wealth and privilege. But neither contingency nor constrained power can be extirpated altogether.

The fact that God does not suffer death has been overread, as if death were the only source of vulnerability. In the words of the biblical scholar Terence Fretheim, "there is not [sic] evidence in the OT that there is a God in himself who is invulnerable to [His] interaction with the world. There is no duality between God in himself and God in his relation to the world; whoever says God, says the God who reveals and acts. There is no other God behind the God who participates in the history of the world."[51] *Contra* Heschel's insistence that divine pathos does not touch the heart of God's essence, biblical and midrashic texts imagine God as prone to shame and hurt.[52] As Hans Jonas put it, "The relation of God to the world from the moment of creation, and certainly from the creation of man on, involves suffering on the part of God." Jonas rightly concludes, "From the very concept of power, it follows that omnipotence is a self-contradictory, self-destructive, indeed senseless concept."[53] The God of Torah and midrash suffers, in many of the same ways as humans, materially and otherwise: God can be humiliated by Israel; God is desecrated when humans engage in wanton violence or mistreat their fellows. God, as the midrashic tradition teaches, suffers exile when the Temple is destroyed and the people of Israel are exiled. God's love for Israel leaves him open to suffering. This vulnerability is the price of responsibility and involvement.

God's capacity for being affected by Israel parallels the vulnerability parents face when they have children. This vulnerability does not negate the sense that one party has "more" power than the other, but it complicates our conception of what greater power truly means. It limits the possibility of reading power outside of its relational context. Regarding God in these terms interrupts the fantasy of God's unbridled power.

This more complex notion of greater power invites attention, finally, to the work of *restraint* in both the divine and the human spheres. Restraint involves the recognition of the potentially catastrophic consequences of exercising unconstrained power. For God, this unconstrained power is vast in scope; for humans, by contrast, it may be a very small sphere indeed that we can call unconstrained: it may exist only in our physical and psychological power over a small child.

Restraint as a Jewish theological concept has a long history, reaching back at least to kabbalah (in the form of *tzimtzum*, or divine self-constriction) and having had its most recent resurgence in the theological reckoning with the

Shoah.[54] Much of the twentieth-century theological discussion of this concept arises out of a philosophical concern with human freedom or out of the sense of divine abandonment in the face of genocide. But the work of restraint, beyond self-constriction *per se*, is unique neither to God nor to the situation of Jewry in the twentieth century. Rather, it is implicit in any relationship of care—and thus of vulnerability—that develops between parties of asymmetrical power. In parenting, restraint implies action with regard to the agentic aspects of one's power: the willed avoidance of violent action toward which children sometimes tempt the parent, or the choice not to complete a difficult task for the child but to let her struggle on her own.

Restraint is not possible, however, when it comes to the nonagentic elements of power. Parents cannot erase their traces—their limitations, constraints, and failures—any more than they can uproot their children's sensory associations with them: their smell, their habits and gestures, the feel of their embraces. Parents mark their children, and God marks God's creation, indelibly and unavoidably, for good and for ill. To face this truth is to face the embeddedness of love in power.

Notes

1. Many such thinkers have focused on reconstructing the marriage metaphor in the prophets, criticizing its patriarchal deployment but also attempting to reclaim it in an egalitarian context. In Jewish theology, see especially Rachel Adler, *Engendering Judaism: An Inclusive Theology and Ethics* (Philadelphia: Jewish Publication Society, 1998).

2. In nonfeminist Jewish theological discourse, the parental metaphor has been examined in terms of God as father and Israel, or the Israelite king, as son, but typically without feminist critique of patriarchal gender expectations and the limitations of fatherhood or sonship; see Michael Wyschogrod, *The Body of Faith: Judaism as Corporeal Election* (New York: Seabury Press, 1983); Jon D. Levenson, *Sinai and Zion: An Entry into the Jewish Bible* (Minneapolis: Winston Press, 1985); Jon D. Levenson, *The Love of God: Divine Gift, Human Gratitude, and Mutual Faithfulness in Judaism* (Princeton, NJ: Princeton University Press, 2015); Yair Lorberbaum, *Disempowered King: Monarchy in Classical Jewish Literature* (New York: Continuum, 2010); Moshe Idel, *Ben: Sonship and Jewish Mysticism* (New York: Continuum, 2007). Naturally, attributing masculinity to parent and child does not *a priori* rule out engagement with the material, embodied work of raising children. However, in practice, none of the extant discussions of fathers and sons have sought to go beyond patriarchal models of paternal power, by which a "father" is not merely the male correlative of a mother, but a role defined by an authority that is separate from that earned by providing daily care for children. Sara Ruddick, among many others, has argued for the nonparallelism of "mothers" and "Fathers" (which she indicates through this deliberately unconventional orthography). Ruddick connects this nonparallelism to the different manifestations of parental authority: "the point about—or against—Fathers is that their authority is not earned by care and indeed undermines the maternal authority that is so earned" (Sara Ruddick, *Maternal Thinking: Toward a Politics of Peace* [Boston: Beacon Press, 1989], 42).

3. Cf. the chapter called "Disability" in Andrew Solomon, *Far from the Tree: Parents, Children and the Search for Identity* (New York: Scribner, 2012).

4. The imbalance in the social, economic, and political power between men and women widens when women become mothers. It is clear that having a child renders women even more vulnerable to economic marginalization than they are without children, in large part due to the inaccessibility of affordable medical care, paid parental leave, and childcare. Thus women who become mothers typically experience a diminution in their economic power, even as their symbolic power may increase as they fulfill centuries'-old expectations regarding women's *telos* (Michelle J. Budig, "The Fatherhood Bonus & the Motherhood Penalty: Parenthood and the Gender Gap in Pay," *Third Way*, 2014 last updated September 2, 2014, accessed November 8, 2017, http://www.thirdway.org/report/the-fatherhood-bonus-and-the-motherhood-penalty-parenthood-and-the-gender-gap-in-pay; Deborah A. Jeon et al., "Amicus Curiae Brief of the American Civil Liberties Union and a Better Balance, Et Al., in Support of Petitioner" [2014]). These facts are, of course, not inevitable but come about through the a variety of means, including deeply entrenched assumptions that both women and men share about the extent to which having and caring for children should influence their lives; governmental policies that regard having children as a matter individuals must navigate (often at their own financial peril) rather than as a matter of public investment; legal limitations on women's access to reproductive care and autonomy; and workplace policies and ethoi that, in effect, systematically punish women for childbearing by failing to implement reasonable leave policies.

5. For example, see Val Gillies, *Marginalised Mothers: Exploring Working-Class Experiences of Parenting* (New York: Routledge, 2007).

6. Differences in the cultural authority of mothers in various communities, specifically as differentiated by race, suggest alternative models of maternal power that should be investigated in their own right. See especially Patricia Hill Collins, *Black Feminist Thought: Knowledge, Consciousness, and the Politics of Empowerment*, Rev. 10th anniversary ed. (New York: Routledge, 2000); Annelise Orleck, *Storming Caesars Palace: How Black Mothers Fought Their Own War on Poverty* (Boston: Beacon Press, 2005); Irene Oh, "Motherhood in Christianity and Islam: Critiques, Realities, and Possibilities," *Journal of Religious Ethics* 38, no. 4 (2010); Donna Bassin, Margaret Honey, and Meryle Mahrer Kaplan, *Representations of Motherhood* (New Haven: Yale University Press, 1994).

7. On the importance of boundaries for the mutual flourishing of parents and children (but especially of children) in religious ethics, see Cristina L. H. Traina, *Erotic Attunement: Parenthood and the Ethics of Sensuality between Unequals* (Chicago: University of Chicago Press, 2011).

8. Ta-Nehisi Coates, *Between the World and Me* (Melbourne: Text Publishing Company, 2015), 16–17.

9. Ruddick, *Maternal Thinking*, 35.

10. Physical power can, of course, be inversely related to authority; a parent may hit her child precisely when she feels most fearful or out of control. This same phenomenon applies in religious life; see John D. Carlson, "Religion and Violence: Coming to Terms with Terms," in *The Blackwell Companion to Religion and Violence*, ed. Andrew R. Murphy (Malden, MA: Wiley-Blackwell, 2011).

11. Jewish ethical and theological treatments of inflicting abuse include David R. Blumenthal, *Facing the Abusing God: A Theology of Protest* (Louisville, KY: Westminster/John Knox Press, 1993) and Catherine Madsen, "Notes on God's Violence," *Cross Currents* 51, no. 2 (2001).

12. Michel Foucault, *Discipline and Punish: The Birth of the Prison*, trans. Alan Sheridan (New York: Vintage Books, 1995); *The Birth of the Clinic: An Archaeology of Medical Perception*, trans. Alan Sheridan (New York: Pantheon Books, 1973).

13. On the power of the cared-for in relationships between adults and their children, see, among others, Jessica Benjamin, *The Bonds of Love: Psychoanalysis, Feminism, and the Problem of Domination* (New York: Pantheon Books, 1988), 45; Nel Noddings, *The Maternal Factor: Two Paths to Morality* (Berkeley: University of California Press, 2010), 46, 127; Traina, *Erotic Attunement*.

14. Some theorists propose, instead, a "distributive" model of power, in which power is a resource that can be distributed evenly or unevenly (e.g., Susan Moller Okin, *Justice, Gender, and the Family* [New York: Basic Books, 1989]). Others, following Foucault, emphasize the relational aspect of power, in that it "exists only in action, and thus must be understood dynamically, as existing in ongoing processes or interactions" (Amy Allen, "Feminist Perspectives on Power," in *The Stanford Encyclopedia of Philosophy*, ed. Edward N. Zalta (2016)). See also Iris Marion Young, *Justice and the Politics of Difference* (Princeton, NJ: Princeton University Press, 1990).

15. Max Weber defines power as "the probability that one actor within a social relationship will be in a position to carry out his own will despite resistance" (Max Weber, *Economy and Society: An Outline of Interpretive Sociology*, 2 vols. [Berkeley: University of California Press, 1978] 53). Foucault argues, "if we speak of the structures or the mechanisms of power, it is only insofar as we suppose that certain persons exercise power over others" (Hubert L. Dreyfus and Paul Rabinow, eds., *Michel Foucault: Beyond Structuralism and Hermeneutics*, 2nd ed. [Chicago: University of Chicago Press, 1983], 217). See also Amy Allen, "Feminist Perspectives on Power," in *The Stanford Encyclopedia of Philosophy*, ed. Edward N. Zalta (Summer 2014 Edition).

16. Mary Daly, *Beyond God the Father: Toward a Philosophy of Women's Liberation* (Boston: Beacon Press, 1973), 13. Daly's logic gave a feminist and gendered angle to Geertz's influential claim that religion simultaneously provides "models for" and "models of" a culture (Clifford Geertz, "Religion as a Cultural System," in *Interpretation of Cultures: Selected Essays* [New York: Basic Books, 1973]).

17. Audre Lorde, "Uses of the Erotic: The Erotic as Power," in *Sister Outsider: Essays and Speeches* (Trumansburg, NY: Crossing Press, 1984), 56.

18. Lorde, "Uses of the Erotic: The Erotic as Power," 58.

19. Kathleen M. Sands, "Uses of the Thea(o)Logian: Sex and Theodicy in Religious Feminism," *Journal of Feminist Studies in Religion* 8, no. 1 (1992): 11.

20. This generation of feminists often emphasized mututality as a corrective, as in Beverly Wildung Harrison's report: "I shudder to think how many times during my years of theological study I came upon a warning from a Christian writer not to confuse real, Christian love with 'mere mutuality'" (Beverly Wildung Harrison, "The Power of Anger in the Work of Love: Christian Ethics for Women and Other Strangers," *Union Seminary Quarterly Review* 36 [1985]: 51).

21. Adler, *Engendering Judaism*, 132. See also Judith Plaskow: "When the erotic is understood not simply as sexual feeling in the narrow sense but as our fundamental life energy, the owning of this power in our lives is even more threatening to established structures" that seek to repress or control it (Judith Plaskow, *Standing Again at Sinai: Judaism from a Feminist Perspective* [San Francisco: HarperCollins, 1991], 202).

22. For an insightful analysis of the problems in much of this literature for feminist theological considerations of sex, and how these problems map onto public feminist discourse about sex, see Sands, "Uses of the Thea(o)Logian."

23. Adler (like Buber) acknowledges briefly structurally asymmetrical relationships. However, neither thinker focuses on these relationships or on the problems they present for the ideal of mutuality (Adler, *Engendering Judaism*, 94; Mara H. Benjamin, "Intersubjectivity Meets Maternity: Buber, Levinas, and the Eclipsed Relation," in *Thinking Jewish Culture in America*, ed. Ken Koltun-Fromm (New York: Lexington Books, 2014). Rachel Adler, in her brief consideration of structurally asymmetrical relationships, argues that "good mentors and good parents take pride in the developing powers of those in whom they have invested themselves and look forward eagerly to their full flowering." But beyond this acknowledgment, Adler does not explore such relationships.

24. Virginia Held, *Feminist Morality: Transforming Culture, Society, and Politics*, Women in Culture and Society (Chicago: University of Chicago Press, 1993), 209. On this point, consider Mary Dietz's observations concerning the structural hierarchies that define family life. Aristotle's political philosophy, she argues, grounds a critique of using "maternal thinking" for civic life, including the "politics of peace" that Sara Ruddick proposed (Mary G. Dietz, "Citizenship with a Feminist Face" in *Turning Operations: Feminism, Arendt, Politics* [New York: Routledge, 2002]).

25. Traina, *Erotic Attunement*, ch. 7.

26. Virginia Held, for instance, asserts that a feminist critique of oppressive theories of power is grounded in maternal practice: "the capacity to give birth and to nurture and empower could be the basis for new and more humanly promising conceptions than the ones that now prevail of power, empowerment, and growth" (Held, *Feminist Morality*, 137). Such an outlook is implicit in the care ethics that can be traced to Carol Gilligan, *In a Different Voice: Psychological Theory and Women's Development* (Cambridge: Harvard University Press, 1982).

27. Here I rely on the insightful reading of the Song of Songs in Ilana Pardes, *Countertraditions in the Bible: A Feminist Approach* (Cambridge: Harvard University Press, 1992). As a counterpoint, Rachel Adler grounds her sexual ethics and her theology in the mutuality she finds in the Song of Songs in particular, a text she argues "celebrates mutuality" (Adler, *Engendering Judaism*, 135).

28. I am influenced here by the definition of tragedy offered in Kathleen Sands's work on the tragic and religious feminism. Sands examines tragedy as a narrative genre that grapples with events that have caused a rupture in the ability to form a coherent worldview. I move away from the literary referent point for the tragic to extract from it, as Sands does, the challenge of the tragic to dominant strains of religious feminism. See especially Sands, "Uses of the Thea(o)Logian"; "Tragedy, Theology, and Feminism in the Time after Time," *New Literary History* 35, no. 1 (2004).

29. Some Christian feminist theologians read this inevitability of "failure" in terms of original sin, as in Bonnie J. Miller-McLemore, *Also a Mother: Work and Family as Theological Dilemma* (Nashville, TN: Abingdon Press, 1994).

30. Many parents of children with cognitive or physical needs that demand greater parental care and involvement, thus complicating the expectation of eventual self-sufficiency, struggle with an even more fraught identity as parents. See Solomon, *Far from the Tree*.

31. As in the statement attributed to R. Abdimi from Haifa: "Since the day when the Temple was destroyed, prophecy has been taken from the prophets and given to the wise" (Baba Batra 12a). David Stern, *Midrash and Theory: Ancient Jewish Exegesis and Contemporary Literary Studies* (Evanston, IL: Northwestern University Press, 1996), 81. Stern notes that anthropomorphism in Bible and midrash only became troubling to Jewish philosophers in the medieval period.

32. Lamentations Rabbah, *petihta* 24, cited in Stern, *Midrash and Theory*, 82.

33. As Stern points out, the climax of these midrashim in Lamentations Rabbah is God's being schooled by the matriarch Rachel, who grieves for her children (Stern, *Midrash and Theory*).

34. See discussion in John Wall, *Ethics in Light of Childhood* (Washington, DC: Georgetown University Press, 2010), 41.

35. Such is the heart of the famous story of Sigmund Freud learning of his father's "impotence" in the face of antisemitic humiliation; see Peter Gay, *Freud: A Life for Our Time* (New York: W. W. Norton, 1988), 11–12.

36. See, e.g., Eva Feder Kittay, *Love's Labor: Essays on Women, Equality, and Dependency* (New York: Routledge, 1999).

37. Elizabeth O'Donnell Gandolfo, *The Power and Vulnerability of Love: A Theological Anthropology* (Minneapolis, MN: Fortress Press, 2015).

38. Both Kelly Brown Douglas and Dolores Williams, for instance, argue that Christology needs to be formulated not primarily with reference to atonement but rather with specific awareness of how many "understandings of Jesus ... have often aided and abetted black women's oppression." By contrast, "a womanist christology must also affirm black women's faith that Jesus has supported them in their struggles to survive and be free" (Kelly Delaine Brown, "God Is as Christ Does: Toward a Womanist Theology," *Journal of Religious Thought* 46, no. 1 [1989]: 14). See also Delores S. Williams, *Sisters in the Wilderness: The Challenge of Womanist God-Talk* (Maryknoll, NY: Orbis Books, 1993), ch. 7.

39. Sarah Coakley, *Powers and Submissions: Spirituality, Philosophy and Gender* (Oxford: Blackwell Publishers, 2002), xv.

40. Coakley, *Powers and Submissions*, 4–5.

41. Reinhold Niebuhr, *The Nature and Destiny of Man: A Christian Interpretation*, 2 vols. (New York: Charles Scribner's Sons, 1946).

42. Wall, *Ethics in Light of Childhood*, 39.

43. Wall, *Ethics in Light of Childhood*, 40. See also Sands, "Uses of the Thea(o)Logian."

44. Pesiqta deRav Kahana 12.6

45. Benjamin, *The Bonds of Love*, 32.

46. On the rich feminist biblical investigation into Hosea, see Gerlinde Baumann, *Love and Violence: Marriage as Metaphor for the Relationship between YHWH and Israel in the Prophetic Books* (Collegeville, MN: Liturgical Press, 2003); Athalya Brenner and Carole R. Fontaine, *A Feminist Companion to the Latter Prophets*, The Feminist Companion to the Bible (Sheffield, England: Sheffield Academic Press, 1995). On the problems of Hosea for constructive Jewish theology, see Adler, *Engendering Judaism*.

47. Exodus Rabbah 2:5.

48. Abraham Joshua Heschel, *The Prophets* (New York: Perennial, 2001), II:100. See the discussion of the issue of divine pathos and the relationship between pathos and God's power in Shai Held, *Abraham Joshua Heschel: The Call of Transcendence* (Bloomington: Indiana University Press, 2013), ch. 4.

49. Held, *Abraham Joshua Heschel*, 10.

50. Heschel, *The Prophets*, II:265. This issue and passage are discussed in Held, *Abraham Joshua Heschel*, 156ff.

51. Terence Fretheim, "The Repentance of God: A Key to Evaluating Old Testament God-Talk," *Horizons in Biblical Theology* 10, no. 1 (1988): 69n30. See discussion, building on Fretheim, in Held, *Abraham Joshua Heschel*, 155–158, 282n141.

52. Only such a concept of God can explain the effectiveness of Moses's appeal to God not to wipe out Israel when he argues that God's reputation will be ruined (Ex. 32:12), or that

the Egyptians and the other nations will conclude that God was powerless (*mibilti yekholet YHVH*) (Num. 14:16). Medieval Jewish commentators on this verse articulate the logic (attributed to the other nations) that a sense of powerlessness is related to violence: God killed the Israelites not out of hatred for them, but because he was unable to bring them into the land. See Rashi ad loc. Num. 14:16; Rashbam ad loc. Gen. 32:13.

53. Hans Jonas, "The Concept of God after Auschwitz: A Jewish Voice," *The Journal of Religion* 67, no. 1 (1987): 6, 8.

54. Jonas, "The Concept of God after Auschwitz"; Zachary Braiterman, *(God) after Auschwitz: Tradition and Change in Post-Holocaust Jewish Thought* (Princeton, NJ: Princeton University Press, 1998).

CHAPTER 4

Teaching

A ONE-YEAR-OLD SITS in a high chair, exploring the food on the tray. She catches sight of an object on the tray and lets go of the sippy cup she was about to bring to her mouth. The sippy cup drops to the floor. The child notices her parent reaching down to retrieve it; her attention now moves from the object on the tray to the movement near the floor, and to the sudden disappearance, and then reappearance, of this figure. Her eyes blink as the pieces of the puzzle fit together: the connection between the falling object and the adult's movement. Her experiment in cause and effect begins as she casts another object off the tray.

This drama, endlessly fascinating for the child, is usually less so for her mother. Enacted multiple times a day, the scene recedes to the realm of the unremarkable. But each episode requires lightning-quick calculations and responses on the part of the mother: whether to pick up the fallen object or leave it be, to ignore or verbalize what she sees.

A few months pass. Instead of absent-mindedly letting the spoon drop, the baby casts a utensil to the floor. She looks up in anticipation. The parent's calculation is a slightly altered, factoring in the child's different developmental stage: If she retrieves the spoon, will her child learn that she exists solely to clean up messes? When does she show her child that this game is tiresome? Perhaps it's time to teach her about eating with others. Maybe she's no longer hungry and it's time to take her out of the high chair.

This parental calculus involves factors well beyond the baby herself: being tired or satisfied or bored after a day of work; being happy or unhappy or preoccupied. While the child in the high chair eats, her mother also eats, talks on the phone, chats with others at the table, pays bills, or attends to others. Rarely is her focus entirely on the child.

The majority of what we teach, and how we teach, lies below the surface of cognition. As parents, we use our bodies: to pick up or not pick up the spoon, to smile or furrow our brow or turn back to our other activity after hearing a clatter. Our bodies are primary instrument of teaching, the medium through which we act and convey meaning to children. Through them, we teach our children about the social worlds we inhabit, about appetite and food, about relationships, about who we are and who they are.

* * *

Two young children sit side by side in a hut, pounding a small rock on a larger one, smoke from what is presumably the cooking fire wafting above them. Both children focus intently on their work, the younger child occasionally looking to the older one, who acknowledges the gaze. One reaches for an old plastic bottle on the dirt floor and the other tries to grab it back. Thwarted, she bites the first child, who then cries and lightly slaps the biter. Both of them still hold the small rocks. We hear an adult woman's voice utter a few words; after a few moments in which the small child continues sobbing, we hear more words, and the crying child stands and walks out of the frame. The older child takes possession of the plastic bottle, briefly investigates an object in the dirt, and returns to pounding rocks.

We are not privy to this mother's calculations, state of mind, or activity. But the inferences the viewer draws from this first scene in the documentary *Babies* cannot but surprise viewers who inhabit a world of Cheerios, high chairs, and what Annette Lareau has called "concerted cultivation."[1] No adult is present in the frame. The off-screen woman is only revealed by voice, in a casual intervention that follows several minutes of a child's audible distress. The camera remains still, focused only on the children as they work alongside, quarrel with, and model action for one another. The mother does not move into the frame toward the child but rather encourages the child to come to her to receive consolation. Her teaching lies in her blithe response to the quarrel, her staying out of it, her tone of voice and her light presence a source of comfort.

The second scene shows the torso of a pregnant woman who is beating one small rock against a larger stationary one, producing a red powder she mixes with water. The woman rubs the red paste on her belly and breasts; later, she will rub this paste onto the baby's freshly-shaved head. We instantly understand the children pounding rocks in a new light: at a year of age, give or take, they are engaged in purposive activity. Without verbal instruction, their mother has been teaching them all along.[2]

* * *

Daily life turns parents into teachers. The work of intimate, material caregiving demands that parents endlessly repeat the lessons of constancy and responsiveness. They attend to their children's changing abilities and modify their actions accordingly. They model and correct behavior. They circle back to earlier lessons, refining and reinterpreting the teachings they and their culture have transmitted. The psychological, cognitive, and social aspects of this parental curriculum depend on the somatic, the sensory, and the material. Quotidian parental work is teaching at its most expansive: it involves teaching a child to be a recognizable member of the human community.

The notion of parents as teachers finds expression in diverse cultures, ancient and modern. The textual records, which typically reflect the viewpoints of the male, educated elite, often juxtapose parents' work as instructors to that of the formal instructional institutions of the culture. Sometimes, parents are viewed as inadequate teachers, and formal educational settings are envisioned as a corrective for parents' deficiencies. Kant, for instance, argued that education should be delegated to institutions outside the family, since parents "exercise forethought for the home," but do not "have for their ultimate aim the good of the world."[3] Many Confucian theorists, by contrast, imagine a more harmonious relationship between the moral cultivation of small children that occurs in familial settings, on the one hand, and the cultural competence children should ultimately achieve through formal institutions, on the other.[4] When parental teaching is viewed in terms of the quotidian, ephemeral actions associated with mothers (feeding, wiping, comforting), the contrast between what parents do and the work of schooling becomes even more stark. Responding to a spoon dropped from the high chair or making a soothing paste: these are legible *as teaching* only to the extent that these activities are seen as imparting privileged cultural traditions, values, and norms.

The classical rabbinic tradition exemplifies this tendency in that it privileges the study of Torah and defines parental work as teaching only insofar as it specifically cultivates this activity. The sources I examine below posit teaching as a key paternal obligation, perfected in the sage who teaches his disciple. The relationship between master and disciple became the critical template for rabbinic creativity and, as such, was a site of considerable cultural investment. Master and disciple, bound by their mutual devotion to explicating Torah, formed a relationship that was to mediate and transform the teachings of the elders for the current and future community of rabbinic Jews. But this rabbinic project of reformulating Torah within a new discipleship community also reshaped a variety of social institutions. The new rabbinic ideal of Torah study had profound effects on the conception of the family and, especially, on the core meaning of child-rearing.[5]

The sages, particularly those of the influential Babylonian community, formed a semi- (or aspirationally) ascetic, homosocial discipleship community, a community *in tension* with women and with the familial and worldly responsibilities marriage signified, even as the rabbinic sages formally endorsed the fulfillment of their duties toward wives and children.[6] An unavoidable friction thus emerged in classical Jewish thought, as it does in other discipleship communities, regarding the relative priority of the family and the sage. In such a setting, as Martin Jaffee has argued, "Teachers are not biologically the mothers or fathers, the grandparents, uncles, or aunts of their pupils, and they do not normally relate to their pupils as kin. But in a system of discipleship the teacher bears for each student a responsibility appropriate to that of kin—particularly the father or mother—or even replacing it."[7] The aptness of Jaffee's description of the rabbinic project is evident in the parental metaphors that recur throughout rabbinic literature to describe the relationship between master and disciple, and the recurring hermeneutic habit by which the sages read parents and children as sages and disciples. For instance, in Sifre on Deuteronomy (*Va'ethanan* §34) we encounter the following claim: "Your children [or: sons] (Deut. 11:19): these are your pupils. And thus you find you find that pupils are always called sons, as it says, AND THE SONS OF THE PROPHETS THAT WERE IN THE HOUSE WENT OUT TO ELISHA (II Kings 2:3). Were these the prophets' sons? [No!] They were their pupils! From this we know that pupils are called sons ... and just as pupils are called 'sons,' so the master is called 'father.'"[8] Where the biblical text speaks of *children* (or sons [*baneikhem*]), the Sifre insists that *students* are really indicated. This midrash exerts little exegetical effort to claim that the biblical text "really" speaks about the sage and his disciples rather than about children and fathers; it is self-evident to the sages that this must be so.

The assertion of the sage as the true parent of the disciple in rabbinic literature generated a corollary claim: that the familial parents provide merely the raw material for life; the master, by contrast, brings their creation to its ultimate purpose, namely, Torah. Many early rabbinic traditions explicitly assert the sage's role to be equivalent to or even greater than that of the familial parent, and that the sagely community, not the "natural" family, constitutes the locus of proper (re)socialization. Early halakhic (practical/legal) literature demonstrates the pervasiveness of this construct and the diminution of the significance of the familial parent: for example, in a conflict between giving priority to one's father and one's teacher, mBaba Metzia 2:11 asserts that one owes primary responsibility to one's teacher.[9] Furthermore, when a father of a young child is not himself learned in Torah, he is expected to arrange for a man who *is* learned to teach his son as the father's proxy; in this case, the teacher acquires a stature and honor for the son that is analogous to that of the father (bQiddushin 30a). Daniel Boyarin has summarized the rabbis' approach by arguing that for them, "the production of spiritual children, those who will follow in the moral and religious ways of the parent, is claimed ... as more important than the production of biological children."[10]

This rabbinic appropriation of parenthood as a category that actually refers to the rabbinic teacher renders invisible actual parental labor and, especially, parental teaching not explicitly focused on Torah transmission. The familial father is judged successful as a father only to the extent that he can replicate or mimic the sage's identity within the family.[11] The complementary cultural construct of the rabbinic sage as father, then, is the construct of the lay *pater familias* as would-be sage, the father who will ritually teach his sons Torah so as to reproduce the mimetic Torah learning of the sage with his disciples. The master and disciple form the primary dyad, compared to which the dyad of unlearned layman and son is derivative, and in relation to which a mother and child are utterly irrelevant.

The rabbinic ideal of Torah study, originating among the sages and replicated among laymen, is a gendered ideal: male masters transmitted Torah to male students; fathers, not mothers, were to replicate this ideal within the familial unit. Fathers are visible as teachers, but only to the extent they teach their children Torah. Mothers, by contrast, do not "teach" anything. The rabbis assume but do not explicitly articulate mothers' obligations to their children. Diapering, feeding, comforting, and so on are tasks they associated with natural instinct. As such, these activities are not raised to the status of obligation.[12] When the everyday care of a young child remains largely invisible, it can hardly be recognized as teaching.

The categorization of maternal work as instinctual and paternal work as properly educational characterizes not only rabbinic literature but also modern Western philosophical, political, and educational traditions. Until very recently, "mothers" and "fathers" were only nominally parallel terms; "mothering," even today, connotes an altogether different kind of work than does "fathering."[13] With few exceptions, modern liberal thinkers (who invariably assume a heterosexual parental couple) argue that fathers instruct and mothers nurture.[14] Among modern Western thinkers who are most generous in their imagining of maternal teaching, such as John Dewey, mothers are envisioned as conveying "the ways of behavior, the language, and much of the transmitted wisdom, of their group and people" to children.[15] But more typical is the formulation of Jean-Jacques Rousseau, who argues that mothers merely provide the sustenance on which children depend; fathers do the work of education, laying the ground on which formal education builds.[16]

The rabbis, like modern Western thinkers, regard as valuable that which reinforces a set of cultural values crafted and perpetuated by male elites. In a text that became the *locus classicus* for the Talmudic discussion of paternal responsibility, paternal obligations reinforce a set of "covenantal obligations":[17] "Our Rabbis taught: A father is obligated to his son (*ha'av ḥayyav bivno*): to circumcise him, to redeem him [if he is a firstborn], to teach him Torah, to find him a wife, and to teach him a craft" (tQiddushin 1:11).[18] This

Tosefta forms the basis for the amoraic discussion of a father's obligations toward his son (bQiddushin 29a), presenting, in the order of a boy's developmental stages, the paternal tasks necessary to ensure the son's participation in and replication of the covenantal community. (Alternatively, this delineation of the father's responsibility to his son centers on the cultivation of the social, intellectual, and economic skills the son would need in order for the covenantal community to replicate itself.[19])

This abbreviated list of mitzvot incumbent on the father leaves out the bulk of caretaking work, what Adrienne Rich called "the small, routine chores of socializing a human being."[20] The Tosefta "is not interested in the day-to-day nurturing, the feeding and clothing of the child";[21] indeed, the text imagines a boy who has already been born, cared for, and sustained in the variety of material ways necessary for the culturally valued activities of Torah, marriage, and work to be available to him as an adult. It does not imagine the woman or women who have gestated, fed, and cared for him (nor does it imagine girls, who will never be formally entered into the covenantal community).[22]

But alongside this constricted meaning of Torah as the property of scholars, a number of Pentateuchal narratives and their midrashic embellishments present Torah as that which is transmitted by a caretaking parent who feeds, carries, swaddles, and cleans her young child. In these texts, God is the maternal teacher of her beloved children, the people of Israel. In others, the sage is figured as a mother who feeds the disciple words of Torah. These narratives invite us to reimagine the daily work of intimate caregiving as Torah in the broadest sense, and the parents who perform it as the true sages. To understand this intimate care of young children as teaching—teaching in a specifically Jewish manner—requires both a consciousness of this history and a look ahead, to possibilities that lie beyond the strictly gendered texts of the past.

* * *

The central narrative of the Pentateuch as a whole, Israel's journey from slavery in Egypt through the wilderness to the Promised Land, continually suggests analogies to birthgiving and the earliest stages of childrearing.[23] The plagues in Egypt, coming wave upon wave with momentary reprieves, suggest painful labor contractions. Israel's passage through the "narrow straits" and the Red Sea evoke the breaking of the waters and the journey through the birth canal.[24] These allusions to childbirth, only implied in the Penateuchal text itself, are made explicit in the Prophets and later midrashic literature, where God is imagined as birthing woman (Isa. 42:14), as midwife attending the birth of Israel (Yalkut Shimoni 828), and as adoptive parent who cares for an abandoned infant (Ez. 16:4–6).[25]

God's maternal *teaching*, however, consists not primarily in birthgiving but also in the nurturing, tedious, and frustrating work of caring for the

newborn nation. The most developed of the biblical narratives focuses on episodes of feeding. The infant Israel is sustained on a diet of manna, the miracle
food that rains down on them during their forty years of wandering in the
desert. The manna becomes a focal point through which midrashic resources
imagine the sometimes burdensome, sometimes delightful work of feeding as
teaching Torah.

Although manna is named as "bread" in Exodus 16, a number of midrashic
traditions liken it instead to mother's milk, the Israelites' first food after their
"birth" as a nation:[26] "The taste of it was the taste of a cake [leshad] baked with
oil [Num. 11:8]. Rabbi Abbahu said: Just as an infant, whenever he touches the
breast [shad], finds many flavors in it, so it was with manna. Whenever Israel
ate it, they found many flavors in it" (bYoma 75a). An eleventh century tradition,
building on the same wordplay between leshad (cake) and shad (breast), reads
this nourishment as the paradigm for all other food: "Like the breast (shad) in
which the baby tastes all sweet things, so too was the manna to Israel. Just as
the breast is the primary food for the baby, and all other food is secondary, so
too the manna was primary and all other food was secondary" (Pesikta Zutarta
Bamidbar Beha'alotekha).[27] The divine food that sustains Israel every day, these
midrashic traditions imply, is best understood in terms of the miraculous yet
ubiquitous fact of birthgiving women nursing their children. This connection
lays the foundation on which manna is imagined simultaneously as sustenance
and as Torah: God becomes the maternal teacher whose acts of feeding are the
medium through which Israel absorbs her teaching. In fact, manna is explicitly
named as a means of introducing Israel to Torah: "Then YHVH said to Moses: 'I
will rain down bread for you from the sky, and the people shall go out and gather
each day that day's portion—that I may thus test them, to see whether they will
follow My Torah or not'" (Ex. 16:4).

"Torah" in its narrow sense—the instructions not to gather more manna or
go out on the seventh day—functions as a gateway into "Torah" in a more expansive sense. Before the people arrive at Sinai and receive God's full revelation,
the manna offers Israel a literal first taste of divine instruction, preparing the
groundwork for additional, sometimes more complex and more abstract, teaching. If the manna is also God's "milk," God's feeding prepares Israel to receive
the fullness of divine instruction. A mother whose infant tests his new teeth on
her breast reminds him "no biting," and so instructs him about his own body
and the subjectivity of others; God's limits on collecting manna on the seventh
day becomes a means of acclimating Israel to the Sabbath and God's teaching as
a whole.

But, as with the milk a mother feeds her child, manna does not have merely
an instrumental value. Its substance itself is precious; as the Mekhilta suggests,
the manna is not only an introduction to Torah, but it is Torah itself. The people

of Israel who eat it literally take God's Torah into their bodies: "The Holy One Blessed be He did not bring them directly to the land of Israel but [brought them] by way of the desert, saying: If I bring them there now, immediately each man will seize his field, and each man his vineyard and they will neglect Torah study. Rather, I will keep them in the desert forty years, eating manna and drinking from the well, and the Torah will be absorbed in their bodies" (Mekhilta de-Rabbi Ishmael ad loc. Ex. 13:17).[28] God feeds the mother's milk of Torah to the infant Israel in its most vulnerable state. This feeding is, in itself, a transmission of divine teaching.

As if to forestall the fantasy of ever-harmonious synchronicity between nursing mother and suckling child, these biblical and midrashic narratives recognize a sometimes discomfiting gap between the infant's experience of being fed and the parent's physical and emotional experience of feeding. By imaginatively inhabiting the position of the feeding mother, and not only that of the suckling Israel, these narratives consider the disjuncture between the experience of the person feeding and that of the person being fed. Manna is associated with Israel's experience of munificence and nurture, but it simultaneously signifies the uniquely challenging work for the divine or Mosaic parent. The infant Israel longs to return from the wilderness to the apparent security of Egypt, which God interprets as forsaking the manna-Torah; God asks, "How long will you refuse to obey My commandments and My teachings?" (Ex. 16:28) when her baby takes too much at the wrong time. In Numbers 11:12, manna again becomes the occasion for an eruption of divine rage—here, between the two caregivers over the recalcitrance of their child, as Moses asks God rhetorically, "Did I conceive all this people? Did I birth them, that you should say to me, Carry them in your bosom, as the nurser ['omen] carries the suckling, to the land that you swore to their fathers?"[29] Israel's desire triggers Moses's frustration rather than generosity.

The child Israel is nourished on divine foodstuffs, yet feeding and being fed are fraught activities. Rather than a site of pacific mutual exchange, the manna exposes underlying tensions about giving and desire, where the child Israel's longing for "adult" food (i.e., meat, Num. 11:4); its "rejection of the breast" (Num. 11:6) cause distress and fury. As Pardes expresses it, the "children's resistance to the manna triggers simultaneous giving and withholding, the episode with the meat leading to explosive violence." In this portrayal of God's maternal subjectivity, the work of feeding is a "pedagogical undertaking," but one that, as Pardes notes, is "excruciatingly slow," ripe with the potential for violent outbursts.[30] Like maternal love, maternal feeding-as-teaching includes rage and frustration alongside giving and nurture. The strife over feeding and specifically over manna in the Pentateuch are all too familiar for nursing mothers and their newborns: the baby wants milk precisely when her exhausted mother lies down to sleep; the infant sucks away greedily while the nursing mother grimaces in pain. The (sometimes) satisfaction and joy that comes from feeding one's child are lodged within the many daily trials of mismatched needs and desires.

Such moments, in life as in scripture, challenge the fantasy in which teaching primarily concerns cultural propagation. This fantasy animates another midrash that links breastfeeding to the transmission of Torah. Song of Songs Rabbah (on Song of Songs 4:5, "Your breasts are like two fawns / Twins of a gazelle, browsing among the lilies") reads: "Just as these breasts are the splendor and glory of a woman, so too Moses and Aaron are the splendor and glory of Israel.... Just like these breasts are full of milk, Moses and Aaron fill Israel with Torah. And just as with these breasts, all that a woman eats, the baby eats and nurses from them, so too all of the Torah that Moses learned he taught to Aaron. This is what is meant by MOSES TOLD AARON ALL OF THE WORDS OF GOD" [Exodus 4:28]. Women's breasts, beautiful and life sustaining, transmute ordinary food into nurturing milk. The unique alchemy within the lactating breast serves as an ideal metaphor for Torah and its transmission to the people of Israel.[31] For the rabbis who produced such an image, the homosocial *beit midrash* held just such a dual capacity: the study hall pulsed with eros and sustaining culture in the face of dispersion.[32] The unfortunate price of this analogy is its appropriation of the physical aspects of biological motherhood and parental labor for the exclusively male terrain of the sages.[33] This irony, however, should not blind us to the constructive possibilities latent within these midrashim. Inverting the signifier and signified, we can see that the caretaking parent engaged in daily routines with her child is the sage whose primary, bodily teaching should be aspirational for all who would transmit Torah.

In the metaphors that link manna, breastmilk, and Torah, the children of Israel internalize the external: Torah/manna, as divine teaching, comes from the outside; the people of Israel are to absorb it into their bodies, and once internalized, it is only indirectly perceptible. But in the work of helping their children become capable performers in their culture, parents attend not only to the internal, but also to what is visible and performative. As with the mother making dye in her hut, or the parent whom the child observes using a spoon long before she can hold one herself, parents perform their culture and then refine their children's performances.

In rabbinic texts, disciples seek out the embodied teaching of the sage, as in the saying attributed to the disciple of the Hasidic Maggid of Mezerich: "I came to the Maggid not to listen to his discourses, nor to learn from his wisdom; I came to watch him tie his shoelaces."[34] Late antique texts testify to this understanding of the role of embodied action as a defining element of Torah that the devoted disciple seeks out, even to the point of transgressing personal boundaries. Consider a Talmudic passage that describes a series of incidents in which one sage follows his teacher into various spaces usually understood to be "private" and reports what he observed and why he undertook this observation.

The passage (bBerakhot 61b) begins with a baraita: "Our sages taught: one who relieves himself: if in Judea, he should not face East or West, but North or South; if in Galilee, he should only face East or West." In the series of short vignettes that follow this curious matter of rabbinic toileting norms, the text goes on to describe two rabbis who follow their teachers to the outhouse; when questioned about their impudence, each student states, "It is Torah and I must learn it" (bBerakhot 62a).[35] This Talmudic outhouse scenario suggests a rabbinic program of "toilet training" in which the sage models correct behavior, much as parents allow their children to watch them at the toilet long before the explicit work of toilet training begins.

As these anecdotes suggest, for the classical rabbinic community, the sage *embodies* Torah, and students are to emulate this embodied Torah as a means to internalize it. Just as in the realm of intellectual formation discussed above, the rabbis' notion of embodied teaching paralleled, and thus stood in tension with, the primary, familial mode of bodily emulation. As Jaffee explains, "Whereas the child is formed through emulation of the adult kin, the disciple's task of emulation involves absorbing the teaching of a master in such a way as to embody the master's own human achievement."[36] In the context of rabbinic Judaism, face-to-face transmission and mimetic learning enabled the promise of Oral Torah to be realized. When successful, "the Rabbinic Sage was Torah transformed into an embodied form of human being.... The Sage, then, the person of the living Master, is our last crucial text of Torah."[37] The ultimate test of the success of all Torah transmission, for the rabbis, lay in its ability to become embodied in a human being, and in the possibility of a disciple "reading" the text that his master had become.

Parents' bodies, actions, and movements are the foundational teaching that their children absorb.[38] Engaged in ordinary, day-to-day moments of care and responsibility, a mother becomes a "living scroll" whose embodied Torah the child learns to read. This teaching, unlike intellectual teaching or factual knowledge, cannot be superseded; it becomes the ground of all that follows. What Jews call "Torah" is, in this sense, the universal embodied teaching all parents transmit to their children.

For the rabbis, as for others who position themselves as caretakers rather than innovators of a culture, the imitative ideal of learning goes hand in hand with the work of transmission. The task, as the self-styled rabbinic "caretakers" conceived of it, emphasizes the critical role of socializing the natals of a group to understand and care for the world into which they were born. Hannah Arendt's subtle discussion of education emphasizes conservation as a core meaning of education:

> Insofar as the child is not yet acquainted with the world, he must be gradually introduced to it; insofar as he is new, care must be taken that this new thing comes

to fruition in relation to the world as it is. In any case, however, the educators here stand in relation to the young as the representatives of a world for which they must assume responsibility, although they themselves did not make it, and even though they may, secretly or openly, wish it were other than it is. This responsibility is not arbitrarily imposed upon educators; it is implicit in the fact that the young are introduced by adults into a continuously changing world. Anyone who refuses to assume joint responsibility for the world should not have children and must not be allowed to take part in educating them.[39]

This view of education, which emphasizes the "world" (or what we may call the culture) into which children must be brought, necessarily grants a privileged place to imitative learning. Parental caregiving includes this kind of teaching, since parents raise children within a world and are their primary mediators of it.

But imitation is only one side of parental teaching. The other side involves a parent's recognition of difference, that is, the constitutional or dispositional impossibility of one's child fully "imitating" her parent. This recognition of a child's difference from oneself means that teaching, fully imagined, is known not only through children's absorption and recapitulation of their parents' bodily, intellectual, and even moral habits. Parental teaching is also located in those moments in which a parent faces the unassimilable difference of her child from herself and the need to think beyond what is intuitive or recognizable to her. Those moments shed light on the innovative, spontaneous, and creative work of teaching. Just as the vitality of Torah depends on reinterpretation, parental teaching depends on bridging the distance between parent and child without collapsing it.

Let us recall the larger context in which the rabbis conceived of their enterprise of transmission. As a number of scholars have noted, the rabbis' appropriation of familial metaphors for the relationship between master and disciple sought to harness the cultural authority once enjoyed by the priesthood. In Boyarin's account, "the Rabbis ... created a sort of meritocracy to replace the religious aristocracy that the Bible ordains [i.e., the priesthood]. Filiation is no longer from father to son but from teacher to disciple.... But the desire that genetic replicability be homologous with pedagogical replicability persists."[40] This tension between the powerful fantasy of filiation-as-imitation, on the one hand, and the recognition, in Boyarin's formulation, that "people do not reproduce each other" creates crises within Talmudic accounts of the relationships between sages and disciples.

For most parents, by contrast, intimate familiarity and involvement with one's child cannot avoid what we might call "the anxiety of filiation." But this intimacy usually makes clear the extent to which "replicability" is a fantasy. Daily caregiving is a mode of teaching that occurs in the nexus between the familiar and the strange, and which must wrestle with the ongoing persistence of the "different," with the *inability* to turn a child into the reproduction of the "same." To attend to a child continuously is to encounter the temperament, abilities, and disposition of someone different from the self.

The physical and emotional intimacy comprising the most elemental substance of maternal teaching engenders a familiarity that is not mastery but rather the constant surprise of difference and strangeness within the familiar. Out of palpable closeness comes the possibility of recognizing subtle but sudden changes in gait or expression or shape of the face, and with them, many other gaps between expectation and present reality.[41] Recognition of this difference lies at the deepest core of all teaching, which is successful or not to the degree it acknowledges the impossibility and ultimate undesirability of shaping the child, or the student, in one's own image. If biological or intellectual paternity, in the rabbinic shorthand, symbolizes identity and replicability, the actual work of attending to one's children constantly demands confrontation with the unexpected, new, and unfamiliar in a creature whom we may anticipate to be familiar. The language of "reproduction," implying that a child replicates the parent, thus testifies to a fantasy. Children cannot be directly traced to their genetic or social parents, even if their shared hair color or gestures would suggest as much.

This recognition of difference enables parents to learn from, and not only teach, their children. In this respect, parents resemble teachers in formal educational settings who speak of learning from their students, as in the famous saying of Rabbi Ḥanina: "I have learned much from my teachers, and from my colleagues more than my teachers, and from my students more than all of them" (bTa'anit 7a). But unlike the intellectual exchange that is the presumed context of Rabbi Ḥanina's statement, the daily, intimate care of young children demands a form of learning that reaches through and beyond intellectual engagement. The learning in which parents engage in the course of transmitting their own Torah to their children touches the core of how parents understand themselves and their world. Such a process lies at the heart of the creative work of interpretation.

The model of sage as the parent who embodies divine instruction suggests that the practice of ritual and intellectual Torah study is derivative. Ritualized Torah study reaches for a more basic and embodied practice of attention, care, and openness epitomized in the active care that mothers have, for generations, undertaken for their children. Moving from a past defined along gendered lines toward a more open future, we might say that the true disciple, or *talmid ḥakham*, gains Torah through more than the type of study typically valorized in Jewish cultures. The fully realized meaning of Torah is grasped and transmitted in the quotidian work of caring for young children, and the *talmid ḥakham* is one who disciplines the mind, heart, and body to engage in this work.

In the repetitive, often tiresome and exasperating labor of attending to one's child, we find a primal teaching practice. In it, teaching does not demand detachment from but rather invites attention to the body; the one-taught retains her otherness; and the teacher herself is destabilized and re-created. The Torah of care and obligation finds its source again.

Notes

An earlier version of this chapter was published as "On Teachers, Rabbinic and Maternal," in *Mothers in the Jewish Cultural Imagination*, ed. Marjorie Lehman, Jane Kanarek, and Simon Broner, 359–76. Liverpool, UK: Littman Library of Jewish Civilization, 2017.

1. Annette Lareau, *Unequal Childhoods: Class, Race, and Family Life*, 2nd ed. (Berkeley: University of California, 2011); Thomas Balmes, "Babies," (France, 2010).

2. David Lancy argues in his cross-cultural anthropological study that parental teaching is primarily mimetic and only exceptionally interventionist: "Active or direct teaching/instruction is rare in cultural transmission, and ... when it occurs, it is not aimed at critical subsistence or survival skills" (David F. Lancy, *The Anthropology of Childhood: Cherubs, Chattel, Changelings*, 2nd ed. [New York: Cambridge University Press, 2014], 205–206). This indirect or implicit instruction, however, doesn't just happen by itself; it relies on specific actors, especially (in many cultures) mothers.

3. Jeffrey Blustein, *Parents and Children: The Ethics of the Family* (New York: Oxford University Press, 1982), 26.

4. Erin M. Cline, *Families of Virtue: Confucian and Western Views on Childhood Development* (New York: Columbia University Press, 2015).

5. On Western philosophical understandings of parents as educators, see Blustein, *Parents and Children*. Hebrew does not have an equivalent term for "parenting": the closest term would be "raising children" [*legadel banim*], which lacks the quality of activity associated with the English term. As discussed in the introduction, the gender-neutral verb "parenting" is of recent vintage. Lofton notes, "Prior to the twentieth century, the verb *to parent* appeared rarely in the English lexicon, and as a noun it referred almost exclusively to a genealogical description (a person who is a progenitor of a child); before the nineteenth century, few invocations of parenting as a practice of cultivation exist, with an exponential increase in such usage after the 1920s" (Kathryn Lofton, "Religion and the Authority in American Parenting," *Journal of the American Academy of Religion* 84, no. 1 [2016]: 806–841).

6. Daniel Boyarin, *Carnal Israel: Reading Sex in Talmudic Culture* (Berkeley: University of California Press, 1993); Eliezer Diamond, *Holy Men and Hunger Artists: Fasting and Asceticism in Rabbinic Culture* (New York: Oxford University Press, 2004); Steven D. Fraade, "Ascetical Aspects of Ancient Judaism," in *Jewish Spirituality*, ed. Arthur Green (New York: Crossroad, 1986); Michael L. Satlow, "'And on the Earth You Shall Sleep': *Talmud Torah* and Rabbinic Asceticism," *Journal of Religion* 83, no. 2 (2003); Jonathan Wyn Schofer, *The Making of a Sage: A Study in Rabbinic Ethics* (Madison: University of Wisconsin Press, 2004). In spite of this attention to ascetic ideas within the rabbinic community, the sages lived among and met with each other within typical familial spaces and communities. The lack of a formal monastic structure within rabbinic Judaism thus created a tension for the sages, who counseled symbolic separation from familial life and the porous, vulnerable body. See Cynthia M. Baker, *Rebuilding the House of Israel: Architectures of Gender in Jewish Antiquity* (Stanford: Stanford University Press, 2002); Catherine Hezser, *The Social Structure of the Rabbinic Movement in Roman Palestine* (Tübingen: Mohr Siebeck, 1997); Jonathan Wyn Schofer, *Confronting*

Vulnerability: The Body and the Divine in Rabbinic Ethics (Chicago: University of Chicago Press, 2010); Alexei Sivertsev, *Households, Sects, and the Origins of Rabbinic Judaism* (Boston: Brill, 2005).

7. Martin Jaffee, "A Rabbinic Ontology of the Written and Spoken Word: On Discipleship, Transformative Knowledge, and the Living Texts of Oral Torah," *Journal of the American Academy of Religion* 65, no. 3 (1997): 530.

8. See also Gerald J. Blidstein, *Honor Thy Father and Mother: Filial Responsibility in Jewish Law and Ethics* (New York: Ktav, 1975), 138.

9. This Mishnah discusses a conflict over whether a father's or a teacher's lost object should be returned first; the teacher takes precedence "because his father brought him into this world; his teacher, who taught him wisdom, brings him life in the world to come. If his father is a sage, his father takes precedence." See bBaba Metzia 33a for additional exploration of this principle. For an extensive discussion of this Mishnah, see Blidstein, *Honor Thy Father and Mother*, 141–143, 215–217.

10. Boyarin, *Carnal Israel*, 217. Rachel Bowlby writes of similar claims to the superiority of metaphorical offspring over biological offspring for writers as diverse as Plato and Virginia Woolf: "What is desirable is a form of parenthood that exceeds—and thereby demotes—the physical reproduction of ordinary mortals. The creative person generates babies that are so much better than the ones that appear in everyday life; but babies is what he (or she) generates, and a parent, intellectual rather than bodily, is what the maker is, in relation to his or her creative productions" (Rachel Bowlby, *A Child of One's Own: Parental Stories* [Oxford: Oxford University Press, 2013], 11).

11. Elizabeth Shanks Alexander has argued that Torah study is presented as a means for the lay *pater familias* to replicate the (male) sagely community; see Elizabeth Shanks Alexander, *Gender and Timebound Commandments in Judaism* (New York: Cambridge University Press, 2013), 184–188. This means, however, that familial fatherhood is best accomplished when it consists in the work of teaching one's own child Torah; when such work is not done, fathers "merely" provide the raw material for a child's conception. (Fraade briefly notes, but does not fully consider, the possible negative implication of this ideological structure for the biological father; see Steven Fraade, *From Tradition to Commentary: Torah and Its Interpretation in the Midrash Sifre to Deuteronomy* [Albany: State University of New York Press, 1991], 257; Blidstein, *Honor Thy Father and Mother*.)

12. Among these tasks, mKetubbot 5:5 names only feeding an infant as a woman's responsibility. But this obligation, as I discuss in chapter 6, is conceived as a wife's duty to her husband, not a mother's duty to her child. On the implications of this legal formulation, see Elisheva Baumgarten, *Mothers and Children: Jewish Family Life in Medieval Europe* (Princeton: Princeton University Press, 2007), 119–154. The Talmud contains nothing comparable to the Tosefta's list of paternal obligations found in bQiddushin 29a for the obligations that mothers owe their children; neither can we find a comparable normative statement on what daughters should be given or taught by parents of either gender.

13. For this reason, a number of feminist theorists have rejected the term "parenting," even as many of them recommend that men care for infants and young children in the ways traditionally associated with mothers. See Virginia Held, "The Obligations of Mothers and Fathers," in *Mothering: Essays in Feminist Theory*, ed. Joyce Trebilcot (Totowa, NJ: Rowman & Allanheld, 1984); Sara Ruddick, *Maternal Thinking: Toward a Politics of Peace* (Boston: Beacon Press, 1989).

14. Confucian texts, by contrast, assign great weight to the mother's role as moral teacher; see Cline, *Families of Virtue*, 138.

15. John Dewey, *The Later Works, 1925–1953*, vol. 7 (Carbondale: Southern Illinois University Press, 1981), 40, quoted in Cline, *Families of Virtue*, 138.

16. As Rousseau writes in *Emile*, "As the true nurse is the mother, the true preceptor is the father" (Jean-Jacques Rousseau, *Emile: Or, on Education*, trans. Allan Bloom [Basic Books, 1979], 48). As Cline puts it, for Rousseau, "although most mothers desire the happiness of their children, most women are not smart enough to raise them properly" (Cline, *Families of Virtue*, 127–128).

17. The term comes from Lawrence A. Hoffman, *Covenant of Blood: Circumcision and Gender in Rabbinic Judaism* (Chicago: University of Chicago Press, 1996), 80–81.

18. In the Bavli, the discussion of this passage is framed by a discussion of the gendered nature and requirements of various *mitzvot*. There, women's exemption from all time-bound positive mitzvot is deduced from their exemption in *tefillin*. For a few of the many treatments of the relationship between women's exemption from time-bound mitzvot and the exclusion of girls from *talmud Torah*, see Alexander, *Gender and Timebound Commandments*; Judith Hauptman, *Rereading the Rabbis: A Woman's Voice* (Boulder: Westview Press, 1998); Natan Margalit, "Priestly Men and Invisible Women: Male Appropriation of the Feminine and the Exemption of Women from Positive Time-Bound Commandments," *AJS Review* 28, no. 2 (2004).

19. The Gemara recognizes the *mitzvah* of education/training (*ḥinukh*) a son in mitzvot incumbent on the father. *Ḥinukh* does not refer to "socialization" per se but rather specific ritual acts construed as positive commandments, such as fasting on Yom Kippur (bYoma 82a) or blowing the shofar (bRosh Hashana 32b–33a). bNazir 28b–29a establishes that a father is obligated to train his son, but not his daughter, and that a mother is not obligated to train her son (nor, we may infer, her daughter).

20. Adrienne Rich, *Of Woman Born: Motherhood as Experience and Institution*, 10th anniversary ed. (New York: Norton, 1986), 33.

21. Margalit, "Priestly Men and Invisible Women," 310.

22. On the issue of women in the "covenantal community," see Shaye J. D. Cohen, *Why Aren't Jewish Women Circumcised?: Gender and Covenant in Judaism* (Berkeley: University of California Press, 2005).

23. Ilana Pardes has explored this idea at length in *The Biography of Ancient Israel: National Narratives in the Bible* (Berkeley: University of California Press, 2000).

24. Michael A. Fishbane, *Sacred Attunement: A Jewish Theology* (Chicago: University of Chicago Press, 2008), 28. On the "birth of a nation" metaphor see Pardes, *The Biography of Ancient Israel*, 16.

25. On God as midwife: The midrash on Deut. 4:34 ("Has God ever ventured to go and take himself one nation from the midst of [*mi-kerev*] another") asks: "What is the force of ONE NATION FROM THE MIDST OF (lit., from the innards [*kerev*] of) ANOTHER NATION? Like a person who extracts a fetus from the bowels of the mother animal, God brought Israel out of Egypt." See Avivah Gottlieb Zornberg, *The Particulars of Rapture: Reflections on Exodus* (New York: Doubleday, 2001), 84–85; Gwynn Kessler, *Conceiving Israel: The Fetus in Rabbinic Narratives* (Philadelphia: University of Pennsylvania Press, 2009); Inbar Raveh, *Feminist Rereadings of Rabbinic Literature*, trans. Kaeren Fish (Waltham: Brandeis University Press, 2014).

On God as adoptive parent of abandoned child: See Pardes, *The Biography of Ancient Israel*; Marc Zvi Brettler, "Incompatible Metaphors for YHWH in Isaiah 40–66," *Journal for the Study of the Old Testament* 23, no. 78 (1998): 115–118; Mayer I. Gruber, *The Motherhood of God and Other Studies*, vol. 57 (Atlanta: Scholars Press 1992); Tikva Simone Frymer-Kensky, *In the Wake of the Goddesses: Women, Culture, and the Biblical Transformation of Pagan Myth* (New York: Free Press,

1992), 163–167; Sarit Kattan Gribetz, "Metaphors of Childbirth: Revisiting Women's Experience in Feminist Scholarship," (lecture, Society for Biblical Literature, Atlanta, 2015).

26. Others liken the manna to water and bread; see Géza Vermès, "'He Is the Bread': Targum Neofiti Exodus 16:15," in *Post-Biblical Jewish Studies* (Leiden: Brill, 1975); Jordan Rosenblum, *Food and Identity in Early Rabbinic Judaism* (New York: Cambridge University Press, 2010), 58–63; Ivan G. Marcus, *Rituals of Childhood: Jewish Culture and Acculturation in the Middle Ages* (New Haven, CT: Yale University Press, 1996).

27. In commenting on Joshua 5:12 ("And the manna ceased on the morrow, after they had eaten of the produce of the land; neither had the children of Israel manna any more; but they did eat of the fruit of the land of Canaan that year"), Rashi also draws the parallel between manna and infant food: "Therefore, they ate from the land. If they had manna, they wouldn't have eaten the fruit of the land, because the manna was easy for them. An appropriate parable is: One says to a child, why do you eat barley bread? Because he has no wheat bread. Therefore it says AND THERE WAS NO MORE [MANNA]" (Rashi ad loc. Joshua 5:12).

28. See discussion of this text in Vermès, "'He Is the Bread'," 142; Rosenblum, *Food and Identity*, 58–63. In Wisdom's invitation in Prov. 9:5 ("Come, eat of my bread, and drink of the wine which I have mingled") the rabbis also interpret the "bread" and "wine" as various elements of Torah. The Gospel of John (6:30 ff.) turns on the same imperative to ingest the Logos, as discussed in Vermès.

29. See chapter 6 for discussion of the *'omen*.

30. Pardes, *The Biography of Ancient Israel*, 51. Although my reading differs from Pardes's in naming this explosive anger as maternal, rather than paternal, rage, I am in agreement with her overall gloss on this verse and its difference from its retelling in Deuteronomy (cf. Pardes, *The Biography of Ancient Israel*, 55).

31. Raveh argues that a number of midrashim portray a gender conflict in which the male God is victorious over breastfeeding women. In this midrash, she argues, this gender contest continues: "The midrash goes to great pains to emphasize that 'just as' in the case of the female paired organ, there is no difference between Moses and Aaron in terms of greatness or importance. This is in itself quite surprising, considering that a discussion of the symmetry—or, more accurately, the discovery of asymmetry—in the appearance of actual female breasts is to be found in various halakhic contexts dealing with the development of the signs of puberty" (Raveh, *Feminist Rereadings*, 27).

32. For a comparative and theoretical perspective on men's appropriations of maternal imagery in a religious context, see Caroline Walker Bynum, "Jesus as Mother and Abbot as Mother: Some Themes in Twelfth-Century Cistercian Writing," in *Jesus as Mother: Studies in the Spirituality of the High Middle Ages* (Berkeley: University of California Press, 1984); *Holy Feast and Holy Fast: The Religious Significance of Food to Medieval Women* (Berkeley: University of California Press, 1987).

33. Ivan G. Marcus, *Rituals of Childhood: Jewish Culture and Acculturation in the Middle Ages* (New Haven, CT: Yale University Press, 1996), 85, 86, and 91. See also tHorayot 2:7: "He who teaches his fellow Mishnah is considered to have formed [*yitzro*] him, wove [*roqmo*] him, and brought him into the world." The master of Torah lays claim to quintessentially maternal activities, here evoking the physical dimension of "knitting together" the fetus in the womb along with birthgiving.

34. Elie Wiesel, *Souls on Fire: Portraits and Legends of Hasidic Masters*, trans. Marion Wiesel (New York: Random House, 1972), 61.

35. The same is Rav Kahana's response when his master, Rav, questions him for hiding under his marital bed, listening to his master's sexual activity and "pillow talk": "It is Torah

and I must learn it." (Boyarin, *Carnal Israel*, 122ff.). Simon-Shoshan considers the potential problems of the what he calls the rabbinic exemplum, the embodied sage whose exemplary acts are understood to "bridge the gap between lived experience and legal principles by bringing the exemplar's actual living deeds into the legal discourse" (Moshe Simon-Shoshan, "'People Talking without Speaking': The Semiotics of the Rabbinic Legal Exemplum as Reflected in Bavli Berakhot 11a," *Law & Literature* 25, no. 3 [2013]: 464).

36. Jaffee, "A Rabbinic Ontology," 530.

37. Jaffee, "A Rabbinic Ontology," 541–542.

38. I am grateful to Elizabeth Shanks Alexander for suggesting using Jaffee's insight this way.

39. Hannah Arendt, "The Crisis in Education," in *Between Past and Future: Eight Exercises in Political Thought* (New York: Penguin Books, 1977), 189.

40. Boyarin, *Carnal Israel*, 208, 10–11. In Boyarin's account, the rabbis were caught in the tension between their "desire on the one hand to pass on the mantle of Torah from father to son and the anxiety that, in a profound sense, *people do not reproduce each other ...*" (ital. in original).

41. Note that the discourse of replicability and sameness often, in androcentric texts, remains focused on physical resemblance: does the child "look like" his or her father to the paternal or nonparental observer. Such a focus befits a patriarchal anxiety about the adequate control of women's sexuality. For discussions of this issue with regard to rabbinic literature and in comparative religious perspective, see Kessler, *Conceiving Israel*; Kathryn Kueny, "Marking the Body: Resemblance and Medieval Muslim Constructions of Paternity," *Journal of Feminist Studies in Religion* 30, no. 1 (2014).

PART II

PART I

CHAPTER 5

The Other

For mothers, children simultaneously embody enmeshment and separation; merging and conflict; difference and identity; mine and not-mine. The oscillations between these modes of relation recur within the daily work of child-rearing. Parents participate in children's ongoing formation and discovery of themselves as unique individuals whose alterity, or "Otherness," is situated within recognizable patterns.

Witnessing and participating in a child's development over time does not leave parental selves untouched. Involvement in children's daily lives presents myriad opportunities for parents, too, to be re-formed, even transformed. Adrienne Rich notes that adults themselves are still "in process" as human beings when they become parents: "Most of the literature of infant care and psychology has assumed that the process toward individuation is essentially the *child*'s drama, played out against and with a parent or parents who are, for better or worse, givens. Nothing could have prepared me for the realization that I was a mother, one of those givens, when I knew I was still in a state of uncreation myself."[1] All adult selves remain in various "states of uncreation" throughout their lives. The persistent literary tendency to identify with the child, not the parent, has obscured the radical implications of Rich's insight: mothers are not merely the stable background against which the individual distinguishes himself; mothers are beings in formation.[2] Intimate involvement with a child lends a unique urgency, relentlessness, and intensity to the process of ongoing human growth.

Modern Jewish religious thinkers give us some of the tools with which to understand the theological significance of the fact that we are formed by our encounters with others. In a trajectory that spans twentieth-century Jewish thought, the relationship between an individual human being and an Other (or a "Thou") attained a place of centrality as philosophers attempted to chart new connections in the understanding of how relationships with other people shed light on God and vice versa. Hermann Cohen, Franz Rosenzweig, Martin Buber, and Emmanuel Levinas each formulated a distinctive notion of intersubjectivity, the phenomenon of the meeting between two subjects. Buber, building on themes in Rosenzweig, used "dialogue" to speak about authentic encounter between two human beings. Levinas, on the other hand, spoke of this encounter in terms of radical alterity, or otherness. In each case, however, the notion of certain dyadic encounters as constitutive of existential and ethical selfhood offers a promising start for articulating the existential significance of parent's relationship with her child.[3]

At the same time, the key models to emerge from the modern Jewish discourse have limitations that inhibit their ability to speak about maternal subjects. For instance, Jewish thinkers consistently speak of the "encounter" with the Other, implying a fleeting moment. But the relationship between parents and children brings with it duration and history, within which any momentary "encounter" is situated. In this chapter, I seek to both enrich and complicate the modern Jewish discourse on intersubjectivity by taking the relationship between mother and child as the paradigmatic example.

*　*　*

One of the critical axes of experience in the encounter with one's child is the interplay between encountering my child as "like me" and as "different from me." Each of these modes of relationship contains a distinctive understanding of what it means to confront a fellow person. While these different understandings have often been read as contradictory, or even opposed, to one another, most if not all parent/child relationships oscillate between these modes of being with other people. Neither can be fully disentangled from the other. This common but complex element of relationship between parents and children yields implications for broader issues of relationality as a whole that have all too often been read as utterly incompatible ethical and existential claims.

Children are a complicated kind of "Other." In the very moment of becoming a parent, my child's "otherness" asserts itself immediately and repeatedly, first and foremost in the fact of her bodily existence. The materiality of a newborn child seems to violate the law of the conservation of matter: suddenly there is something where nothing was before. Today, technologies may mitigate the absolute strangeness of one's child: sonograms make visible the previously invisible and unknowable; expanded networks of communication can give adoptive parents information about the sometimes faraway, unknown children to whom they will become parents.[4] But even so, the persistence of this uncanny otherness of another human being cannot be completely eradicated.

We may notice our children's separateness from us especially in those moments when their needs conflict with our own: the baby needs to be changed, fed, or rocked at the very instant that her mother needs to sleep, eat, or use the toilet. But the experience of my child's otherness is apparent not only in moments of conflict; it also occurs in moments of simple *difference*. From the beginning, one's child asserts her otherness in a thousand ways daily. She does this by making demands on her parent, literally, metaphysically, and ethically. John Wall speaks of these demands in terms of "disruption" of the self, in which "the fact of a child's existence, whether upon birth or otherwise, obliges persons and communities to undergo constant and unanticipated self-trans-formation."[5] Moments of existential disruption occur in the most prosaic and ordinary of ways, sometimes in anticipation of a child's arrival (looking for the first time at the location of parks and schools in relation to one's home) but often in response to the particular needs and desires of this particular child: he loves dogs, so I now take him to visit the neighbor's dog; she is autistic and disturbed by too much noise, so I seek out calm environments and avoid cha-otic places.

In revealing the way she comes to make sense of the world and responds to it, my child surprises me, annoys me, teaches me, oppresses me, and pulls me up short. Any and all of these moments remind me that she is *not me*. This sense of my child's difference is what I will refer to as her "otherness." The valence of this "not me-ness" can shift dramatically even within the course of a day: I may experience my child's being "not me" as a relief, a burden, a delight, or a startling mystery. Unlike the difference of other others—a spouse, a neighbor—my child is the other to whom I am tethered and the one who is abjectly and materially dependent on me. To be a parent, as Andrew Solomon has written, is to be in "a permanent relationship with a stranger."[6]

This gap pulls parents up short. We have a deeply rooted understanding of our children as not only *known*, but also as *ours, of us*. As Solomon documents in his investigation of children whose social and physical identities create a "horizontal" social identity that differs from that of their parents, experiences of a child's alter-ity can be difficult because of the omnipresent assumption that children "take after" their parents. The assumption that one's child extends or even replicates the self makes manifestations of difference particularly charged.

The drive to connect parents and children as the "same" is expressed in the most prosaic of ways. New parents and their kin, for instance, routinely remark that the baby "looks like" biologically related family members. More than con-firming an objective reality, this "resemblance talk" is a means of seeking out, affirming, and creating a sense of belonging that mitigates the otherness of one's child.[7] This symbolism of belonging, of which resemblance talk is just one example, is both something parents *feel* as one element of their relationships with their children and something they may *feel compelled to feel*. When both biologi-cal and nonbiological parents look to a familiar gesture or a verbal expression, they are seeking to establish and affirm a common participation in a shared and recognizable reality, in which "you belong with me and I with you."

Resemblance talk is a way of speaking about the legibility of two people as kin, as parent and child. The omnipresence of visual resemblance can be painful or difficult as well as the occasion of delight and reassurance. Parents who are not biologically related to their children but who bear a passing likeness to their children face internal as well as external questions of whether to openly respond to or redirect resemblance talk. Parents whose looks differ enough from their children to forestall resemblance talk, as in transracial adoption, may long for strangers to recognize them and their children as belonging together, and may take more deliberate measures to make clear their status as kin. Same-sex parental couples may experience heightened awareness of the difficulty of achieving the sense of belonging together that strangers' recognition of them as family confers. Biological parents whose hair texture, shade of skin, body type, or facial expression don't seem to "match" their children's find themselves needing to account for this discrepancy.[8]

All of these emotional valences point to the force of the notion that one's child participates in something of the parent. In contemporary America, this understanding of participation is heavily weighted toward a strong sense of parental responsibility for who children become. Parents are endowed with a decisive role in shaping their children and attending to their individual talents and proclivities, rather than merely guarding them as they unfurl along more or less typical paths of development.[9] The growing research into genetic and other biological and environmental explanations for children's personalities, abilities, and dispositions have not yet shifted this entrenched sense that deliberate parental activity constitutes the primary factor in shaping children's character. Mothers in particular are implicitly tasked with the crucial role in child formation, freighting the work of recognition and resemblance with the weight of moral responsibility.

The almost inevitable grappling with visual resemblance suggests a much more profound set of questions about connection and belonging, with which parents, perhaps especially contemporary American parents, struggle. To raise a child is not merely to watch from the sidelines as an infant unfolds into an adult, but to *participate* in that person's development in ways that will always remain too deeply imbricated with environmental elements to disentangle.

The heavy burden of parental, especially maternal, responsibility for children reflects a peculiarly modern and American sensibility. As David Lancy has argued, the Puritans "were the first society to create a truly comprehensive theory of childrearing," one that reflected a growing sense of children's malleability, and which informed future Americans' understanding of the inordinately powerful responsibility of parental work.[10] Lancy writes, "The Puritans were perhaps the first anxious parents, fearing they might fail and their children would turn out badly. Many migrated to found new communities in order to isolate their children from the harmful effects of nonbelieving peers, much like parents today moving to a neighborhood because it has 'good' schools."[11] Although the characteristically Puritan understanding of children as sinful and animalistic has been replaced by secular and comparatively rosy beliefs, parental implication in children's eventual character remains strong in many corners of American culture. Modern Western societies' increasing understanding of genetic predispositions, capacities, and limits has not replaced this sense of the parents' capacity to mold their children, and most parents internalize the sense that their children will perforce bear traces of themselves that go beyond the "passive" transmission of genetics.

Paradoxically, those people who "know" their children best through this intimate care are the ones who are best able to appreciate those children's instability and alterity. The material activities of caring for young children take place within a context of participatory recognition and difference. Parents who acquire a lexicon of their children's bodies develop an increasingly intimate knowledge of their child. Yet the very activities of feeding and diapering and comforting that child—the immersive classroom in which adults learn their children's particular somatic vocabulary—reveal an unstable, dynamic, unmasterable language. The infant who was content to gaze at the mobile now reaches for it; the toddler who was startled at the noise of a pot clanging now wants to bang it herself; the preschooler whose fingers tightened in fear at the sight of a dog now releases our hand and runs toward the animal excitedly. Our child's somatic language changes before we can ever hope to gain fluency in it. And like the bodily expressions we decode, cognitive awareness and emotional complexity, too, are always in flux, as are our children's needs and capacities. The physical intimacy that is the most elemental substance of maternal care engenders a familiarity that is not mastery, but rather the constant surprise of difference and strangeness *within* the familiar. Out of tactile closeness comes the possibility of recognizing the subtle but sudden change in gait, in expression, in shape of the face, in gesture, and thus of noticing the gap between expectation and present reality.[12] Within the familiar and the known, difference constantly asserts itself; yet otherness, in this case, is inextricable from recognition and participation.

This oscillation between sameness and difference offers a case in which the opposition between unity and alterity reveals distinct elements of an existential truth. Intimate involvement with one's small child reveals that a theory of intersubjectivity rooted in the parent/child dyad must include the ethical challenge of Otherness. But otherness is not the only truth of these relationships. A sense of belonging and familiarity—even if it is only partial, episodic, and constantly subject to the irruption of difference—is inevitable for people who spend long periods of time helping children develop into themselves. Belonging and sameness, mystery and alterity: as distinctive as they are from each other, they can in fact only be articulated in relation to one another.

* * *

This paradoxical interweaving of difference and participatory "sameness," so evident in common parental experience, teaches broader theological and ethical truths. The theological, political, and ethical stakes of questions of alterity, or radical difference, on the one hand, and interconnectedness, on the other, have animated the core of Jewish thought and modern religious thought throughout the modern period. The philosophers who approached these questions of difference and sameness primarily through the lens of theology and politics typically present them as mutually exclusive alternatives. But the co-presence of these different modes in a single experiential reality, which is particularly acute in the experience of caring for one's own child, offers a point of departure for a corrective to modern Jewish orthodoxies. Rather than insisting on the irreducible alterity of the other, or a monism that denies radical alterity, we find here an intersubjectivity that encompasses both.

In the period during and following the First World War, Jewish and Christian Central European thinkers began to speak of God as "totally Other." Societal and cultural upheaval led the way toward revolution in vast arenas of European culture; in theology, Karl Barth and Franz Rosenzweig articulated God's Otherness in contrast to the approach of nineteenth-century liberal and Romantic thinkers in the model of Schleiermacher and Feuerbach.[13] Revelation—true revelation—could only come from *outside* what humans could devise, not from within; only alterity could intervene against the excesses of claims to "totality"—whether in its Hegelian-idealist or Stalinist-totalitarian forms. For Emmanuel Levinas, who placed alterity at the center of his ethical philosophy, the simultaneous demands of epistemological humility and ethical responsibility spring from the irreducible alterity of the other who commands me.

The theological conception of the Other that gave rise to Levinasian ethics has an analogue in the relationship to one's child. The visceral experience of a child's otherness points to the importance of humility before the mystery that is the other—an other toward whom parents often feel a proprietary "sameness." If I understand my child only as fundamentally "like me," I can too easily fail to reckon with her uniqueness and the unique command she issues to me. What psychologists call projection—the tendency to identify the other's experience with that of the self—can obscure my attention to my child's difference from and claim on me.

However, to consider one's child *only* through the lens of alterity is descriptively inadequate. The parental experience of resemblance and "belonging together" may be hard-won or effortless, fraught or comfortable, a source of pride or of shame, but it is inescapable as a daily, lived question. As I have suggested, the work of parenting engenders not only a sense of one's child's otherness but also moments of somatic and characterological "likeness"—that is, a kind of attunement to the repetition or extension of events in a parent's life to a child, or, conversely, to the interruption of familiar and experienced realities. Whether parents feel this likeness spontaneously or whether they unconsciously seek it out is less relevant for our purposes than the fact that parenting, almost by definition, invites questions of belonging. Thus radical alterity alone cannot be adequate as a conceptual framework through which to understand the particular kind of Otherness that one's own child represents.

In theological discourse, a number of recent theologians, Jewish and non-Jewish, have pointed to the inadequacies of radical alterity alone as a framework for conceiving of God. Models of interconnectivity alongside difference have been offered in order to conceive of the relationships among humans, between humans and nonhuman life, and, especially, of human beings in relation to God. Such models can be useful in thinking about how to map parents' particular relationships with their children. While the roots of this emphasis on interconnection in the modern period reach back to Spinoza, contemporary theologians have harnessed the panentheism that was posited in contradiction to monotheism as a viable Jewish theological option.

The Jewish panentheism of Arthur Green, Marcia Falk, and, most recently, Judith Plaskow emphasizes the interconnection of all beings and the immersion of all humans and the created world within God as well.[14] In contrast to conceiving of God as utterly inaccessible, these thinkers imagine humans as participating, along with the rest of creation, *in* God. As Green argues, "The 'radical otherness' of God, so insisted upon by Western theology, is not an ontological otherness but an otherness of perspective," one that allows for us to perceive reality as unitive.[15] These theologians differ in how they find this panentheistic perception of reality adequately expressed (or not) in our inherited God-language, and especially the language of a personal God. But in each case, the difference between Creator and creation is not conceived as dualistic; the contradiction exists only in human perception.[16] Thus rather than radical alterity, these theologians propose nonoppositional difference to constitute the distinctions among humans, among tribes or peoples, and between humans and God.

Especially for feminist theologians, a panentheist approach challenges the radical otherness that has been so problematic for women and other subjugated peoples. Panentheism, they argue, enables the recognition of difference without the binary opposition that can easily, and has often, become part of the discourse of Otherness. Images such as the spider's web, in Catherine Keller's classic account, convey the links that tie human beings, and indeed all of creation, together. For these thinkers, this mode of connection has a theological as well as a social or natural dimension: the divine is, and is in, the web.[17] These contemporary Jewish panentheists have argued that an impersonal concept of God is most appropriate for contemporary theology: a God who is immanent in creation. Thus we find an emphasis on *participation in* and *connection to* the other; she remains different from me, but never radically so.

Maternal reflection on the experience of ongoing relationship with children reveals otherness, entanglement, ownership, alienation, and collaboration. Children remain opaque and untranslatable to us; in this, they are like any other fellow human. However, they are *also* are subjects whom we know deeply, and people with whom we experience and seek out resemblance. The oscillations between contradictory modes of relationship and the paradoxical co-presence of multiple modes within the same moment require theological models that can contain the difference one's own child presents to a parent, while embedding that difference within a framework of searching for interconnection and participation.

Both sides of this theological fault line engage not only metaphysical but also ethical questions. The latter concern my response, and my responsibility, to the other. If the other is radically other than me, in what sense do I bear responsibility for her? If I am part of all others, to what extent can I imagine myself as separate enough to bear responsibility for any individual?

According to Jewish thinkers who emphasize alterity, only what is truly outside of us can constitute a revelation and a command. In the best-known works of Rosenzweig and Levinas, I do not merely *encounter* the other, but I am also *commanded* by him—whether that other is God (as for Rosenzweig) or another person (as for Levinas). *The Star of Redemption*, Rosenzweig's magnum opus, presents God's command as precisely that which brings humans out of their "self-enclosure" as individuals and, eventually, as a whole. Only God can "interrupt" human self and instigate revelation, and God can do so only because he is utterly irreducible to what humans can conceive. This insistence on the specifically divine locus of alterity characterizes what some scholars have dubbed Rosenzweig's theocentrism.

Levinas built on Rosenzweig's framework but translated his notion of existential encounter into the interhuman sphere: not God but my fellow human, in her defenseless need, shatters my illusions of self-contained, autonomous agency, interrupting and making demands on me.[18] The face of the other, Levinas writes, "imposes itself ... precisely by appealing to me with its destitution and nudity— its hunger—without my being able to be deaf to that appeal."[19] The other *solicits* me, yet also stands "above" me, as it were, with an extreme and irreducible moral authority (what Levinas calls "infinity"): "This infinity, stronger than murder, already resists us in his face, is his face, is the primordial expression, is the first word: 'you shall not commit murder.'"[20] This primordial "command," as Levinas suggests, issues from the face of the other, who will always remain utterly other to me; the command not to murder is a command not to obliterate the ethical demand the Other makes by his presence.

Yet if the alterity of my child cannot be apprehended without the backdrop of the familiar and vice versa, so too might we say that the command my child issues and the responsibility I have toward her can only be comprehended through intimacy. My child's "first word," in Levinas's existential-ethical sense, may indeed be "you shall not commit murder;" yet this single existential commandment emerges as a multiple-times-daily "command" to locate difference (the mysterious that always remains beyond my grasp) within the familiar, and familiarity (what I recognize as having a claim on me) within difference. Children's needs and abilities can be plotted in the abstract, but the distinctive needs of any given child determines the command she issues. The specific command can only be heard in the immediacy of one's particular child at a particular moment.

In other words, a child does not merely issue a single *abstract* existential command, *contra* Levinas's portrayal of the paradigmatic encounter, but issues embodied and variable commands that are just as existentially significant as "do not murder." Discernment and error are constant companions in the effort to enact my responsibility to this particular other. Responding to the command requires deliberative work and not merely the adoption of a posture of service. Responsibility need not derive only from radical alterity, but can emerge as the inevitable result of my participation—and thus my implication—in the embedded experience of the world of my child and of the world we share together.[21]

The participatory origin of responsibility is underscored when we consider how parents' responsibility for their children changes over the course of months and years, periodically shifting and realigning. What parents and children experience over time is not a progressive movement in the direction of "equality," but usually something much more complex: parents retain their "parenthood" even when they become increasingly dependent physically or emotionally on others, including their children. The parent is never "just another person," even for children who grow into independent adulthood and whose capabilities or achievements may equal or exceed their parents'. An adult child's care for an aging parent cannot be mapped as a reciprocal relationship, or as "payback" for the parent's care for that child, without flattening the emotional and social complexities of this quasi-inversion of care.

Nevertheless, an indirect, oblique goal of mutuality may nonetheless inform what many parents seek for their children, a mutuality that will not be recompensed to the parents themselves but will only be manifested in relation to a different set of recipients. As the first Jewish "memoirist" Glikl of Hameln underscores at the beginning of her text, wise parents do not strive to recoup any direct return on the investment of child-rearing. Glikl recounts a fable in which a father bird transports his fledglings over dangerous waters. He tests them by demanding the fledglings to swear that they will care for him as he has for them. The first two fledglings so swear, but the father calls them liars and drops them into the raging waters. Glikl concludes,

> Finally he set out with the third fledgling, and when he asked the same question, the third and last fledgling replied, "My dear father, it is true that you are struggling mightily and risking your life on my behalf, and I shall be wrong not to repay you when you are old, but I cannot bind myself. This though I can promise: when I am grown up and have children of my own, I shall do as much for them as you have done for me." Whereupon the father bird said, "Well spoken, my child, and wisely; your life I will spare and I will carry you to shore in safety."[22]

In the post-industrial West, as for Glikl, parents generally strive to raise children who are socially, economically, and in other respects independent; "mutuality" and "reciprocity" (let alone "reversibility") are not usually thought of as ideals for the eventual relationship between parent and child, at least not in any simple sense.[23] Rather, children are expected to show their future children the care from which they themselves benefited.[24] A critical piece of the parent's task is welcoming and encouraging the development of a child's capacity for mutuality in relationship, knowing that the relationship with one's child will never be directly "reversible" or "reciprocal."[25]

Parents' simultaneous sense of *responsibility for* and *implication in* their children suggests that the Other need not be figured as utterly outside of oneself in order to issue a command, nor as simply as an extension of oneself in order to be perceived as a co-participant in a common reality. So too for the divine Other. The interconnection, difference, and responsibility that characterizes the asymmetrical relationship between God and human beings is given texture by the work of caring for and raising a child.

The resulting theological insight ultimately may not be best articulated by a strict panentheism, but by a modification of the theology of radical alterity such that intimacy and mystery can be seen as dialectically related. In a comment written several years after *The Star of Redemption*, Rosenzweig looked askance at the theological insistence on God as radically other. Speaking of contemporaneous Protestant theologians like Karl Barth (but implicating the theology of his own earlier volume as well), Rosenzweig scoffed, "We have it now: that God is Wholly Other, that to talk about Him is to talk Him away, that we can only say what He does to us."[26] But *experientially*, Rosenzweig argued, people know what it is to feel divine nearness *and* absence, and thus "the faraway God is none other than the near God, the unknown God none other than the revealed one.... Even in the most dreadful nearness the human can look away and then does not know in the least what has happened to him. And in the farthest distance the glance of God and of the human can burn into one another."[27] The human being who understands herself as a matter of divine concern cannot have theological intimacy without theological mystery and vice versa.

Child-rearing is a daily practicum in this complex form of relationality. To be immersed in the work of caring for a child is to experience harmonious oneness and radical rupture, to know resemblance and alienation on a cellular level. In doing so, we viscerally encounter the religious sensibility Rosenzweig describes, of "dreadful nearness" and farthest distance that cannot but command our concern.

Notes

An early version of this chapter appeared as "Intersubjectivity Meets Maternity: Buber, Levinas, and the Eclipsed Relation," in *Thinking Jewish Culture in America*, ed. Ken Koltun-Fromm, (New York: Lexington Books, 2014), 261–284.

1. Adrienne Rich, *Of Woman Born: Motherhood as Experience and Institution*, 10th anniversary ed. (New York: Norton, 1986), 17.

2. Susan Suleiman, writing about this tendency in psychoanalytic literature, puts it simply: *Mothers don't write, they are written* (Suleiman, "Writing and Motherhood," in *Mother Reader: Essential Writings on Motherhood*, ed. Moyra Davey ([New York: Seven Stories Press, 1985], 117).

3. For one feminist assessment of this legacy, which connects these thinkers' work on intersubjectivity to the ethics of care, see Leora Batnitzky, "Dependence and Vulnerability: Jewish and Existentialist Constructions of the Human," in *Women and Gender in Jewish Philosophy*, ed. Hava Tirosh-Samuelson (Indianapolis: Indiana University Press, 2004).

4. The "knowledge" these technologies offer are hardly neutral; they participate in consumerism, the attack on women's reproductive freedom, and the politics of race and disability. See for instance Janelle S. Taylor, "A Fetish Is Born: Sonographers and the Making of the Public Fetus," in *Consuming Motherhood*, ed. Janelle S. Taylor, Linda L. Layne, and Danielle F. Wozniak (New Brunswick: Rutgers University Press, 2004); Erik Parens and Adrienne Asch, *Prenatal Testing and Disability Rights*, Hastings Center Studies in Ethics (Washington, DC: Georgetown University Press, 2000). Sara Dubow reminds us, however, that technological advances in prenatal imaging are embedded in a broader history: "Although it is true that ultrasound technology has familiarized a particular visual image of the fetus, that image is only one moment along the historical continuum of Americans' encounters with the fetal body" (Sara Dubow, *Ourselves Unborn: A History of the Fetus in Modern America* [Oxford: Oxford University Press, 2011], 6).

5. John Wall, *Ethics in Light of Childhood* (Washington, DC: Georgetown University Press, 2010), 90.

6. Andrew Solomon, *Far from the Tree: Parents, Children and the Search for Identity* (New York: Scribner, 2012), 1.

7. Gay Becker, Anneliese Butler, and Robert D. Nachtigall, "Resemblance Talk: A Challenge for Parents Whose Children Were Conceived with Donor Gametes in the Us,"

Social Science & Medicine 61, no. 6 (2005); Karín Lesnik-Oberstein, *On Having an Own Child: Reproductive Technologies and the Cultural Construction of Childhood* (London: Karnac Books, 2007).

8. Solomon explores the flip side of the reign of "resemblance" in his chapter on children conceived through rape, documenting the pain some biological mothers experience in sensing a child's perceived resemblance to the biological father; see Solomon, *Far from the Tree*, ch. 9.

9. The effects of this hegemonic ideology of parental responsibility for the development of a child's personhood go beyond specific class practices, but are particularly pronounced in the middle and upper class practices of "concerted cultivation" in contemporary America. See Annette Lareau, *Unequal Childhoods: Class, Race, and Family Life*, 2nd ed. (Berkeley: University of California, 2011). Cross-cultural, transhistorical, and cross-class studies reveal the peculiarity of this practice, such as Erin M. Cline, *Families of Virtue: Confucian and Western Views on Childhood Development* (New York: Columbia University Press, 2015) and Steven Mintz, *Huck's Raft: A History of American Childhood* (Cambridge, MA: Belknap Press, 2004).

10. David F. Lancy, *The Anthropology of Childhood: Cherubs, Chattel, Changelings*, 2nd ed. (New York: Cambridge University Press, 2014), 152–153. See also Mintz, *Huck's Raft*, 71.

11. Lancy, *The Anthropology of Childhood*, 153, quoting C. John Sommerville, *The Rise and Fall of Childhood* (Beverly Hills, CA: Sage Publications, 1982), 112–113.

12. Note that the discourse of replicability and sameness often, in androcentric texts, remains focused on physical resemblance, that is, whether the child "look like" his or her father to the paternal or nonparental observer. Such a focus befits a patriarchal anxiety about the adequate control of women's sexuality. For discussions of this issue with regard to rabbinic literature and in comparative religious perspective, see Gwynn Kessler, *Conceiving Israel: The Fetus in Rabbinic Narratives* (Philadelphia: University of Pennsylvania Press, 2009) and Kathryn Kueny, *Conceiving Identities: Maternity in Medieval Muslim Discourse and Practice* (Albany: State University of New York Press, 2013).

13. On the comparison and differences between Rosenzweig and Barth, see Randi Rashkover, *Revelation and Theopolitics: Barth, Rosenzweig, and the Politics of Praise* (London; New York: T&T Clark, 2005); Mara H. Benjamin, *Rosenzweig's Bible: Reinventing Scripture for Jewish Modernity* (New York: Cambridge University Press, 2009). On Jewish engagement with the idea of God as "totally Other," see Samuel Moyn, *Origins of the Other: Emmanuel Levinas between Revelation and Ethics* (Ithaca, NY: Cornell University Press, 2005), ch. 4.

14. Marcia Falk, *The Book of Blessings: New Jewish Prayers for Daily Life, the Sabbath, and the New Moon Festival* (San Francisco, CA: HarperSanFrancisco, 1996); Arthur Green, *Radical Judaism: Rethinking God and Tradition* (New Haven, CT: Yale University Press, 2010), 18; Judith Plaskow and Carol Christ, *Goddess and God in the World: Conversations in Embodied Theology* (Minneapolis, MN: Augsburg Fortress, 2016).

15. Green, *Radical Judaism*, 18.

16. Like Green, Falk suggests that we can overcome the divisions between God and "world" or "creation" in moments of perceiving a transcendence embedded within immanence: "Speaking personally, I would describe my own experience of the divine as an awareness, of a sensing, of the dynamic, alive, and unifying wholeness within creation—a wholeness that subsumes and contains and embraces me, a wholeness greater than the sum of its parts" (Falk, *The Book of Blessings*, 419).

17. Catherine Keller, *From a Broken Web: Separation, Sexism, and Self* (Boston: Beacon Press, 1986).

18. Roger Burggraeve has suggested the crying infant as an example: the infant overwhelms the carer's illusions of self-sufficiency; she interrupts the self-containedness

of the parent (Burggraeve, "The Ethical Voice of the Child: Plea for a Chiastic Responsibility in the Footsteps of Levinas," in *Children's Voices: Children's Perspectives in Ethics, Theology and Religious Education*, ed. Annemie Dillen and Didier Pollefeyt [Leuven: Peeters, 2010]).

19. Indeed, many parents involved in caring for young children might be the ones most likely to endorse Levinas's later formulation that this particular Other holds me hostage. Derrida explores the meaning of the language of "hostage" (in Levinas, *Otherwise than Being*) in Jacques Derrida, *Adieu to Emmanuel Levinas*, Meridian, Crossing Aesthetics (Stanford: Stanford University Press, 1999), 56–63.

20. Emmanuel Levinas, *Totality and Infinity: An Essay on Exteriority*, trans. Alphonso Lingis (Pittsburgh, PA: Duquesne University Press, 1969), 199–200.

21. As panentheist and monist thinkers argue, the implications of my necessary connection to the world within which I am embedded extend beyond the social, to the environmental level as well.

22. Glückel, *The Life of Glückel of Hameln, 1646–1724*, ed. Beth-Zion Abrahams (Philadelphia, PA: Jewish Publication Society, 1962), 8–9.

23. Christine Gudorf has remarked, in the context of her critique of agape in Reinhold Niebuhr, "With our own children we realized very clearly that though much of the early giving seemed to be solely ours, this was not disinterested, because the children were considered extensions of us, such that our efforts for them rebounded to our credit. Failure to provide for them would have discredited us. And we had expectations that giving would be mutual. This led to the most revealing lesson the children taught us: that complete agape as either intention or as result is impossible" (Gudorf, "Parenting, Mutual Love, and Sacrifice," in *Women's Consciousness and Women's Conscience: A Reader in Feminist Ethics*, ed. Barbara Hilkert Andolsen, Christine E. Gudorf, and Mary D. Pellauer [San Francisco: Harper & Row, 1985], 181–182).

24. The corresponding expectation is also widely shared: children who are not given proper care as youngsters will be unable to (or will at least have a much harder time learning to) parent properly in adulthood.

25. That having been said, the expectation of children to provide—directly or indirectly—for elderly parents is a topic important both in classical religious texts and in contemporary considerations of filial responsibility. For an example of each in a Jewish context, see bQiddushin 30b–32a and Gerald J. Blidstein, *Honor Thy Father and Mother: Filial Responsibility in Jewish Law and Ethics* (New York: Ktav, 1975), 60–74.

26. Franz Rosenzweig, "The Far-and-Near One," in *Franz Rosenzweig and Jehuda Halevi: Translating, Translations, and Translators*, ed. Galli (Montreal: McGill-Queen's University Press, 1995), 205.

27. Barbara E. Galli, *Franz Rosenzweig and Jehuda Halevi: Translating, Translations, and Translators* (Montreal: McGill-Queen's University Press, 1995), 204–206. Rosenzweig here comments on a poem by the medieval writer Yehuda Halevi, which Rosenzweig referred to as "The Far-and-Near One." See also the discussion in Moyn, *Origins of the Other*, 158–160.

CHAPTER 6

The Third

Some moments in the work of child-rearing are clearly dyadic in nature. But these episodic experiences of dyadic intimacy are nestled in more complex webs of relationship. Parenting demands an intersection with many others on whom a parent relies and whose presence shapes the life, mind, and selfhood of one's child. Privileging the felt, but also the idealized, experience of dyadic intimacy often comes at the expense of recognizing the many other people involved in the work of having and raising children.

In this chapter, I examine the implications for theology of the nonparental adults who participate in intimate caregiving within and beyond the domicile: the nanny, the close aunt, the day care provider. I refer to this category of person as the "Third." This designation acknowledges both the dyadic elements that can characterize parent/child encounters and how the parent/child couple, as it were, is constructed in so much contemporary literature on parenting.[1] This term also gestures toward Emmanuel Levinas's concept of "the third party." For Levinas, the "third party" refers to a person who lies beyond the Self and Other, and whose presence signals ethical and political dimensions beyond what can be found within the dyad itself.[2] As in Levinas's work, the singular term (the Third) should not imply that there is only one "third party"; rather, each dyadic relationship has many "thirds." My analysis, however, is not a Levinasian account of the Third; instead, I offer a textual and theological account of the nonparental adults who are intimately involved in the daily material and spiritual care of specific children.

Contemporary theologies of parental care typically elide the presence of these Thirds, but biblical and rabbinic texts help us conceptualize the theological significance of caregiving beyond the nuclear family. Jewish textual traditions recognize other actors who share responsibility for the proper cultivation of children. As Erin Cline's cross-cultural study of child-rearing in religious ethics demonstrates, sophisticated systems for allocating child-rearing responsibility within and beyond the family vary widely across traditions.[3] Substantial debate regarding "who should bear primary responsibility for the child-rearing task" likewise occurs within cultures and religious traditions.[4]

Contemporary American social and political policy allocates child-rearing to the so-called "private sphere" of parents and their hired substitutes. This allocation suggests that children are not "a collective good ... but a good assigned to individual parents."[5] Beyond a general critique of this problematic arrangement, feminists face an additional imperative to take non-parental caregivers seriously in any discussion of parental care and parental subjectivity. The feminist revolution that opened up the professional classes to women left what has been called an "unfinished agenda:" the burden of childcare shifted from parents (usually mothers) to hired workers without improving the situation for the workers, most of whom are working class women.[6] In the majority of households in the contemporary United States, childcare is provided by a person other than the child's parent for significant periods before children reach school age; indeed, in some households, children spend many more waking hours with these caregiving adults than with their parents.[7] These adults include grandparents, stepparents, aunts, nannies, day care workers, neighbors, au pairs, and long-term babysitters. Recognizing the true allocation of caring labor reveals the inadequacies of the hegemonic model of childcare within the nuclear family.

This chapter aims to develop a richer vocabulary for the role and meaning of the Third, especially the paid nonfamilial caregiver, in the construction of a theological account of maternal subjectivity. While many feminist theorists have aimed to integrate recognition of what I am calling the Third into a variety of fields—such as economic and political analysis of labor within the household, or in psychological and educational analysis of child development—I explore the moral, theological, and existential significance of the Third for parental caregiving. In locating the Third in of biblical and rabbinic texts, we can simultaneously destabilize the parent/child "couple" and fashion a lexicon with which to articulate her role.

* * *

For many middle-class, upper-middle-class and upper-class families, the Third is represented primarily by the nonfamilial, usually female, adult who is paid by the parent(s) for her time, labor, and affection. The seemingly straightforward arrangement of caregiver as employee, however, masks a complex reality of relationships that develop between parent and hired caregiver (and, of course, with the child or children cared for). Caregiving by definition creates often long-lasting affective relationships, distinct from many other forms of service work. Childcare workers often develop strong bonds with the children for whom they care (and sometimes with their employing parents). But unlike relatives, who are understood to be permanent members of an extended family, paid nonfamilial caregivers are resident aliens, as it were, within a family rather than full citizens in it. Even caregivers who spend many years with a given household know that they can be dismissed from it and that their authority is circumscribed. This peculiar combination of emotional ties and explicit economic contracting produces a confusing liminal space in which employing parents, in particular, struggle to articulate the contradictions of the "accidental family" they have created.[8]

A range of conceptual possibilities undergirds the relationships parents develop with Thirds. A Third may be conceived as "subcontractor" to whom parents "outsource" caregiving tasks. In this paradigm of delegated care, a nanny feeds the child instead of the parent doing it himself; a schoolteacher is conceived as a substitute for the educational work that is properly performed by the parent.[9] This model speaks to the real economic effects of caring for children: parents who care for their own children typically cannot hold a job outside the house; a paid caregiver frees up the parent's labor for her own paid work.

But viewing such arrangements only as economic transactions is unsatisfactory. The Third cannot be reduced to a (fungible) substitute for the (irreplaceable) parent. The Third(s) within any given family become part of the caregiving landscape within which specific children are raised. In addition, transactional accounts of the Third typically assume that she is a substitute caregiver for the wife/mother, as if caregiving were privately subcontracted out to relieve women of their burden of caregiving. If so, then childcare remains a *mother*'s duty, not a father's, much less that of a neighborhood, a community, a municipality, or a society.[10] Finally, this model cannot account for the domestic worker's own children and family obligations, resulting in the "poignant irony" that "domestic workers must leave their children so that they can ensure that 'other people's children' receive the proper care."[11] The worker seen merely as a "substitute mother" for the employing parent is one whose own webs of relationship and obligation, and indeed whose own subjective experience of her caregiving, remain invisible.[12]

An alternative paradigm of Third as "partner" or "additional parent" in child-rearing addresses some of the problems with the subcontractor model. Children who receive care from paid caregivers, and the parents who employ them, rely on the caregivers' love and attachment, qualities associated with parenting itself. Valuing the work of nonparental caregivers as additional "partners" in child-rearing recognizes the real and lasting meaning of nonparents in caring for young children.

But neither is this conceptual model fully adequate. The trouble stems from the fact that, although both employing parents and domestic caregivers may look to this model to describe the ideal caregiving arrangement, the two parties often have incompatible ideas of what "partnership" in child-rearing involves. In her recent study, Cameron Macdonald shows that parents typically speak of the paid caregivers as "third parent" when they wish to indicate a quality of affection they hold for caregivers.[13] By contrast, nannies and au pairs invoked this language when they "meant that they wanted to be a valued, if transient, member of the family team in raising children. They were not seeking literal parental status. Lacking a socially acceptable term for individuals who love young children for pay, however, they fell back on the language of parenthood."[14] This difference in meaning, when left unaddressed, allows parents to ignore the differential power characteristic of the relationship between parents and caregivers and, especially, the potential for exploitation in such relationships.[15]

Jewish religious sources from the Hebrew Bible onward acknowledge the presence of delegated care and nonparental caregivers, and in doing so, confront many of the challenges inherent in both models I have presented. Narratives from the Tanakh, legal deliberations from the Talmud, and midrashic texts map a range of possible ways to view the Third, in each case adding new tools with which to articulate the Third's moral and religious significance. The categories of nonparental caregivers these texts present do not fully correspond to the common forms of caregiving labor in contemporary North America, and the economic, social, and moral assumptions of the texts differ from ours. Nonetheless, the categories through which the sources speak and the questions they raise enable us to create a more expansive understanding of how today's parents raise their children.

The *Shifḥa*

The familial narratives of Genesis constitute, in Jewish tradition, the stories of the patriarchs and matriarchs of the people of Israel. Tensions over inheritance and lineage characterize each of these stories. In a number of them, the narrative hinges on a nonkin adult female, a *shifḥa* (female slave), within the family.[16] Hagar, the foreign slave who is both surrogate and mother, represents what it is to be part of the family and yet also to be separated, and ultimately expelled, from it.

The particulars of Hagar's story are unique, but the presence of the *shifḥa* is taken for granted within biblical narrative and law. Etymologically, the title *shifḥa* conjures *mishpaḥa* (family), suggesting that domestic service lies at the heart of the clan.[17] The presence of the *shifḥa* belies contemporary normative understandings of the family's boundaries and its true members. In contrast to the concept of the "accidental family" created by live-in nannies, the biblical *shifḥa* is constitutive for the Israelite family. She reveals the inner workings of the family as a set of relations that spill over (*sh.f.ḥ.*) the categories of licit and illicit, official and unofficial. The *shifḥa* is not a category I wish to retrieve.[18] But the *shifḥa* is good to think with, for she lays bare aspects of inequality and subordination among family members that our own caregiving constellations often reproduce.

The most developed biblical narrative we have concerning a *shifḥa*, Hagar's story illustrates a key component of the Third in contemporary familial arrangements. Questions of power, agency, and resistance, we see, are formative to its contours—starting with the fact that Hagar is structurally marginal in the story of Abraham and God's covenant with him that is the biblical author's primary concern.[19] Hagar, whose name means "the stranger," is a figure defined as the subaltern.

Hagar's service is of the most intimate kind: Sarai, who cannot conceive, introduces Hagar to Abram as a surrogate: "Go in, I pray thee, unto my handmaid; it may be that I shall be built up through her" (Gen. 16:2).[20] When Hagar conceives, Sarai fears the balance of power has shifted, since Hagar's fertility elevates her status: Hagar's ability to produce the valuable commodity of (male) children adds a complicating layer to her low standing as a slave. The text insists on relating Hagar's agency and subjectivity: when Hagar saw she was pregnant, "her mistress [Sarai] was devalued [*vateqal*] in her eyes" (Gen. 16:4). Sarai torments her (*vate'aneha*), but Hagar runs away (Gen. 16:6).

In the wilderness to which she escapes, Hagar meets "an angel of YHVH." But her encounter with the angel does not end her suffering. In fact, the angel seemingly sanctions Hagar's subordination and victimization: "And the angel of YHVH said unto her: 'Return to thy mistress, and submit thyself under her hands'" (Gen. 16:9). Hagar knows she has been seen by God and even hints that she has seen the divine (Gen. 16:13), but this knowledge neither redeems her suffering nor removes her from it. Hagar knows both exploitation and theophany; neither cancels out the other. This insistence on subjectivity and resistance within brutal conditions has made her an evocative figure for womanists grappling with "slavery, poverty, ethnicity, sexual and economic exploitation, surrogacy, rape, domestic violence, homelessness, motherhood [and] single parenting."[21]

Like Abram, Sarai, and Hagar, we live in society in which class status, racial or ethnic identity, geography, and gender structure a set of interlocking power relations that mark all of us. These power relations include figures within the family and the intimate others who intersect in substantive ways with it. These factors in our social lives do not preclude the interruption of the transcendent; as suggested in Genesis 16, divinity enters into the conditions of human sociality in all its painful limitations. The text's interest in Hagar's prophetic vision, which occurs from within a life of suffering, invites recognition that our own social reality is marked both by injustice and by the possibility of agency and even transcendence within it.

The insistence on divine presence within exploitation and suffering is most familiar to Jews from the story of the exodus from Egypt, in which Jews identify with the slaves who are ultimately redeemed. But in the story of Hagar, Jews must identify with the oppressor in an inverted situation: the foremother Sarai torments the Egyptian slave. In this sense, Genesis 16 is, perhaps, a prehistory of the Exodus story, and one in which the protagonists of the narrative, Abram and Sarai, are the perpetrators rather than victims of oppression.[22] For a moment, at least, the reader's gaze is focused on the foreign slave girl, the surrogate, the exploited domestic laborer, the woman who is obligated materially and morally to her own child even as she is conscripted in another family's labor.[23] Hagar, the oppressed stranger, sits at the heart of the origin story of the people of Israel. To consider her in this light destabilizes the liturgical narrative of victimization familiar to Jews and reaches toward a narrative that integrates the injustices within the "family" of Israel itself.

In our own intimate spheres, just as for Hagar and Sarai, competition and collaboration intertwine and cross boundaries of class and race without erasing them. Here, the Third exists both within and outside a family of her own. No universal ethical imperatives or straightforward policy implications flow from reading her story. In the project of creating a more capacious understanding of parents, children, and the Third, the most compelling aspect of Hagar's narrative for us is the text's inclusion of her experience: of suffering, of gloating, of choosing to flee, of submission, of naming God. Sarai and Hagar "have no place in the text *as it stands* for resolving their plight," but the text invites us to recognize the presence of its dynamics in our own world.[24]

The 'Omen/et

If the *shifḥa* is defined by her birthing labor and liminal status within the family, the biblical *'omen* ("nursemaid") and *meneqet* ("wet nurse") are imagined more expansively. The *'omen/et*, from the root aleph-mem-nun, is the (usually) female caregiver and educator; as Deena Aranoff has argued, that meaning arises from the root indicating "constancy" or "faithfulness" (*'emuna*) and affirmation (*'amen*).[25] Implicit within this etymologically connected cluster, Aranoff suggests, is a recognition that constancy is the *sine qua non* of the work of caretaking.[26]

In biblical literature, the *'omen/et* shoulders the material and spiritual burdens of caring for a child but is specifically *not* the biological parent. The term is used in masculine and feminine forms, indicating that both men and women could, potentially, care for and rear children in this embodied, material, quotidian sense.[27] In some cases, the *'omen/et* is portrayed as subcontractor, in others, as coparent.

Two examples from the biblical corpus mark out this range of experience and the *'omen/et*'s self-understanding. Numbers 11:12 characterizes the work of the *'omen/et* as unrewarding: he or she has the burdens of the material care without the recognition or authority enjoyed by the parent. Moses protests against being saddled with the unsavory task of leading Israel to the Promised Land with two rhetorical questions: "Have I conceived (*hariti*) these people? Have I birthed it, that you should say unto me: Carry them in thy bosom, as an *'omen* carries the suckling (*yoneq*), unto the land which you did swear unto their fathers?" Implicitly, since God "conceived" the people, God ought to both sustain the people and "carry" them to the land. But God has not done so; God delegated this caregiving to Moses as if Moses were the *'omen*, sticking him with the material burdens of feeding and "carrying" a whiny, ungrateful people. It is the *'omen*, not necessarily the parent, who shoulders the burden of the material care. And sometimes that work—all drudgery, no glory—is unpleasant indeed.

By contrast, the *'omenet* at the end of the book of Ruth is recognized as a kind of co-parent who shares in the joys of having a child with the birthgiving mother. The embittered, bereft Naomi, whose daughter-in-law will not leave her alone, becomes a woman fully integrated into a family and a community as a coparent: "And the women said to Naomi, 'Blessed be the LORD, who has not withheld a redeemer from you today! May his name be perpetuated in Israel! He will renew your life and sustain your old age; for he is born of your daughter-in-law, who loves you and is better to you than seven sons.' Naomi took the child and held it to her bosom, and became his *'omenet*. And the women neighbors gave him a name, saying, 'A son is born to Naomi!' They named him 'Oved; he was the father of Jesse, father of David" (Ruth 4:14–17).[28] Naomi claims the child born to Ruth and Boaz not with words, but with actions. With a gesture, she becomes the child's *'omenet*. In doing so, Naomi does not *displace* Ruth (who "loves" and "sustains" Naomi) but becomes a co-mother with her. The female neighbors recognize the significance not only of Naomi's relationship to the child but also that of her relationship to Ruth.

The idyllic, even utopian, character of the ending is indicated by the genealogy in the final verses, which points to the messianic redemption.[29] But beyond the ending, the joy and dignity in Naomi's actions have a redemptive quality. Naomi is a woman for whom the status of *'omenet* is freely chosen. Clearly, this is not the operative reality for most nannies and babysitters; their role will only rarely, if ever, be as fully integrated into the self-perception of the family as is Naomi's with Ruth, Boaz, and the larger social world of their community. The nanny may be a *de facto* co-mother or even primary mother in her own eyes and in the eyes of the child for whom she cares—but is not officially recognized as such by the parents or the social world beyond them.

The idyll of Naomi and Ruth reorients our vision. To take the narrative seriously is to envision a different social world than one that is, like ours, organized around exploitation. With Ruth and Naomi, we envision world in which a person might choose to care for a child *alongside* its parents, and in which the parents and the larger society would recognize caring labor as creating familial bonds.

The biblical *'omen/et*, in both of these cases, remains a subject whose frustration and delight with the child for whom s/he cares are given vocal expression in biblical narratives. The interactions, harmonious and difficult, with the recognized parent are a crucial part of the *'omen/et*'s affective relationship with the child. We today do not have a single term in English that offers the full semantic range of meanings of the *'omen/et*. Yet this figure has not disappeared from contemporary life. Today's *'omen/et* generates complex relationships, not only with the parents but also with the children whom they love. By looking at this role today through the lens of biblical narrative, we find language with which to articulate the nature of their caregiving.

The *Meneqet* and the *Meniqa*

Halakhic and aggadic rabbinic texts do not use the term *'omenet*. Instead, rabbinic sources use a different designation: the *meniqa*, the woman who breastfeeds. This rabbinic term has a prehistory in the biblical term *meneqet*, or "nursemaid." Just as the word "nurse," in English, can mean both "to breastfeed" and "to attend to someone" (as in "he nursed her back to health"), the biblical *meneqet* can refer to a woman who suckles a child or to a caretaker more generally. In the contemporary West, most Thirds do not breastfeed other people's children; however, texts concerning wet nursing in the Bible and rabbinic texts help us think through the tensions in employing others to care for children, as the role of wet nurse in ancient times is likely analogous to that of Thirds today who give infants bottles of formula or pumped milk.

Both terms derived from the root meaning "to suckle" [*y.n.q*], *meneqet* and *meniqa*, place the activity of suckling at the core of caregiving. There is, therefore, a potential for the identity of the *meneqet* and the *meniqa* to be reduced to lactation, with the result that breastfeeding becomes alienated labor. This potential consistently surfaces in both biblical and rabbinic texts, revealing a tension that we in our own time have resolved no better than the rabbis: can care be detached from the personhood of the caretaker?

Two key biblical stories of the *meneqet* confront this possibility, but both reject the temptation to read the *meneqet* as "mere" food source. In Exodus 2, Moses's sister offers to fetch a Hebrew *meneqet* to suckle the infant Moses for Pharoah's daughter. She retrieves Moses's own birth mother, whom Pharoah's daughter now pays to breastfeed (her own) child. The ironic subterfuge in Exodus 2 depends, in other words, on the ability to strip down the function of the *meneqet* to breastfeeding; Pharoah's daughter sees the woman only as a nutrition-delivery system, that is, as commodified labor. But the reader understands, as Pharoah's daughter does not, that this arrangement enables Moses's mother to be reunited with the three-month-old child she relinquished.[30]

Likewise, the *meneqet* Devorah is mentioned in two biblical verses. On a strictly etymological reading, Devorah would merely be Rebekah's wet nurse. But she is mentioned as part of the adult matriarch Rebekah's entourage: "And they sent away Rebekah their sister, and her *meneqet*, and Abraham's servant, and his men" (Gen. 24:59). It is impossible to explain why a girl of marriageable age would need her *meneqet* when she goes forth to her husband's home if the *meneqet* is defined solely as wet nurse, with no other caretaking function or caring relationship with a child. We see, then, that the *meneqet* is no mere disposable service provider. She is a lifelong caretaker and member of the family unit. Her death is mourned: "Deborah, Rebekah's nurse, died, and was buried under the oak below Bethel; so it was named 'the oak of weeping'" (Gen. 35:8).[31] The *meneqet* has become sufficiently integrated into the family of Jacob that not only is her death recorded, but so too the grieving that accompanied it.[32] The multilayered narrative depends, for its full effect, on imagining the *meneqet* as an integrated member of the household.

Whereas the biblical *'omenet* and *meneqet* are imagined as governesses who wet-nurse and love specific children, the rabbinic *meniqa* simply designates the woman who is paid to breastfeed; usually, but not always, she is not the biological mother of the children she nurses.[33] The dominant assumption in rabbinic discussions of the *meniqa* is that breastfeeding can be subcontracted.[34] Such an assumption informs a number of the treatments of the *meniqa* in legal texts, where the rabbis address a variety of questions that might arise from a wet nursing arrangement, among them: when and whether a woman breastfeeding a certain child may be married to a man who is not that child's father (bKetubbot 60b); the permissibility of contraceptive use for a breastfeeding woman (bYevamot 12b); and the conditions under which a non-Jewish wet nurse may breastfeed Jewish children and vice versa (bAvodah Zara 26a–27a).[35] (Medieval commentators on the latter topic explicitly consider what parents today would call the family day care provider: a woman paid to watch other people's children in her own domicile, in contrast to the domestic worker who works in the home of the employing parent.[36])

These Talmudic discussions generally presume that the "hired breastfeeding woman" is not the mother of the child she breastfeeds. But whereas we today typically make a firm linguistic distinction between the "mother" and the "wet nurse," many halakhic texts do not insist as strongly on differentiating between the woman who nurses her own child and the woman who nurses another woman's child. The line of connection between mother and child is typically subordinate, for the rabbis, to the connection between father and child or between husband and wife.[37] This lamentable patriarchal organizing principle, however, produces an unexpected possibility: the privileging of biological and even familial ties is diminished, as the breastfeeding woman can be either the mother or a "hired substitute." The silver lining, as it were, of the law's disinterest in the mother/child tie is a new framework for rethinking the Third.

A Talmudic story in Ketubbot offers a fruitful site for exploring this new conceptual model. The story concerns a woman who does not want to breastfeed her child, but who is obligated to do so. For the rabbis of the Mishnah and the Talmud, breastfeeding a child is a domestic labor (one among others) that a wife owes her *husband*. Breastfeeding, in mKetubbot 5:5, is thus legally constructed not as a relationship between a mother and child, but between a wife and husband: "These are the labors which the woman does/must do for her husband. She grinds, and bakes, and launders. She cooks, and nurses her child. She makes his bed and works with wool. If she brought one maidservant [from her father's home], she does not [need to] grind, bake, or wash. [If she brought] two [maidservants], she does not [need to] cook or nurse her child."[38] Building on this mishnah, the rabbis of the Gemara then ask: what if the woman is divorced? Is she still obligated to nurse her child—the child who is, in halakhic terms, the child of her former husband? What if a woman has taken a vow not to breastfeed—can she be compelled to do so anyway (bKetubbot 59a)?

According to Beit Shammai, a divorcée cannot be forced to breastfeed. But Beit Hillel, by contrast, holds the following position: "He [the husband] compels her and she nurses him [the child]. He cannot compel the divorcée [to breastfeed], but if he [the child] recognizes her, he [the husband] pays her a wage and forces her to breastfeed because of the danger [to the infant]." The question then becomes, at what point does a child recognize her, and, by implication, refuse to nurse from a woman other than the one to whom it is accustomed?

> Once [a divorcée who did not want to nurse her son] came to Shmuel, who said to Rav Dimi son of Yosef: "Go and check her [the woman]." He went and placed her among a row of women and, taking hold of her child, carried him in front of them. When he came up to her, [the child] looked at her face with joy, but she turned her eyes away from him [or: covered her eyes]. "Lift up your eyes," he called to her; "come, take away your son." How does a blind child know [its mother]? Rav Ashi said: By the smell and the taste (bKetubbot 60a).

In its own context, this is a story about a legal/halakhic question of whether breastfeeding (on which, it must be remembered, an infant's life depended in the ancient world) can be forced.[39] If a woman's obligation to nurse her child is established solely through marriage, she should not have to nurse the child once she is divorced. The story wrestles with the recognition of breastfeeding labor as, on the one hand, like all other kinds of labor—it can be outsourced or exchanged on the marketplace—and, on the other hand, as unique in its tendency to overflow the category of ordinary commodity exchange. This awareness gives poignancy to the conundrum in the story: what if the child, now attached to his mother, won't accept a substitute?

In the Talmud, patriarchal control wins out: Rav Shmuel's assertion is uncontested; women are "checked" and ultimately can be compelled to nurse. In the context of the question at the heart of our inquiry, however, I suggest an alternative reading from which we can learn about how intimate labor establishes relationships.

The biological motherhood of the woman in this story is essentially irrelevant; none of what transpires hinges on her maternal status vis-à-vis the child. Through divorce, this woman has become a Third, a hired caregiver. This woman does not want to nurse the child and refuses to do so. The storytellers neither ask why the woman does not want to breastfeed nor show surprise at her response. Instead, Rav Shmuel and Rav Dimi bar Yosef arrange a line-up. This setting simultaneously stages and subverts fungibility: we imagine a row of lactating women, any of whom might breastfeed the child. Ultimately the child is being called upon to pick out the woman he recognizes. The sages, in this story, "police" the relationship between the woman and the child. With their intervention, the child—perhaps an infant, perhaps a toddler—reaches out to the woman in question with a look for recognition. By revealing his own desires, the child conscripts this Third to continue breastfeeding. The Third likewise exercises her agency by hiding her eyes. But ultimately, the woman—or her breastfeeding body, against her will—has created a relationship of obligation. The coda reinforces the fact of her distinctiveness: the rabbis declare that although a blind child cannot recognize the woman who breastfeeds him by sight, the sensory apparatus of her body and her milk mark her as unique.

Intimate labor creates relationships. The woman who performs intimate domestic labor, whether as (unpaid) mother or as (paid) *meniqa*, cannot remain an anonymous service provider. She has become unique. That fact in itself obligates her to this particular child—even, for the rabbis, against her will. In the end, this story comprehends what the Mishnah had obstructed: the tie of obligation between a woman and a child, unmediated by father/husband. That this tie comes at the expense of violating the woman's own desire is a painful price to pay for the establishment of a nontriangulated connection between woman and child.

This Talmudic narrative challenges the assumption that the role of the paid/nonparental caregiver is *a priori* distinct from and lesser than that of the parent. It suggests that the domestic caregiver or day care provider gives material, intimate care and thereby establishes an irreplaceable relationship. Wet nursing may be the embodied intimate service *par excellence*, but it is not far removed from other physical labors that each person conducts in her own distinctive style and with the stamp of her own body.[40] The mundane activity of feeding infants with formula or pumped milk makes a caregiver the object of a child's unique attachment—an attachment that only grows over time as caregiving activities grow. Each act carries the signature of its author: the particular feel of the caregiver's hand or embrace; the sound of her voice; the feel of her skin. The person who cares for a child in the most intimate and material ways becomes unique to that child, whether that person is the child's parent or not. Having become unique, the caregiver cannot simply withdraw without emotional consequence for the cared-for.

Maternal fears of being replaced or usurped by the loving caregiver are a familiar trope; as Barbara Katz Rothman has argued, the problem is, "Women want good child care, want deeply someone the child can feel secure with, feel love for—and yet feel threatened by that love."[41] The Talmudic story, as I read it, offers an acknowledgment of the tendency of paid labor in the intimate sphere to overflow the category of market exchange. This labor creates relationships that by definition go beyond the capacity of a single actor to contain them. This recognition does not deny that market forces are and remain at work within the establishment of caregiving labor. But this labor is also distinct from other kinds of services one can buy and sell on the market. As Joan Tronto has argued, "Insofar as the work of domestic service is care, one of the 'products' of care is that it creates ongoing relationships among the care givers and care receivers."[42] Those relationships, in turn, mark their participants—sometimes against their will.

The talmudic story of the divorced breastfeeding woman whom the child recognizes breaks down the wall, so treasured in contemporary child-rearing, between the parent and the Third. A logic that differentiates care as paid versus unpaid, parental versus substitute, is impoverished. The intimate labor of the Third establishes a relationship no less than does the labor of the parent, albeit a relationship that social and cultural conventions and economic policies systematically dishonors. In the talmudic story, the infant establishes the meaningfulness of care, beyond its economic analysis as household labor, when he looks with anticipation and joy at the woman from whom he receives milk, warmth, and familiar presence. If this is the child's elemental reality, then parents hold the responsibility of expanding their own framework to accommodate it.

* * *

I have argued that considering the Third as "outsourced" labor acknowledges the economic function of hired caregivers within and beyond the family, but is limited in that it cannot comprehend the subjectivity of the caregiving laborer. That laborer may be mistreated and exploited, like Hagar, or may be embraced as a co-mother, like Naomi. A purely economic lens on the Third cannot help us understand her role in shaping a child's world and views on relationships, or in shaping parents' own understanding of their tasks in child-rearing as employing caregivers and as caregiving workers.

But neither does the language of "partnership" fully address the significance of nonparental caregivers. Such language can too easily whitewash the power inequalities between the employing parent and the paid caregiver; the difficult

dynamics between the parental and other caregivers; and the parents' consciousness of the differences between the teaching of the day care worker and the values
of the parents themselves.

If parenting is a God-like identity, as I have argued in this book, the fact of
Thirds in child-rearing suggests that parents are not the only gods. As we know
from countless Pentateuchal episodes, the singular authority of God is a contested rather than a settled matter.[43] Many episodes in the Pentateuch offer clear
recognition of the existence of multiple gods: the gods of Egypt, who are van-
quished by the God of Israel (Ex. 12:12, Num. 33:4); the gods whom the Israelites
are forbidden to worship (Ex. 20:3; 23:32–33), and many others.

The multiplicity of gods is thus inscribed—albeit grudgingly or polemically—
into the most foundational layer of Jewish religious texts, the Hebrew Bible. Most
biblical scholars today understand these passages to indicate ongoing "culture
wars" *within* Israelite religious life rather than the triumphant suppression of
polytheistic worship.[44] The outright recognition of the gods of others, and the
(condemnatory) recognition of those gods by the people of Israel, demonstrates
an ongoing religious and cultural struggle that continued long after the biblical
texts themselves were written. Later communities of biblical interpreters, both
Jewish and Christian, continued to wrestle with the inherently plural nature
of religious experience, long after the closing of the biblical canon.[45] As Peter
Schäfer has argued, the scholarly task is "to expose Jewish and Christian monotheism as a construct that encompasses more than the alleged end product, as
a process continuously in flux, moving between the poles of a broad and varied
spectrum."[46] Reckoning with the always-indeterminate status of God's primacy
lays important theological groundwork for recognizing multiplicity itself within
the cosmic order.[47]

The significance of the ongoing traces of multiplicity within scripture and
the struggles over the establishment of divine singularity reveal tremendous
anxiety about whether God is the only god, a question that the biblical authors
portray as deeply vexing for God himself: "For thou shalt bow down to no other
god; for YHVH, whose name is Jealous, is a jealous God" (Ex. 34:14). The singularity, the lonely supremacy, of God, can never be established with finality, but
remains subject to being undone by the worship practices of his followers. For
Israelites, on the other hand, the recognition of multiple, if unequal, gods is not
threatening; it simply acknowledges their having had an *'omenet* or a *meneqet* in
their quest to love God, the "true" parent.

The contested monotheism of the Hebrew Bible invites theorizing of the
multiple others involved from the very beginning in the work of child-rearing.
Like God, contemporary parents may indulge in the fantasy of self-sufficiency
and supremacy vis-à-vis their children and may struggle to recognize the role
of multiple others in their own work. The much-famed jealousy of God finds its

analogue in a parent's threatened sense of authority or anxiety about being less loved than the paid caregiver. This threat, in turn, may account for the paucity of language with which to integrate the others with whom parents contend, and on whom they rely, into their conceptions of their own role. Like the other gods grudgingly recognized in the Hebrew Bible, the Third represents those whose work can usually be recognized only at the cost of disparagement.

Yet if we look for traces of the repressed others throughout the later history of Jewish thought, we find them surely enough: in the preexistent Torah of the Wisdom literature; in the *Shekhina* who accompanies the children of Israel through their exile; in the emanations of the ten-fold Godhead of mysticism.[48] Over the course of several decades, a number of feminist Bible scholars have uncovered the gender politics of the supreme, incontestably male, singular God who absorbed the pantheon of pagan gods and goddesses in ancient Israel.[49] The recognition, and sometimes retrieval, of multiplicity as the suppressed other of the One has been understood by some feminists to be in itself a form of theological activism.[50] Informed by these investigations, I suggest that rather than seeking out a monotheism in which these articulations of otherness must be only acknowledged as mere facets of the One God, we are better served by a theological paradigm in which we might affirm the multiplicity that persists *alongside* God.[51] God's supremacy and primacy only are intelligible, in other words, in the context of plurality.

The work of acknowledging multiplicity within the parental and familial realm is not unlike the intervention so many feminist scholars have recommended in the theological realm. The figure I have been calling the Third is nearly ubiquitous as a participant in the work of parental care, even if she is too rarely acknowledged. Rather than collaborating in the project of subsuming this care within a framework in which the parent reigns supreme and alone, our task requires recognizing the many Thirds who stand alongside the parent. When we acknowledge what is already reality, we disrupt the dominant logic of the family—not to make the parent irrelevant, but to interrupt the fantasy of singularity.

Notes

1. On the "romantic" analogues of the parent/child couple, see Penny Munn, "Mothering More Than One Child," in *Motherhood: Meanings, Practices, and Ideologies*, ed. Ann Phoenix, Anne Woollett, and Eva Lloyd (London: Sage Publications, 1991).

2. Robert Bernasconi, "The Third Party: Levinas on the Intersection of the Ethical and the Political," *Journal of the British Society for Phenomenology* 30, no. 1 (1999).

3. Erin M. Cline, *Families of Virtue: Confucian and Western Views on Childhood Development* (New York: Columbia University Press, 2015).

4. John Wall, "Animals and Innocents: Theological Reflections on the Meaning and Purpose of Child-Rearing," *Theology Today* 59, no. 4 (2003): 578.

5. Joan C. Tronto, "The Nanny Question in Feminism," *Hypatia* 17, no. 2 (2002): 48.

6. Tronto, "The Nanny Question," 34.

7. See the Bureau of Labor Statistics for current information.

8. Joan C. Tronto, "'The Servant Problem' and Justice in Households," *Iris: European Journal of Philosophy and Public Debate* 2, no. 2 (2010).

9. While contemporary Western parents do not typically consider the schoolteacher in this role, that is precisely the conception we find in rabbinic texts (see ch. 4) and in texts from other religious/cultural traditions (Wall, "Animals and Innocents;" Cline, *Families of Virtue*). Much educational theory during and since the Enlightenment, by contrast, considers schooling to be in the state's interest; hence the development of public schools and the conceptualization of citizenship as one of the values schools inculcate or cultivate.

10. The gender coding of such discussions reinscribe a pattern of female responsibility for children, an assumption borne out in the unfortunate reality that men's economic and social status does not significantly change with the addition of a child, whereas women suffer economically when they become mothers. A number of researchers have argued that professional men's economic and social capital actually *grows* with the addition of a child, whereas women's typically decreases. See Michelle J. Budig, "The Fatherhood Bonus & the Motherhood Penalty: Parenthood and the Gender Gap in Pay," Third Way, 2014, last updated September 2, 2014, accessed November 8, 2017, http://www.thirdway.org/report/the-fatherhood-bonus-and-the-motherhood-penalty-parenthood-and-the-gender-gap-in-pay; Tronto, "The Nanny Question"; Cameron Lynne Macdonald, *Shadow Mothers: Nannies, Au Pairs, and the Micropolitics of Mothering* (Berkeley: University of California Press, 2010); Barbara Katz Rothman, *Recreating Motherhood: Ideology and Technology in a Patriarchal Society*, Revised ed. (New York: Rutgers University Press, 2000). A particularly memorable episode illustrating this phenomenon was the derailment of not one but two potential Attorneys General because it was discovered that they had employed nannies "off the books." It was not incidental that these indiscretions derailed two *female* employers' eligibility for political office; to date, no male seeking political office has been thought disqualified due to his hiring practices regarding domestic laborers. (Eventually the position of Attorney General went to Janet Reno, who held the unimpeachable credential of being childless.)

11. Tronto, "The Nanny Question," 38. Tronto here builds on Mary Romero, *Maid in the U.S.A* (New York: Routledge, 1992) and "Who Takes Care of the Maid's Children: Exploring the Costs of Domestic Service," in *Feminism and Families*, ed. Hilde Lindemann Nelson (London: Psychology Press, 1997). In previous centuries, the reigning models of domestic servitude reflected the actual or normative assumption that such servants (most of whom began their service as teenage girls) would not have their own "legitimate" families. In Jewish communities in medieval and early modern Europe, for example, the right of marriage was usually severely restricted; paid servants were unlikely ever to be granted such a right and were thus unlikely to have children born in wedlock for whom to care. Other children born to these women were often relinquished, hidden, or killed (Elisheva Carlebach, "Fallen Women and Fatherless Children: Jewish Domestic Servants in Eighteenth-Century Altona," *Jewish History* 24 [2010]; ChaeRan Y. Freeze, "Lilith's Midwives: Jewish Newborn Child Murder in Nineteenth-Century Vilna," *Jewish Social Studies*, n.s. 16, no. 2 [2010]).

12. Kimberly Wallace-Sanders, *Mammy: A Century of Race, Gender, and Southern Memory* (Ann Arbor, MI: University of Michigan Press, 2008); Tamara Mose Brown, *Raising Brooklyn: Nannies, Childcare, and Caribbeans Creating Community* (New York: New York University

108 | The Obligated Self

Press, 2011); Mary Romero, *The Maid's Daughter: Living inside and outside the American Dream* (New York: New York University Press, 2011).

13. Macdonald, *Shadow Mothers*, ch. 7.

14. Macdonald, *Shadow Mothers*, 132.

15. As Macdonald argues, "the third-parent ideal has its own self-defeating characteristics" that result from this mismatch between the content of the "third-parent ideal" for caregivers and for employing parents.

16. On Abraham as founder of a family, not a faith, in rabbinic Judaism, see Jon D. Levenson, *Inheriting Abraham: The Legacy of the Patriarch in Judaism, Christianity, and Islam* (Princeton, NJ: Princeton University Press, 2012).

17. This etymological connection is listed as "questionable" in Ludwig Köhler and Walter Baumgartner, *The Hebrew and Aramaic Lexicon of the Old Testament* (Leiden: Brill, 1994), but Klein argues for a connection; see Ernest Klein and Baruch Sarel, *A Comprehensive Etymological Dictionary of the Hebrew Language for Readers of English* (New York, NY: Macmillan, 1987).

18. Cf. the chilling rehabilitation of the biblical *shifḥa* as a dystopian possibility in Margaret Atwood, *The Handmaid's Tale* (New York: Anchor Books, 1998).

19. On household structure in Genesis, see Leo G. Perdue, *Families in Ancient Israel* (Louisville, KY: Westminster John Knox Press, 1997); Naomi A. Steinberg, *Kinship and Marriage in Genesis: A Household Economics Perspective* (Minneapolis, MN: Fortress Press, 1993); Jennie R. Ebeling, *Women's Lives in Biblical Times* (New York: T. & T. Clark, 2010); Ken M. Campbell, *Marriage and Family in the Biblical World* (Downers Grove, IL: InterVarsity Press, 2003); William G. Dever, *The Lives of Ordinary People in Ancient Israel: Where Archaeology and the Bible Intersect* (Grand Rapids, MI: W.B. Eerdmans, 2012). On contemporary readings of Hagar, see the overview in Delores S. Williams, "Hagar in African American Biblical Appropriation," in *Hagar, Sarah, and Their Children: Jewish, Christian, and Muslim Perspectives*, ed. Phyllis Trible and Letty M. Russell (Louisville, KY: Westminster John Knox Press, 2006) and *Sisters in the Wilderness: The Challenge of Womanist God-Talk* (Maryknoll, NY: Orbis Books, 1993); Renita J. Weems, *Just a Sister Away: A Womanist Vision of Women's Relationships in the Bible* (San Diego, CA: LuraMedia, 1988).

20. On this text and its relevance for contemporary discussions of assisted reproduction and surrogacy, see Laurie Zoloth and Alyssa A. Henning, "Hagar's Child: Theology, Ethics, and the Third Party in Emerging Reproductive Technology," in *Third-Party Reproduction: A Comprehensive Guide*, ed. James M. Goldfarb (New York: Springer, 2013).

21. Williams, *Sisters in the Wilderness*, 4. See also Phyllis Trible, *Texts of Terror: Literary-Feminist Readings of Biblical Narratives* (Philadelphia, PA: Fortress Press, 1984), 9–35; Weems, *Just a Sister Away*; Diana L. Hayes, *Hagar's Daughters: Womanist Ways of Being in the World*, Madeleva Lecture in Spirituality (New York: Paulist Press, 1995).

22. See Ramban and Radak on Genesis 16:6; see also Martin Buber, *On the Bible: Eighteen Studies*, trans. Nahum Glatzer (New York: Schocken Books, 1968), 39.

23. See Romero, "Who Takes Care."

24. Phyllis Trible, "Ominous Beginnings for a Promise of Blessings," in *Hagar, Sarah, and Their Children: Jewish, Christian, and Muslim Perspectives*, ed. Phyllis Trible and Letty M. Russell (Louisville, KY: Westminster John Knox Press, 2006), 61.

25. Deena Aranoff, "The Biblical Root 'MN: Retrieval of a Term and its Household Context," in *Mothers in the Jewish Cultural Imagination*, ed. Marjorie Lehman, Jane L. Kanarek, and Simon J. Broner (Liverpool: Littman, 2017).

26. In Meir Gruber's felicitous observation about another reference to a male *'omen* (Is. 49:23) and a male whose breasts give suck (Is. 60:16), he remarks that "Deutero-Isaiah

suggests that Gentile kings will be the male deliverers of child care, presumably changing Israel's metaphoric diapers" (Mayer I. Gruber, "Breast-Feeding Practices in Biblical Israel and in Old Babylonian Mesopotamia," *Journal of the Ancient Near Eastern Society* 19 [1989]: 82).

27. On the male *'omen*, see also Brenda Forster, "The Biblical *'Omen* and Evidence for the Nurturance of Children by Hebrew Males," *Judaism* 42, no. 3 (1993). Esther 2:7 explains that Mordecai was a "nursemaid" (*'omen*) to his niece/cousin Esther because (*ki*) "she had neither father nor mother." Midrashic traditions push this meaning, with Mordecai not only taking Esther under his wing (which is the implication of Esther 2:20), but also suckling her at his lactating breasts (Gen. Rabbah 30:8). On these midrashim, see Marc Bregman, "Mordecai the 'Milk-Man': Sexual Ambivalence in a Provocative Midrash," in *The Faces of Torah: Studies in the Texts and Contexts of Ancient Judaism in Honor of Steven Fraade* (Göttingen: Vandenhoeck & Ruprecht, 2017). I set aside this intriguing midrash and the example of Mordecai for the present discussion because he is presented here as a *substitute* for the dead parents rather than a Third who cares for a child *alongside* the parents.

28. Translation adapted from JPS 1985.

29. Ilana Pardes has analyzed the "idyllic revisionism" that characterizes the book of Ruth in *Countertraditions in the Bible: A Feminist Approach* (Cambridge: Harvard University Press, 1992), 98–117.

30. Curiously, the event of Moses's weaning is not mentioned, unlike those of Isaac and Samuel, whose weanings serve as transitional moments in their narratives.

31. Levenson, writing in the *Jewish Study Bible* commentary, notes that "a midrash, ingeniously connecting oak (Heb *'alon*) with a form of the Greek word for 'other' (*alon*), reports that while still mourning Rebekah's nurse, Jacob received the news of another death, that of Rebekah herself (Genesis Rabbah 81:5)—an event strangely unreported in the Torah. Another midrash gives a reason for this omission: Her funeral was held at night so that 'everybody would not say, Cursed be the breasts that suckled a person like this [i.e., her wicked son Esau]' (*Tanḥuma, ki-tetze* 4)" (Adele Berlin, Marc Zvi Brettler, and Michael Fishbane, eds., *The Jewish Study Bible: Featuring the Jewish Publication Society Tanakh Translation* [New York: Oxford University Press, 2004], ad loc. Gen. 35:8.).

32. Martha T. Roth, "Deborah, Rebekah's Nurse," *Eretz-Israel: Archaeological, Historical and Geographical Studies* 27 (2003).

33. A parallelism suggests that by the time of Deutero-Isaiah, the two different terms were understood to be harmonious with one another: "Kings shall tend your children, Their queens shall serve you as nurses [*'omnayich*]" (Isaiah 49:23). Note that in this verse the term *'omen* is used in the masculine.

34. The rabbis assume (and perhaps prefer) breastfeeding as the default, or at least the common, practice for biological mothers: "The ordinary pregnant woman (*stam me'uberet*) nurses [her child]" (bYevamot 42a). At the same time, breastfeeding is a marker of low class status for the woman who does it, whether she is the child's biological mother or a wet nurse: when considering whether a woman whose family custom is to hire a wet nurse has the obligation to breastfeed if she marries a man whose family custom it is not to hire out breastfeeding, the rabbis conclude, "she [the wife] goes up [in terms of social status] with him [the husband], but she does not go down [in status] with him" (bKetubbot 61a). This logic explains why she is not obligated to nurse the child herself. Most women were part of what we today might call the "99%"; they were not wealthy enough to subcontract out breastfeeding. Mayer Gruber argues that ancient Israelite sources suggest that "the tendency, encouraged by cultic law, was for women to nurse their own children" (Gruber, "Breast-Feeding Practices," 79). The same cannot be said of the alignment between class and the hiring of wet nurses in later periods of Jewish history. For an excellent treatment of wet nursing in medieval

Ashkenaz, with reference to practices in other parts of medieval Jewish Europe, see Elisheva Baumgarten, *Mothers and Children: Jewish Family Life in Medieval Europe* (Princeton, NJ: Princeton University Press, 2007), ch. 5.

These rabbinic discussions do not address whether breastfeeding one's own child was, in general, desirable *for mothers themselves*. Our texts assume that individual preference varied and, in addition, that individual preference was relevant to legislating practice (bKetubbot 61a). On the question of women's desire for and pain in breastfeeding, see Miriam-Simma Walfish, "Upending the Curse of Eve: A Reframing of Maternal Breastfeeding in BT *Ketubot*," in *Mothers in the Jewish Cultural Imagination*, ed. Marjorie Lehman, Jane L. Kanarek, and Simon J. Broner (Liverpool: Littman, 2017).

35. For an account of the differences between the Bavli's account of the latter question and comparative discussions in Palestinian sources, see Christine Hayes, *Between the Babylonian and Palestinian Talmuds: Accounting for Halakhic Differences in Selected Sugyot from Tractate Avodah Zarah* (New York: Oxford University Press, 1997).

36. Note also the discussion in Tosafot (bAvodah Zara 26a, s.v. *'ovedet kochavim meniqa*) on the common practice of leaving one's child in the home of the wet nurse.

37. See also tNiddah 2:3 and discussion in Walfish, "Upending the Curse of Eve."

38. Note the mishnah refers to "her child," not "his child"—a striking contrast to the substance of the mishnah, which treats the child as the father's (not the mother's) for halakhic purposes. A vast scholarly literature has analyzed this text's construction of a gendered marriage and household economy, including Miriam Peskowitz, *Spinning Fantasies: Rabbis, Gender, and History* (Berkeley: University of California Press, 1997); Naftali Cohn, "Domestic Women: Constructing and Deconstructing a Gender Stereotype in the Mishnah," in *From Antiquity to the Postmodern World: Jewish Studies in Canada*, ed. Daniel Maoz and Andrea Gondos (London: Cambridge Scholars Publishing, 2011); Jordan Rosenblum, "'Blessings of the Breasts': Breastfeeding in Rabbinic Literature," *Hebrew Union College Annual* 87 (2017); Gail Labovitz, "'These Are the Labors': Constructions of the Woman Nursing Her Child in the Mishnah and Tosefta," *Nashim: A Journal of Jewish Women's Studies & Gender Issues*, no. 3 (2000); Judith Romney Wegner, *Chattel or Person? The Status of Women in the Mishnah* (New York: Oxford University Press, 1988). Walfish claims that Bavli Ketubot showcases the subjugated status of the wife through a discussion of breastfeeding while Bavli Niddah highlights a nurser's obligation to the infant she is nursing (Walfish, "Upending the Curse of Eve").

39. Note that "the length of expected nursing [breastfeeding] does not vary whether the one nursing the infant is its biological mother or a wetnurse" (tNiddah 2:4); on this point, see Rosenblum, "Blessings of the Breasts," 173.

40. Here I bracket the question of breastmilk as "spiritual transmission," an important theme in ancient and medieval rabbinic conceptions of breastfeeding. Some of the rabbinic groundwork for the anxiety around breastmilk as a form of spiritual transmission is laid in bAvodah Zarah 26a and following, on the question of whether a non-Jewish wet nurse may nurse a Jewish child. However, the discussion there does not raise this issue explicitly; elsewhere, the discussion of non-Jewish women's milk as "impure" surfaces in a midrash that reads the infant Moses as refusing to nurse from an Egyptian wet nurse (bSotah 12b). For discussion of this sugya, see Rosenblum, "Blessings of the Breasts," 175–178. On the theme of spiritual transmission through breastmilk, see Ellen Davina Haskell, *Suckling at My Mother's Breasts: The Image of a Nursing God in Jewish Mysticism* (Albany: State University of New York Press, 2012). For a treatment of these themes among the Church Fathers, see John Penniman, *Lacte Christiano Educatus: The Symbolic Power of Nourishment in Early Christianity* (Bronx, NY: Fordham University, 2015).

41. Rothman, *Recreating Motherhood*, 140.

42. Tronto, "The Nanny Question," 37.

43. Indeed, the singularity of divine authority is a shifting entity throughout the Tanakh, according to different biblical authors. The variety of the names of God, from YHVH to *'El* to the grammatically plural name *'elohim*, testifies to a multiplicity of visions of God that later biblical authors (and of course midrashic readers, not to mention much later philosophers) struggled to reconcile as a single supreme character (Benjamin D. Sommer, *The Bodies of God and the World of Ancient Israel* [New York: Cambridge University Press, 2009]).

44. For a summary of current research on this point, see Stephen Geller, "The Religion of the Bible," in Berlin, Brettler, and Fishbane, *The Jewish Study Bible*, 2021–2040.

45. On this point, see especially Peter Schäfer, *Mirror of His Beauty: Feminine Images of God from the Bible to the Early Kabbala* (Princeton, NJ: Princeton University Press, 2002); Sommer, *The Bodies of God*; Tikva Simone Frymer-Kensky, *In the Wake of the Goddesses: Women, Culture, and the Biblical Transformation of Pagan Myth* (New York: Free Press, 1992); Jon D. Levenson, *The Love of God: Divine Gift, Human Gratitude, and Mutual Faithfulness in Judaism* (Princeton, NJ: Princeton University Press, 2015), 39.

46. Schäfer, *Mirror of His Beauty*, 3.

47. Laurel C. Schneider, *Beyond Monotheism: A Theology of Multiplicity* (New York: Routledge, 2008); Catherine Keller, *The Face of the Deep: A Theology of Becoming* (New York: Routledge, 2003).

48. Arthur Green, "Shekhinah, the Virgin Mary, and the Song of Songs: Reflections on a Kabbalistic Symbol in Its Historical Context," *AJS Review* 26, no. 1 (2002); Schäfer, *Mirror of His Beauty*; Elliot R. Wolfson, *Through a Speculum That Shines: Vision and Imagination in Medieval Jewish Mysticism* (Princeton, NJ: Princeton University Press, 1994).

49. Frymer-Kensky, *In the Wake of the Goddesses*, 85. The masculinity of the God of the Hebrew Bible, as Howard Eilberg-Schwartz has noted, is complicated by the absence or non-functionality of his phallus. See Eilberg-Schwartz, *God's Phallus: And Other Problems for Men and Monotheism* (Boston: Beacon Press, 1994). On the possibilities of "a divinity 'which is not One,'" see Schneider, *Beyond Monotheism*.

50. By contrast, Frymer-Kensky argues for a far more positive read of Israelite monotheism on feminist grounds (Frymer-Kensky, *In the Wake of the Goddesses*).

51. More recent challenges to the gender politics of the early terms in which these questions were understood. It is no longer as clear that the question of the "many" versus the "one" is coterminous with a contest between a feminist embrace of multiplicity and a "phallocentric" assertion of singularity. See Catherine Keller and Laurel C. Schneider, *Polydoxy: Theology of Multiplicity and Relation* (New York: Routledge, 2011).

CHAPTER 7

The Neighbor

A VAST WORLD of people lies beyond the individuals intimately involved in caring for a child. These other people do not change the child's diapers, soothe the child after she has fallen on the playground, wipe her nose, or teach her to tie her shoes. Rather, they come into contact with a parent and child in the course of ordinary life in society, perhaps in the form of a mail carrier going along her route; a homeless person asking for spare change; a social worker visiting the home; a fellow pedestrian at the corner. These individuals often remain anonymous, even undifferentiated to us; sometimes they become fixtures in our daily routines. But the intersections of these nonintimate individuals with parents and children shape parental experience decisively. Their transient or casual relationship with the parent/child dyad, though not immersive, stretches the social sphere of both parent and child outward.

Co-inhabitants of the world emerge, sometimes insistently, from the background and elicit explicit parental response. The pedestrian on the street, for instance: does he jaywalk (when the child has been taught to wait for the signal)? Does he offer a friendly greeting to the child (who has perhaps been told not to talk to strangers)? Does he visibly differ from others in physical ability or appearance (thus prompting a parent to articulate her own understanding of the meaning of visual difference)? Children's unprompted questions provoke new ways of thinking and seeing and understanding the world for parents, and the unthinking actions of these strangers become part of the long-lasting stories and memories a parent and child share.

Grace Paley's "Midrash on Happiness" connects these transient moments to the work of parenting. In this short story, the main character, Faith, explains her requirements for happiness. The first of these is the companionship of other women, talking and walking together in the city. And then, the narrator writes of Faith,

> For happiness, she also required work in this world and bread on the table. By work to do she included the important work of raising children righteously up. By righteously she meant that along with being useful and speaking the truth to the community, they must do no harm. By harm she meant not only personal injury to the friend the lover the coworker the parent (the city the nation) but also the stranger; she meant particularly the stranger in all her or his difference, who, because we were strangers in Egypt, deserved special goodness for life or at least until the end of strangeness.[1]

Paley's movement from the intimate to the distant other is continuous and harmonious: the narrator travels smoothly from friend, lover, coworker, and parent, outward to bigger social units and then, finally, to "the stranger." The "important work of raising children righteously up" culminates in a gloss on the biblical command to love the stranger. Parenting lies at the foundation of social ethics.

Many parents intuitively understand that learning to share a toy with a sibling or a friend in childhood forms the basis of learning to share time, space, and material resources with others.[2] In Paley's rendition, the resonant voice of scripture articulates the correlation between these two realms. But adults in the thick of parenting understand this connection not primarily as a logical or moral principle. Instead, the work of attentive care over long periods of time enables caregiving adults to bridge the young child's character and that of the adult she becomes. In the daily work of navigating the vast terrain of others and the world of the child, parents help a child become a future inhabitant of the social order. Parents move ceaselessly between their intimate knowledge of their particular children and the awareness that most other people will apprehend those children not in their singularity but as generic persons.

The word "stranger" in Paley's story evokes the charged meaning of "the stranger" in Jewish theological traditions. The "stranger" has been a focal point for ethics in Jewish thought from the Torah to the modern era. The stranger or resident alien, the *ger*, in the Pentateuch is the figure who dwells with and among Israel but is not a member of the community. The Israelite is obligated to the *ger* both negatively and positively: "When a stranger resides with you in your land, you shall not wrong him. The stranger who resides with you shall be to you as one of your citizens; you shall love him as yourself, for you were strangers in the land of Egypt: I YHVH am your God" (Lev. 19:33). The resident alien holds a marginal place and thus requires special mention as the object of ethical concern; the very category of the stranger, as Paley suggests, is inseparable from the terms of ethical obligation in which the Torah inevitably locates him. To find the "stranger" today, in contemporary America, we might look to the undocumented immigrant or the victim of sex trafficking: the person who resides among the citizenry but lacks standing and visibility. The Torah mandates equal treatment of—even love for—for the stranger precisely because he or she is so vulnerable to exclusion and exploitation.

But the Torah offers another category, likewise wrapped up in a moral imperative, that indicates a more proximate, non-intimate other with whom parents and children interact in most of their daily lives: the "neighbor" (re'ekha). By the "neighbor," the Torah indicates a member of civil society: one's fellow householder (Ex. 20:14) or property-owner (Deut. 19:14), one's worker (Ex. 22:25) or simply the person whose land lies adjacent to one's own (Deut. 23:25–26). Whereas the ger by definition occupies a place on the margins of the social order, the re'a does not. The neighbor is the person with whom adults share equivalence in the eyes of law, society, and God (Lev. 19:18); she is "the person with whom one is brought into contact and with whom one must live on account of the circumstances of life."[3] If the neighbor is marginalized, the cause is necessarily circumstantial, not structural.

To translate this category of individual into contemporary terms: neighbors stand at the corner with us waiting (or not) for the light to change; they ride the bus with us; they supervise their children at the playground; they are ahead of us in line at the doctor's office or sitting and reading a magazine in the waiting room. Parents and children encounter what the Torah calls "neighbors" all the time. When parents instruct their children, "don't talk to strangers," they have in mind the category of person the Torah calls the neighbor: a person with whom we participate in a shared life circumstance in the most expansive sense.[4] In our world—as opposed to the world of ancient Israel—the "neighbor" can be a person whom we do not yet know, and whom we most likely will never know intimately. But she is nonetheless the person with whom we create society.[5]

The duty to the "neighbor," for modern Jewish thinkers, has often signified the realm of social ethics as a whole. But if, as I argued in chapter 2, maternity yields a special understanding of love as engagement with a particular person, how can love be rendered to the person whom we do not know and cannot cherish in her particularity? In addressing this basic tension, I offer a meditation on Leviticus 19:18 through a maternal lens.

* * *

God commands, "Love your neighbor as yourself; I am YHVH." The neighbor whom we are to love falls into a generic category of person and lies outside our immediate sphere of concern, but whom we are enjoined to treat him as if he were part of that sphere. Indeed, as worded, the commandment implies that this generic other is not drawn in to intimacy with me, but rather is to be regarded as equivalent to me nonetheless.[6] In explicating this aspect of the commandment, Maimonides remarks, "I should have mercy for and love my brother as faithfully as I love and have mercy for myself. This applies to his financial and physical state, and whatever he has or desires. What I want for myself I should want for him, and whatever I don't want for myself or my friends, I shouldn't want for him."[7] Maimonides's explanation emphasizes the equivalence of the neighbor, but at the cost of recognizing his *difference* from me.

The dynamics of parental love enable us to see the problematic nature of this formulation especially clearly. The activities of daily, embodied care, performed with the expectation of a permanent relationship, create the conditions under which love that is attuned to the other—"attentive love," as Iris Murdoch called it—may emerge.[8] Considering one's own child as the "neighbor" in the terms suggested by the Torah requires us to imagine our children as "generic" others. But this is an impossible task; even people very experienced in caring for children and who have gained a grasp of their general developmental trajectories do not simply plot children along or against those trajectories. The "generic" template can only complement, not replace, an adult's appreciation of any particular child. My child will never be "merely" a generic other to me.

In light of this dilemma, the language of the biblical commandment is intriguing. The verses in Leviticus 19 slip back and forth between the familial and the national: "Thou shalt not hate *thy brother* (*'aḥikha*) in thy heart; thou shalt surely rebuke your fellow-citizen (*'amitekha*) and not bear sin because of him. Thou shalt not take vengeance, nor bear any grudge against the children of thy people (*benei 'amekha*), but thou shalt love thy neighbor (*re'ekha*) as thyself: I am YHVH (Lev. 19:17–18)."[9] The instruction conveys a quality of irreducible sense of obligation—the obligation that parents feel for their children—for "the neighbor." The use of the phrase "your brother," which occurs frequently in the laws concerning one's duty toward the person who has fallen into poverty (Lev. 25) likewise cultivates vicarious intimacy. While "brotherhood" itself does not ensure loving treatment—Cain and Abel, the first brothers, illustrate the point negatively, in Cain's abdication of fraternal responsibility—the language in the legal sections nonetheless conveys an irreducible belonging.

The revelation of becoming a parent was, for me, one of newfound wonder at the miracle of creation and the revelation of my own capacity to love a particular creation intensely and above all others. But the implications of this revelation pulled me in at least two divergent directions. What was I—what are we—to *do* with the new knowledge of love parenthood can bring? How was this love to translate into my regard for other people, and not only for my child?

I see two opposing tendencies as equally likely to flow from the revelation implicit in the love of one's child. One tendency moves in the direction of the particular: it is *this* child whom I cherish; his personhood, unique in all the world, commands, solicits, and seduces me. Under the right circumstances, evolutionary biologists tell us, infants exert a magnetic pull that lures their caretakers into the kind of attention that can yield appreciation and ultimately protection.[10] The tendency to notice and revel in what is uniquely miraculous about *this* child, *my* child, is part of human evolution.

If unchecked or unexamined, the location of the miraculous and the beloved in one's own child leads to a constricted moral life for the parent—a life modern moral philosophers like Kant claim can be barely called moral at all, because it is natural and easy to love "one's own." Imperatives to love what is *not* one's own are necessary precisely because humans have a primal drive that privileges "us" (our children, our tribe) over "them" (their children, their tribe).

But the revelation of the miracle of creation implicit in one's child, and the capacity to love this one in particular, can pull a parent in the opposite direction: toward a vision of all people, and not only this one particular beloved child, as manifesting the divine and issuing a command. Parental love of the unique miracle of one's child overflows banks and transforms the landscape of humanity as a whole. The love and wonder I feel in marveling at my child's existence is both mine alone, and, at the same time, known by many people for *their* children.

This revelation of analogous love uncovers an obligation and responsibility through which I become *more* rather than *less* connected to the world. I see other people as being (or having been) loved in all of their distinctive particularity, and of being perceived (or having been perceived) as a wonder of creation as much as I do my own child.[11] My love for my child enables me to see the divine image multiplied and refracted through many prisms: that of the homeless person who sleeps on the street, the corporate executive, the police officer, the old person leaning on a cane.

Becoming a parent can transform people by enabling them to experience a venerable notion in Jewish ethics: that each distinctive human is an occasion for seeing some aspect of God, since humans are made in the divine image. In one rabbinic formulation: "Rabbi Joshua ben Levi said: When a man walks on the road, an *ikonia* of angels goes before him, proclaiming, 'Make way for the *ikonia* of the Holy One, blessed be He!'"[12] As Yair Lorberbaum explains, this maxim conveys the rabbis' understanding of the divine form as present in human bodies, in keeping with classical notions of the icon.[13] For me, caring for my child made gave this notion an overwhelmingly powerful reality. When I saw, in my child, an image of divinity, I began to newly see others as reflections of the divine as well.

That some people do not receive the care to which their existence entitles them only heightens our attunement to their being so entitled and underscores the poignancy of their not having received the attentive love they should have. All people were once helpless infants, whose abject dependency issued the command "Love me!" Sometimes, these commands are heard and fulfilled by parents and Thirds; many times, these commands are ignored or violated. As in

Rabbi Joshua ben Levi's saying, occasions in which a human being is not properly honored degrade the image of God.

But the midrash also describes an aspect of reality immanent within the structure of maternity, an insight whose latent potential uniquely helps us recognize the divine image in the neighbor. In other words, the parental recognition of other adults having once been children does not require caring for these others as deeply as I care for my own child, but requires engaging in the world such that others people might receive the care that their existence commands. The neighbor occasions an *analogous* revelation to the one my own child occasioned; at the same time, it generates an understanding of my own child as a present or eventual neighbor to others.

The two countervailing tendencies I have outlined here are equally implicit in the experience of parenthood—not only because both possibilities are plausible for any parent, but also because they each contain elements of truth. The visceral encounter with humans' dual nature legitimately pulls parents in opposite directions, sometimes simultaneously, because human beings are in fact both particular *and* generic. The famous teaching in Mishnah Sanhedrin expresses this insight thus: "A man strikes many coins from the same mold, and all the coins are alike. But the king, the king of kings, the Holy One [blessed be He] strikes every man from the mold of the first human ['adam harishon], and yet none of them is like his fellow" (mSanhedrin 4:5). Each individual human being is fashioned with same divine "stamp"—the stamp of the primordial human, created in the image of God—yet each human being is unique. God appreciates individual uniqueness, and the rabbis enjoined this appreciation to inform action in the civil sphere. Parental responsibility for a child tills particularly fertile ground in which this ethical, theological instinct can take root.

Most of the time, however, the neighbor's status as utterly unique recedes into the background of consciousness, and we encounter her as just another "anonymous" person. The neighbor is not unique for me. Sometimes she is hardly even recognizable as an individual, but is merely part of the larger fabric of society in which my child and I participate.[14] Parents recognize the generic quality of the neighbor in order to enable their children to become people who recognize that the humanity of the neighbor does not depend on knowing him or her personally. This is the work of socialization, or "training a child to be the kind of person whom others accept and whom the mothers themselves can actively appreciate."[15] Thus even relatively solitary moments between parents and children involve a parent's navigation among at least three (often conflicting) factors: her own values, her child's wishes and needs, and what she understands to be valued in her culture. We "interact" all the time, literally or figuratively, with people who are "anonymous" to us.

A parent is the *meturgeman*, or translator, of the social world for their young children. In the ancient synagogue, the *meturgeman* translated scripture into the Aramaic vernacular, interpolating his translation as the scroll was read aloud.[16] The work of this figure was also always interpretive, as we know from the written versions of the vernacular oral translations; elaborate additions and telling elisions in the Targumim testify to a great degree of interpretive license.[17] The task, for the ancient *meturgeman*, was not conceived of as the reproduction of the scripture in its exactitude, as we might assume today, but rather the attempt to make contact with the listener.

Parents constantly interpret the social world to their children, making difficult, benign, challenging, and beautiful situations the occasion for instruction. In each case, the parent translates what she sees—and what her child sees—into a language her child can understand. The world itself and its inhabitants are the "scripture" that, like Torah, is received rather than chosen. We find ourselves already in the world, already listening and responsive to it. Parents translate the scripture that is the world into language comprehensible to our children, who will eventually take their place in it without us. The work cannot but be interpretive and selective; we always impose a set of values as we translate. Parents can and do seek to limit certain elements, and to draw out other elements, of the world with which their children come into contact.[18] But the social and natural worlds in which parents and children live impose themselves on even the most vigorous efforts to hermetically seal them off.

Unlike the *meturgeman* of the ancient synagogue, however, the parent's work of translation operates both ways: it involves not only translating the world to one's child, but translating one's young child into the world of populated by neighbors. In the most literal senses, we explicitly explain our child's particularities to other adults and children when needed. But more than that, we interpret the world to our children through the everyday work of socialization. We do so because we recognize that our children, who are unique and irreplaceable to us and to others who know them intimately, also will eventually function as the (generic) neighbor for others.

Maternal subjectivity demonstrates that the trajectory according to which children progressively move from the intimate sphere outwards is insufficient. It neither describes how young children's engagement with the world occurs nor enables us to imagine the subjectivity of the mother who facilitates ongoing engagement. The parent-child dyad, and the intimate work of others (siblings, Thirds) in young children's understanding of the world, remains operative *within* the world of many neighbors. To view the world of neighbors with a maternal lens is not (only) to see a "progression" by which a mother's work is foundational but superseded; it is also to recognize the ongoing, continuous work of translating from child to world and world to child, even when the child becomes a more active agent in the social environment.

This aspect of parenting work arises out of the knowledge that neither I nor my child is unique to the neighbor, and that humans need to be trained to function *as* neighbors. My sense of my child's miraculous nature and uniqueness is precisely that: it is *my* sense. My child is unique *to me*, and to the others who care for her through the vagaries of quotidian life. But to others, she is, or she will eventually simply become, "a neighbor." While I wish for others to see my child through my eyes, I also recognize, at least sometimes, that it is *my* lens of love and appreciation that makes her uniquely beloved; to the neighbor, she is merely another child. My awareness of being a neighbor, and not only the presence of the other as neighbor, modulates my temptation to recognize only my child's uniqueness; seeing her in the world invites me to recognize her as another participant in it.

In this sense, even infants can be considered "neighbors" to others. Who among us has not shared a confined space with someone else's agitated or tantruming child, who becomes for that moment a (very loud) part of the social fabric? Who among us has not noticed someone else's smiley baby and found himself dislodged, if only briefly, from his own preoccupations? As excruciating as the former and delightful as the latter moments can be for the people within whom a child momentarily shares a world, they are all the more so for the mothers who inevitably participate in these interactions by force of internal and external pressures. Mothers, associated with and held responsible for their children by the broader social world, experience their offspring as neighbors to others through the lens of this attributed responsibility. In turn, the dyadic relation is affected by the presence of other neighbors: a mother may bestow an extra kiss on the smiley baby who has triggered a fellow-traveler's momentary delight, and she may lash out verbally or physically at the toddler who has triggered others' expressions of displeasure in a heretofore quiet public space.

The significance of my child as a neighbor to others becomes manifest as children develop into increasingly independent beings. When my children became old enough to play relatively unsupervised at the playground, walk half a block ahead of me, or fetch an item from a different aisle in the supermarket, I realized that I could, for the first time, watch them interact with others without my mediating presence. Witnessing my children in public spaces, I experienced a new curiosity about the place they would take in civil society, a world in which I was not their center, in which they (and not I) were the primary authors of their interactions. I also experienced the anxiety, quite familiar to mothers, about whether my children would behave in ways that reflected well on them and on the adequacy of my parenting: would they be able to navigate unexpected challenges? Would they share playground equipment appropriately? Would they be able to know when and whom to ask for help? But the more they moved and continue to move on their own in the world, the more I become attuned to their "generic" aspect.

In Jewish thought, the formulation of human beings as simultaneously unique and generic derives from the notion of God as the creator of human-kind. Modern central European Jewish thinkers who grappled with this legacy of humans as paradoxically dual in nature found it a powerful resource for articulating the ongoing significance of the particular (i.e., the Jewish people) within a social and political environment bent on an erstwhile "universalism" that demanded the supression of what was perceived as specific and local to the Jews. In response to this ongoing challenge, Jewish philosophical thinkers like Hermann Cohen and his interpreters, gave "the particular" a privileged political, religious and ethical meaning: it was only through encounter with the particular, the individual, and the unique, that the universal could be apprehended.[19]

The idea that the individual emerges only through contact with the other informs much of twentieth-century Jewish thought. Cohen, for instance, argued that the concept of humanity, which is the basis for ethics, fails if it disregards individuals in their singularity. Compassion was the power that could turn the generic other (*Nebenmensch*) into my fellow (*Mitmensch*), the person whose suf-fering affects my moral life: "The observation of another man's suffering is not an inert affect to which I surrender myself, particularly when I observe it not as a natural or empirical phenomenon, but when I make of it a question mark for my who orientation in the moral world."[20] Cohen suggested that being morally oriented by the suffering of the person "near me" enacts a double transformation: the "near one" becomes my "fellow," and I become a moral "I," that is, a person who understands myself as sinful insofar as I am implicated in her suffering. For Cohen, *ethically relevant* suffering was not illness or death, but economic and social suffering, especially as represented by poverty. In encountering the other's suffering, I become an "I," a "self," who suffers with and takes responsibility for others' suffering. Thus Cohen argued, perhaps counterintuitively, that the feeling of compassion by which we recognize the neighbor *precedes* the concept of the self. This conceptual structure oriented the major Jewish religious philosophers who came after Hermann Cohen (even as they departed quite substantially from him): we discover ourselves as selves only by way of encounter with a Thou.[21]

Cohen, Buber, Rosenzweig, and Levinas understood "encounter" to mean something deeper than ordinary, superficial social interaction. A parent's wait-ing in line at the grocery store, surrounded by "neighbors," was not the kind of "encounter" these thinkers had in mind. They dove into a subterranean level of interaction that was undisturbed by the sometimes tumultuous but, for them, largely insignificant disturbances of daily life in the world. These philosophers were interested in the substructure of intersubjectivity, which remained abstract and removed from ordinary social life.[22] Everyday social interactions, along with gender, race, and most other factors that affect social life, were relegated to the level of superficiality.

But quotidian social interactivity overflows with religious and ethical significance, as a maternally inflected account of the social world makes clear. Dominant modern Jewish theologies of the neighbor tend to avoid or even dismiss the realm of shared social space as relevant for ethics, thus disregarding most of what comprises our social lives in public space and as members of a "public." Maternal insight at its best reveals the neighbor riding the city bus or walking to the post office as having once been an infant who issued a command for obligation and attentive love. (It also reveals those neighbors—including the ones who glare at parents trying futilely to calm their screaming babies—as having once been an annoyance to the others with whom they shared space.) This awareness does not occur only in extraordinary moments of existential encounter, but in daily life in places we share, if only temporarily, with others.[23]

The final clause in Lev. 19:18, "I am YHVH," situates the project of social ethics as theological and the project of theological mandate as social.[24] The nature of the connection between the relation to the neighbor and the divine, however, is not at all clear. Leviticus 19:18, rarely invoked as a *legal* principle in rabbinic thought, has instead evoked centuries of commentary and narrative traditions meditating on how to understand God in terms of the other's human experience and vice versa.[25]

I have argued throughout this book that the ultimate theological significance of a maternal intervention into modern and contemporary Jewish thought lies in the new knowledge of the ineffable that emerges through the daily, quotidian work of caring for one's child. In this chapter, I have suggested that neighbors become conscripted into the work of mothering even though by definition they do not participate in direct, material caregiving toward one's own children. Neighbors play a role in this particular, maternal experience of the divine. But their role is ambiguous and complex, not mapping clearly onto the principal approaches we find in modern Jewish thought.

Jewish twentieth-century religious thinkers consider two main alternatives for formulating the relationship between the neighbor and the divine. They divided along the question of whether the encounter with the divine leads to one's fellow human or whether the encounter with our fellow human leads to the divine. The "theocentric" option is best articulated in Rosenzweig's great philosophical work, *The Star of Redemption* (1921). Rosenzweig focuses on the "primary dyad" consisting of the human being, which he calls the "soul," and God.[26] God's revelation transforms the "self" into a "soul" and instigates her love for God. The experience of revelation is simultaneously immanent and transcendent, and in response to it, the soul yearns for a messianic reality—the full presence of God manifest in the world.

But the messianic time has not arrived; God is not fully present in the world. The human being therefore channels her yearning to the neighbor and to the "community," which subsumes the individual and the primary dyad of soul and God.[27] For Rosenzweig, then, love for one's fellow human being inadequately imitates the true, divine source of love, and is best thought of as the "overflow" from an ontologically prior source. Furthermore, the community as Rosenzweig envisions it hardly allowed for difference or tension among the community members; the *Männerbund* he envisioned, with its almost military-style actions performed in unison, evoke a stylized homogeneity rather than offering room for multiplicity and dyadic connection among the members.[28]

In counterpoint to Rosenzweig's theocentrism, Buber and Levinas prioritize the neighbor as the source of encounter with the divine. For Buber, the encounter between an I and a Thou reverberates with the presence of what he calls the Eternal Thou, who is addressed every time a Thou is addressed *qua* Thou. Levinas, even more insistently than Buber, argues that divinity can only be encountered *through* and *within* the neighbor. He effectively reverses Rosenzweig's account by secularizing it: the fellow human being, not God, occasions the revelation of my obligation to her. Levinas emphasizes the immanent nature of his account; it need not invoke God, being self-sufficient as a site for ethics. And yet, for Levinas, encounter with one's fellow human opens up what he calls transcendence, even as this a transcendence, paradoxically, remains "terrestrial."[29]

Neither of these models offers an adequate account of the relationship between the love of neighbor and the knowledge of God as it unfolds in daily experience of mothers with their children. Maternal experience includes the perception, at times, of one's child as the neighbor whom one often loves more dearly than oneself, and whose needs are often prioritized over those of the self—at times easily and naturally, at times out of an internal sense of duty. Maternal experience also includes the perception of both oneself and one's child as "neighbors" for others, or of one's child as an eventual neighbor who acts in her own right toward others, and who we hope will treat others and will be treated with kindness and respect. Whether the other is intimately connected to us or the participant in civil society whose particularity we never come to know, a maternal intervention recognizes the pathway between the divine and our fellows to run both ways: from divine to human and back again.

* * *

One day, my then six-year-old daughter threw a spectacular tantrum on the New York City subway. She flailed and screamed; she banged her umbrella on the floor. I took away the umbrella, and her rage escalated. She was a volcano, and nothing could stop the explosion. My every word of reassurance, and then threat, made it worse. She screamed louder and flailed with more momentum. Consumed by the drama, we missed our stop. The express train bounded onward for ten interminable minutes to the next stop. I tried not to focus on the other people in the car and their annoyance, but I could neither tune out my aware-ness of them nor, in that moment, escape to the greater anonymity of the station platform, the street, or the privacy of our apartment.

The presence of the other riders transformed an unpleasant but (in the case of this child) occasional hazard of child-rearing into a moment that laid bare the dif-ficult, public side of the intimate relationships between parents and children and the role of neighbors within them. There were plenty of empty seats in the subway car, but a fashionably dressed young man working on a laptop chose, inexplicably, to sit within striking distance of my daughter's out-of-control body. Soon her back-pack grazed him. "Excuse me!" he said as he glared at the screen. Again, a moment later: "Excuse me! Watch it!" Beyond the other riders whose eyes I could not meet, a stranger—a neighbor—was now actively involved. I futilely searched my mental toolbox for every trick I knew to make my daughter calm down. Finally, he turned to me after another jostle and asked, "Are you going to pay for a new computer for me when she breaks this one?" Mortified and furious, at my daughter and at this man, I countered, "Why did you choose to sit here? You can see she's having a hard time!" His response: "You're crazy. I can sit wherever I want."

I dragged my still-flailing, still-screaming child to another corner of the sub-way in mounting desperation. A woman a few seats away looked at my daughter pointedly. "SHHH," she commanded. "There are other people here!" I struggled to hold onto my daughter's hands, trying to keep her from hitting me as she hissed a forbidden phrase at me: *you are so stupid!* I turned on the woman. "You must not be a parent," I said, "because if you were, you would not possibly say that to me at this moment." "No," she sniffed. "I am a human being sharing this space. And I am a teacher. I teach a class of 28 students." "Really?" I asked with undisguised fury. "Terrific. Go ahead, Teacher. Make her stop." The woman, seiz-ing the opportunity, alternatively shushed my daughter and barked at her, "This is not all about you! Respect your mother!"

This woman, in fact, gave an exact definition of what it means to be a "neighbor": she was a human being with whom I was sharing physical and social space in civil society. I was this woman's neighbor, as was my daugh-ter. We were all neighbors simply by virtue of being in the same subway car. Although neighbors usually play the tacit role of demonstrating and enforc-ing cultural norms, this woman took on that role explicitly and with gusto. Perhaps she meant to be helpful; more likely, she thought an intervention to be necessary, even warranted, on account of my daughter's obvious violation of the norms of decent behavior—the norms of a civil society in which people are expected to regulate and repress the unruly. In fact, I agreed with her: there *were* other people there, and that fact mandated that loud demonstrations emo-tional expression be contained.

But beyond this woman's poor choice of timing and delivery, I objected to a conception of public space that was so restricted and unforgiving. Sometimes the unruliness cannot be fully controlled. As a consequence of this particular eruption, these two individuals viewed my daughter—and, by extension, me—as "strangers" rather than "neighbors," that is, as interlopers in the civil society of the subway car. And yet the cause of this demotion, my child's the tantrum, was inseparable from the condemnation of these "neighbors"—the people who passively occupied the background of my frame and to whose presumed dismay I was keenly attuned.

God commanded me to love this woman, and the man with the laptop. They—as far as the Torah is concerned—are commanded to love me, and my daughter too. But I hated them. Most likely, they hated me as well.[30]

When the subway finally stopped at the next station, I pulled my daughter off the train, deeply shaken. The tantrum slowly began to decrescendo. Finally, she and I stepped onto the next train. She cried, more quietly now, and I held my breath. A man a few seats away reached into his bag and handed her a tissue. I exhaled with relief and gratitude. This man, too, was my neighbor.

The episode demonstrates the range of possible ways in which neighbors support or undermine another person's parenting, and the stances a neighbor might have toward one of its own: the contemptuous detachment, even provocation, of the man with the laptop; the teacher's counterproductive but clearly earnest concern for the welfare of the social group; and the active solicitude of the man who responded to my daughter's tears. These neighbors were all representatives of the "culture at large" and, at the same time, of the diversity of actors within it.

My daughter's developmental stage was a factor in these neighbors' determination of her existence on the margins of but nonetheless included in society: a screaming infant would likely only have provoked other passengers to more firmly insert their ear buds; a screaming adult would have cleared the car and been written off as "crazy." But an out-of-control kindergartner one without any visible special needs that might exonerate her, invited responses that, each in their way, acknowledged my daughter as a fellow member of society. My child, unlike an infant or a visibly compromised adult, was understood to be a moral subject. I, the person the neighbors rightly took to be her mother, was also held accountable for her moral failures. The parent/child dyad did not get lost in this moment. In the eyes of these neighbors, my daughter was merely a loud extension of me, and I was therefore answerable for her sins.

Unlike the neighbors in the subway car, I experienced the moment also in the context of my ongoing relationship with my daughter, the unique, beloved individual whom it was my job to socialize. She and I talked about the episode the following day. I knew that her behavior on the subway had been out of character; she, being a reflective soul, did too. I explained—interpreted, translated—the reaction of the subway riders. We talked, in terms she could understand, about why her behavior had been a violation of a social compact; we considered what to do next time she felt so extraordinarily overwhelmed by rage. She apologized. We hugged, read a book, and both continued in the endless work of learning to be a human in the world.

After the terrible train ride had ended that day, I dropped off my daughter to play with a friend and slowly walked back to the subway. I took a seat, surrounded by other people, an adult alone, a neighbor amidst other neighbors. I was no longer visibly tethered to my daughter; I was temporarily responsible only for myself. It was a vantage point of disorienting and exhilarating solitariness. I took in the crowded scene: tourists looking at city maps, laborers slouching against poles, elders with shopping bags, young people involved with their phones. My gaze settled on the women tending to children in strollers: mothers, neighbors, human beings.

Notes

1. Grace Paley, "Midrash on Happiness," in *A Grace Paley Reader: Stories, Essays, and Poetry*, ed. Kevin Bowen and Nora Paley, (New York: Farrar, Straus and Giroux, 2017), 313–316.

2. As discussed in chapter 4, the relationship between child-rearing and eventual adulthood as a matter of civic interest occupied liberal political thinkers, who often construed child-rearing either as a domestic matter (associated with women) or as an educational matter (in which the institution might support or correct the work of the home). A key task among feminist political theorists was to reexamine the relationship between the so-called "private" and "public" realms in liberal political thought.

3. Ludwig Köhler and Walter Baumgartner, *The Hebrew and Aramaic Lexicon of the Old Testament*, trans. M. E. J. Richardson and Johann Jakob Stamm, Study ed., 2 vols. (Boston: Brill, 2001), s.v. *re'a*, II:1254. Jacob Milgrom exhaustively documents the significance of each term in the verse, in Milgrom, *Leviticus 17–22: A New Translation with Introduction and Commentary*, The Anchor Bible (New York: Doubleday, 2000), 1646–1656. The Torah is not explicit as to who exactly was to be included in the concept of the *re'a*, either in terms of gender or in terms of "nationality." It is not clear whether Israelite women, Israelite children, and non-Israelites were considered (or excluded) as "neighbors" (See Milgrom, *Leviticus 17–22*, 1654–1655). Implicitly or explicitly, many modern Jewish thinkers responded to the frequent charge of Jewish tribalism by claiming that the command regarding the neighbor was not limited to the treatment of fellow Jews (or Israelites); they argued that the Torah's true intent was universal in scope. The political stakes of this discussion, especially in nineteenth-century and early twentieth-century Germany, were inextricable from the question itself; one can hardly answer the question of the universality or particularity of the Pentateuch's command without still treading on this difficult ground. In terms of gender, the "neighbor," like the implied addressee of the command, is indicated with the masculine singular. In this constructive project, I understand the neighbor as a category that is not defined by a specific gender requirement, nor, obviously, as a category that refers only to fellow "Israelites." However, I retain the meaning of *re'a* as one who is a member of the national-social body, as distinct from the *ger*/stranger.

4. For a useful discussion of a shared life with others in civil society, see Danielle S. Allen, *Talking to Strangers: Anxieties of Citizenship after Brown V. Board of Education* (Chicago: The University of Chicago Press, 2004).

5. Even in ancient Israel, the term *re'a* did not necessarily (or even probably) refer to a person who was known intimately; see Milgrom's comments on *re'ekha* and the parallel terms used in Lev. 19, such as *'amitekha/'amekha* (your people/kinsfolk) and *'aḥikha* (your brother) (Milgrom, *Leviticus 17–22*, 1655).

6. For an additional meditation on the dative formulation ("render love for") in contrast to the accusative formulation, see Paul Mendes-Flohr, *Love, Accusative and Dative: Reflections on Leviticus 19:18* (Syracuse: Syracuse University Press, 2007).

7. Moses Maimonides, *The Commandments: Sefer Ha-Mitzvoth of Maimonides*, 2 vols. (London, New York: Soncino, 1967), s.v. the 206th commandment.

8. See Iris Murdoch, *The Sovereignty of Good* (New York: Schocken Books, 1971), 74. On Murdoch's use of this concept in a maternal context, see Janet Martin Soskice, *The Kindness of God: Metaphor, Gender, and Religious Language* (New York: Oxford University Press, 2007), 7–34.

9. There is no colloquial English equivalent for *'amitekha* (fellow-national). Milgrom translates *'amitekha* as "member of your people," and argues that the "probable intent [of this word in particular] is to include all Israelites, particularly those belonging to other clans." See Milgrom, *Leviticus 17–22*, s.v. Lev. 19:17–18 and s.v. Lev. 25:25.

10. Sarah Blaffer Hrdy, *Mother Nature: A History of Mothers, Infants, and Natural Selection* (New York: Pantheon Books, 1999). Hrdy also usefully explores the contingency of care, that is, the fact that mammalian parents do not invest in all their children equally.

11. On others as "some mother's child," see Eva Feder Kittay, *Love's Labor: Essays on Women, Equality, and Dependency* (New York: Routledge, 1999).

12. Midrash Tehillim 17:8; Deuteronomy Rabbah 4:4. I wish to thank especially Dianne Cohler-Esses and Michael Gottsegen for discussion of this issue.

13. Yair Lorberbaum, *In God's Image: Myth, Theology, and Law in Classical Judaism* (New York: Cambridge University Press), 181; Kittay, *Love's Labor*.

14. Some moments in civil life demand our contemplation of individual uniqueness with special force; the passage quoted above from mSanhedrin 4:5 forms a part of a speech to be delivered to witnesses in a capital case. The aim is to remind the witness, given the irreversibility of the capital punishment, of the importance of truthful testimony. See discussion in Beth A. Berkowitz, *Execution and Invention: Death Penalty Discourse in Early Rabbinic and Christian Cultures* (New York: Oxford University Press, 2006).

15. Sara Ruddick, *Maternal Thinking: Toward a Politics of Peace* (Boston: Beacon Press, 1989), 104.

16. More recently, some scholars have challenged this traditional view that the *meturgeman* came to fill a linguistic "gap;" instead, it is possible that "the two voices . . . functioned in counterpoint as a bilingual text" (Steven D. Fraade, "Rabbinic Views on the Practice of Targum, and Multilingualism in the Jewish Galilee of the Third-Sixth Centuries," in *The Galilee in Late Antiquity*, ed. Lee I. Levine (New York: Jewish Theological Seminary of America, 1992), cited in Tessa Rajak, *Translation and Survival: The Greek Bible of the Ancient Jewish Diaspora* (New York: Oxford University Press, 2009), 150. See also Philip S. Alexander, "Targumim and the Rabbinic Rules for the Delivery of the Targum," in *Congress Volume Salamanca, Supplements to Vetus Testamentum* (Leiden: Brill, 1985).

17. See Avigdor Shinan, "Live Translation: On the Nature of the Aramaic Targums to the Pentateuch," *Prooftexts* 3, no. 1 (1983).

18. This is not only a feature of the most proximate recent period—our own—but is an ideology that emerges in the modern period, especially the presumptions of nineteenth century Western European and American texts on child-rearing. In terms of this ideology as contemporary concerted cultivation, see Annette Lareau, *Unequal Childhoods: Class, Race, and Family Life*, 2nd ed. (Berkeley: University of California, 2011).

19. See Michael Zank, *The Idea of Atonement in the Philosophy of Hermann Cohen* (Providence: Brown Judaic Studies, 2000).

20. Hermann Cohen, *Religion of Reason out of the Sources of Judaism*, trans. Simon Kaplan (Atlanta: Scholars Press, 1995), 18. See also Ketil Bonaunet, *Hermann Cohen's Kantian Philosophy of Religion* (New York: Peter Lang, 2004), ch. 3.

21. In particular, these thinkers rejected Cohen's understanding of God as merely an ethical postulate. See Samuel Moyn, *Origins of the Other: Emmanuel Levinas between Revelation and Ethics* (Ithaca, NY: Cornell University Press, 2005), ch. 4; On some of the most important Jewish and Christian philosophical critiques of Cohen in his later years, see Moyn, *Origins of the Other*, 123–133 and 141–142.

22. Dana Hollander, "Is the Other My Neighbor? Reading Levinas Alongside Hermann Cohen," in *The Exorbitant: Emmanuel Levinas between Jews and Christians*, ed. Kevin Hart and Michael Alan Signer (New York: Fordham University Press, 2010).

23. The merits and disadvantages of "maternal values" for politics and citizenship have been debated elsewhere widely; see especially Jean Bethke Elshtain, *Public Man, Private Woman: Women in Social and Political Thought* (Princeton, NJ: Princeton University Press, 1981); Ruddick, *Maternal Thinking*. One of the incisive critiques of Ruddick's political proposal remains Mary G. Dietz, "Citizenship with a Feminist Face: The Problem with Maternal Thinking," *Political Theory* 13, no. 1 (1985).

24. Scholars of biblical literature in ancient Near Eastern context have, for some time, convincingly described the function of this clause as a function of the biblical transformation of the suzerainty formula. It indicates that for Israel's suzerain, namely God, nothing falls outside the sphere of his concern. See Moshe Greenberg, "Some Postulates of Biblical Criminal Law," in *Essential Papers on Israel and the Ancient near East*, ed. Frederick E. Greenspahn (New York: New York University Press, 1991).

25. Classical Jewish texts only rarely invoke Lev. 19:18 as a legal principle, although the verse is presented in the form of an imperative and is placed among other clear behavioral norms. The few times the verse is used to explain a legal procedure or principle primarily concern capital punishment. In rabbinic discussions of the appropriate methods of execution, such as bSanhedrin 52a, the verse "Love your neighbor as yourself" is invoked and then glossed as: "choose for him [the convict] a nice death." In several other places, the text uses the verse in matrimonial and sexual matters (e.g., Qiddushin 41a and Niddah 17a).

26. Martin Kavka, "Annulling Theocentrism," *Bamidbar* 4, no. 2. Special edition: Gender and Jewish Philosophy, edited by Susan Shapiro (forthcoming).

27. See my discussion in Mara H. Benjamin, *Rosenzweig's Bible: Reinventing Scripture for Jewish Modernity* (New York: Cambridge University Press, 2009).

28. For a strong reading of this issue—and of Rosenzweig's turn from the female soul to the homosocial (quasi-military) collectivity of men (*Männerbund*), see Zachary Braiterman, *The Shape of Revelation: Aesthetics and Modern Jewish Thought* (Stanford: Stanford University Press, 2007).

29. Emmanuel Levinas, *Totality and Infinity: An Essay on Exteriority*, trans. Alphonso Lingis (Pittsburgh: Duquesne University Press, 1969), 202–203.

30. Precisely the capacity to "hate" one's fellow member of society, and the directive not to "nurse a grudge" against him, provides the context in which Lev. 19:18 commands love of one's neighbor.

Epilogue

I BEGAN WORKING on this book not long after my younger child was born, and I am finishing it as my older child becomes, in the eyes of tradition, an agent in her own right. The concurrence of my work's conclusion with a child reaching the age at which she becomes independently obligated by the commandments is fortuitous. But it is a fitting opportunity to note how significantly my status as an obligated self has changed since my children's infancy, and to imagine how it will change as my children, please God, grow into adults.

Jewish tradition has developed a ritual moment to mark the change in parents' obligations toward their children when a child reaches the age of responsibility: her parents recite the blessing, Blessed is the One who has exempted me from this one's punishment (*barukh shepetarani me'onsho shel zeh/zo*). The child's parents have become *patur*: exempted or released, a state that is the opposite of being *mehuyav* (obligated) or *metzuveh* (commanded). The blessing constructs that from which the parents are released in narrow terms: the parents are no longer held responsible for their children's wrongdoings. But if read capaciously, this blessing affirms a moment of transformation in the nature of parental obligation, a transformation triggered not by the parent's readiness for it but, instead, by the child's growth and maturation.

That such a liturgical act exists affirms the premise of this book: caregiving parents of young children inhabit a distinctive posture of obligation. But it also suggests a recognition that the intense, even abject state of obligation does not last forever. Most children are able to eventually care for their own physical bodies, to sustain themselves with a livelihood, to interact independently with other people and the world. All of these changes are typically viewed as the *telos* of child-rearing, and it is toward this state of relative independence that the blessing gestures.

As I look ahead to reciting these words at my own child's bat mitzvah celebration, I recognize the limits of this blessing as a marker of parental transition: it speaks in technical and legalistic terms of transferring the accounts of sin and punishment, not of the bittersweet pride that accompanies the recognition of a child's agency; the blessing is, moreover, incongruous in a world in which my child, like most young American adolescents, still needs parenting. Even if a bar or bat mitzvah celebration marks a child's new form of responsibility, this ritual pronouncement seemingly denies the ongoing relationship characterized by her dependency and my obligation. My children's growing capability for self-sufficiency slackens the tether that binds me to them through material, embodied service but it does not entirely dissolve the tie of obligation.

As my children become increasingly capable individuals, and the pronounced physical intimacy of caring for them recedes, other models in Jewish thought speak to the ongoing but changed nature of my parental obligation. In this new phase, the model of parent as teacher, and teacher as parent, complements the traditional blessing by recognizing that parents can also be released from their status as teachers. At some moments, our children best us, surpassing us as they transform what have given them.

In a famous talmudic midrash, God, the ultimate teacher, witnesses his "children"—the community of sages—claim their authority. The most famous example occurs in a dispute known as the Oven of 'Akhnai (bBaba Metzia 59b). Rabbi Eliezer argues for his position against the majority of the sages. A series of miracles give evidence that Rabbi Eliezer's opinion is correct, but the sages do not budge. Rabbi Eliezer calls on heaven for unequivocal proof:

> [Rabbi Eliezer] said to them: If the *halakha* agrees with me, let proof come from Heaven! A heavenly voice [*bat qol*] cried out: Why do you dispute with R. Eliezer, since the *halakha* always agrees with him! Rabbi Joshua arose and exclaimed: IT IS NOT IN HEAVEN [Deut. 30:12]. IT IS NOT IN HEAVEN—what does that mean? Rabbi Jeremiah said: Because Torah was already given at Mount Sinai, we pay no attention to a heavenly voice, because You already wrote in the Torah at Mount Sinai, AFTER THE MAJORITY INCLINE [Ex. 23:2]. Rabbi Nathan came upon Elijah [the prophet] and asked him: What did the Holy One Blessed be He say when that happened? Elijah said, He laughed and said, "My sons have defeated Me, My sons have defeated Me."[1]

The defeat is real. The children reject God's intervention, purchasing their autonomy by ousting God from the beit midrash—ironically, asserting their independence on the ground given to them long before.

Like God as imagined here, parents remain teachers even when the foundational years of teaching have passed. We reflexively inhabit postures of acute obligation when they are no longer required. At our worst, we resist acknowledgment of how our relationships with our children change. At our best, we accept the daily reminders of our circumscribed power gracefully, even with delight and pride. Never fully released and never fully bound, the work of rearing children discloses our fraught, dichotomous place in the world.

Notes

1. Among the excellent treatments of this narrative, see Charlotte Elisheva Fonrobert, "When the Rabbi Weeps: On Reading Gender in Talmudic Aggadah," *Nashim* 4 (2001) and Jeffrey L. Rubenstein, *Talmudic Stories: Narrative Art, Composition, and Culture* (Bloomington: Indiana University Press, 1999), 34–64.

Bibliography

Ackerman, Susan. "The Personal Is Political: Covenantal and Affectionate Love ('Aheb, 'Ahaba) in the Hebrew Bible." *Vetus Testamentum* 52, no. 4 (October 2002): 437–458.

Adler, Rachel. *Engendering Judaism: An Inclusive Theology and Ethics*. Philadelphia: Jewish Publication Society, 1998.

Alexander, Elizabeth Shanks. *Gender and Timebound Commandments in Judaism*. New York: Cambridge University Press, 2013.

Alexander, Philip S. "Targumim and the Rabbinic Rules for the Delivery of the Targum." In *Congress Volume Salamanca, Supplements to Vetus Testamentum*, 14–28. Leiden: Brill, 1985.

Allen, Amy. "Feminist Perspectives on Power." In *The Stanford Encyclopedia of Philosophy*, edited by Edward N. Zalta, 2016.

Allen, Danielle S. *Talking to Strangers: Anxieties of Citizenship after Brown V. Board of Education*. Chicago: The University of Chicago Press, 2004.

Andolsen, Barbara Hilkert. "Agape in Feminist Ethics." In *Feminist Theological Ethics: A Reader*, edited by Lois K. Daly and Margaret A. Farley, 146–159. Louisville, KY: Westminster John Knox Press, 1994.

Aranoff, Deena. "The Biblical Root 'MN: Retrieval of a Term and Its Household Context." In *Mothers in the Jewish Cultural Imagination*, edited by Marjorie Lehman, Jane L. Kanarek, and Simon J. Broner, 327–341. Liverpool: Littman, 2017.

Arendt, Hannah. "The Crisis in Education." In *Between Past and Future: Eight Exercises in Political Thought*, 173–196. New York: Penguin Books, 1977.

Ariès, Philippe. *Centuries of Childhood: A Social History of Family Life*. Translated by Robert Baldick. New York: Vintage Books, 1962.

Arnold, Bill T. "The Love-Fear Antinomy in Deuteronomy 5–11." *Vetus Testamentum* 61 (2011): 551–569.

Asad, Talal. *Genealogies of Religion: Discipline and Reasons of Power in Christianity and Islam*. Baltimore, MD: Johns Hopkins University Press, 1993.

Atwood, Margaret Eleanor. *The Handmaid's Tale*. New York: Anchor Books, 1998.

Badinter, Elisabeth. *Mother Love, Myth and Reality: Motherhood in Modern History*. New York: Macmillan, 1981.

Baker, Cynthia M. *Rebuilding the House of Israel: Architectures of Gender in Jewish Antiquity*. Stanford, CA: Stanford University Press, 2002.

Balmes, Thomas. "Babies." 79 min. France, 2010.

Bassin, Donna, Margaret Honey, and Meryle Mahrer Kaplan. *Representations of Motherhood*. New Haven, CT: Yale University Press, 1994.

Batnitzky, Leora. "Dependence and Vulnerability: Jewish and Existentialist Constructions of the Human." In *Women and Gender in Jewish Philosophy*, edited by Hava Tirosh-Samuelson, 127–152. Indianapolis: Indiana University Press, 2004.

Batnitzky, Leora Faye. *How Judaism Became a Religion: An Introduction to Modern Jewish Thought*. Princeton, NJ: Princeton University Press, 2011.

Baumann, Gerlinde. *Love and Violence: Marriage as Metaphor for the Relationship between Yhvh and Israel in the Prophetic Books*. Collegeville, MN: Liturgical Press, 2003.

Baumgarten, Elisheva. *Mothers and Children: Jewish Family Life in Medieval Europe*. Princeton, NJ: Princeton University Press, 2007.

———. *Practicing Piety in Medieval Ashkenaz: Men, Women, and Everyday Religious Observance*. Philadelphia: University of Pennsylvania Press, 2014.

Becker, Gay, Anneliese Butler, and Robert D. Nachtigall. "Resemblance Talk: A Challenge for Parents Whose Children Were Conceived with Donor Gametes in the Us." *Social Science & Medicine* 61, no. 6 (September 2005): 1300–1309.

Benatar, David. "Obligation, Motivation, and Reward: An Analysis of a Talmudic Principle." *Journal of Law and Religion* 17, no. 1/2 (2002): 1–17.

Benjamin, Jessica. *The Bonds of Love: Psychoanalysis, Feminism, and the Problem of Domination*. New York: Pantheon Books, 1988.

Benjamin, Mara H. "Intersubjectivity Meets Maternity: Buber, Levinas, and the Eclipsed Relation." In *Thinking Jewish Culture in America*, edited by Ken Koltun-Fromm, 261–284. New York: Lexington Books, 2014.

———. *Rosenzweig's Bible: Reinventing Scripture for Jewish Modernity*. New York: Cambridge University Press, 2009.

Berkowitz, Beth A. *Execution and Invention: Death Penalty Discourse in Early Rabbinic and Christian Cultures*. New York: Oxford University Press, 2006.

Berlin, Adele, Marc Zvi Brettler, and Michael Fishbane, eds. *The Jewish Study Bible: Featuring the Jewish Publication Society Tanakh Translation*. New York: Oxford University Press, 2004.

Berlin, Isaiah. *Two Concepts of Liberty: An Inaugural Lecture Delivered before the University of Oxford on 31 October 1958*. Oxford: Clarendon Press, 1958.

Bernasconi, Robert. "The Third Party: Levinas on the Intersection of the Ethical and the Political." *Journal of the British Society for Phenomenology* 30, no. 1 (Jan 1999): 76–87.

Biale, Rachel. *Women and Jewish Law: An Exploration of Women's Issues in Halakhic Sources*. New York: Schocken Books, 1984.

Bialik, Hayyim Nahman. "Halachah and Aggadah." In *Revealment and Concealment: Five Essays*, 45–88. Jerusalem: Ibis, 2000.

Blidstein, Gerald J. *Honor Thy Father and Mother: Filial Responsibility in Jewish Law and Ethics*. New York: Ktav, 1975.

Blumenthal, David R. *Facing the Abusing God: A Theology of Protest*. Louisville, KY: Westminster/John Knox Press, 1993.

Blustein, Jeffrey. *Parents and Children: The Ethics of the Family.* New York: Oxford University Press, 1982.

Bonaunet, Ketil. *Hermann Cohen's Kantian Philosophy of Religion.* New York: Peter Lang, 2004.

Boswell, John. *The Kindness of Strangers: The Abandonment of Children in Western Europe from Late Antiquity to the Renaissance.* New York: Pantheon Books, 1988.

Bowlby, Rachel. *A Child of One's Own: Parental Stories.* Oxford: Oxford University Press, 2013.

Boyarin, Daniel. *Carnal Israel: Reading Sex in Talmudic Culture.* Berkeley, CA: University of California Press, 1993.

Braiterman, Zachary. *(God) after Auschwitz: Tradition and Change in Post-Holocaust Jewish Thought.* Princeton, NJ: Princeton University Press, 1998.

———. *The Shape of Revelation: Aesthetics and Modern Jewish Thought.* Stanford: Stanford University Press, 2007.

Bregman, Marc. "Mordecai the "Milk-Man:" Sexual Ambivalence in a Provocative Midrash." In *The Faces of Torah: Studies in the Texts and Contexts of Ancient Judaism in Honor of Steven Fraade,* edited by Michal Bar-Asher Siegal, Tzvi Novick, and Christine Hayes, 257–274. Göttingen: Vandenhoeck & Ruprecht, 2017.

Brenner, Athalya, and Carole R. Fontaine. *A Feminist Companion to the Latter Prophets.* Sheffield, England: Sheffield Academic Press, 1995.

Brettler, Marc Zvi. "Incompatible Metaphors for YHWH in Isaiah 40–66." *Journal for the Study of the Old Testament* 78 (1998): 97–120.

Brown, Kelly Delaine. "God Is as Christ Does: Toward a Womanist Theology." *Journal of Religious Thought* 46, no. 1 (Summer/Fall 1989): 7–16.

Brown, Peter. *The Body and Society: Men, Women, and Sexual Renunciation in Early Christianity.* 20th anniversary ed. New York: Columbia University Press, 2008.

Brown, Tamara Mose. *Raising Brooklyn: Nannies, Childcare, and Caribbeans Creating Community.* New York: New York University Press, 2011.

Buber, Martin. *On the Bible: Eighteen Studies.* Translated by Nahum Glatzer. New York: Schocken Books, 1968.

Bucar, Elizabeth. "Dianomy: Understanding Religious Women's Moral Agency as Creative Conformity." *Journal of the American Academy of Religion* 78, no. 3 (September 2010): 662–686.

Budig, Michelle. "The Fatherhood Bonus & the Motherhood Penalty: Parenthood and the Gender Gap in Pay." *Third Way,* 2014, last updated September 2, 2014, accessed November 8, 2017, http://www.thirdway.org/report/the-fatherhood-bonus-and -the-motherhood-penalty-parenthood-and-the-gender-gap-in-pay.

Burggraeve, Roger. "The Ethical Voice of the Child: Plea for a Chiastic Responsibility in the Footsteps of Levinas." In *Children's Voices: Children's Perspectives in Ethics, Theology and Religious Education,* edited by Annemie Dillen and Didier Pollefeyt, 267–291. Leuven: Peeters, 2010.

Burrus, Virginia, and Catherine Keller. *Toward a Theology of Eros: Transfiguring Passion at the Limits of Discipline.* New York: Fordham University Press, 2006.

Bynum, Caroline Walker. *Holy Feast and Holy Fast: The Religious Significance of Food to Medieval Women.* Berkeley: University of California Press, 1987.

———. "Jesus as Mother and Abbot as Mother: Some Themes in Twelfth-Century Cistercian Writing." In *Jesus as Mother: Studies in the Spirituality of the High Middle Ages*, 110–169. Berkeley: University of California Press, 1984.

Cahill, Lisa Sowle. *Sex, Gender, and Christian Ethics*. New York: Cambridge University Press, 1996.

Campbell, Ken M. *Marriage and Family in the Biblical World*. Downers Grove, IL: InterVarsity Press, 2003.

Caputo, John D. *Against Ethics: Contributions to a Poetics of Obligation with Constant Reference to Deconstruction*. Bloomington: Indiana University Press, 1993.

Carlebach, Elisheva. "Fallen Women and Fatherless Children: Jewish Domestic Servants in Eighteenth-Century Altona." *Jewish History* 24 (2010): 295–308.

Carlson, John D. "Religion and Violence: Coming to Terms with Terms." In *The Blackwell Companion to Religion and Violence*, edited by Andrew R. Murphy, 7–22. Malden, MA: Wiley-Blackwell, 2011.

Christ, Carol P., and Judith Plaskow. *Womanspirit Rising: A Feminist Reader in Religion*. Harper Forum Books. 1st ed. San Francisco: Harper & Row, 1979.

———. *Goddess and God in the World: Conversations in Embodied Theology*. Minneapolis, MN: Fortress Press, 2016.

Cline, Erin M. *Families of Virtue: Confucian and Western Views on Childhood Development*. New York: Columbia University Press, 2015.

Coakley, Sarah. *Powers and Submissions: Spirituality, Philosophy and Gender*. Oxford: Blackwell Publishers, 2002.

Coates, Ta-Nehisi. *Between the World and Me*. New York: Spiegel & Grau: Text Publishing Company, 2015.

Cohen, Hermann. *Religion of Reason out of the Sources of Judaism*. Translated by Simon Kaplan. Atlanta: Scholars Press, 1995.

Cohen, Shaye J. D. *Why Aren't Jewish Women Circumcised? Gender and Covenant in Judaism*. Berkeley: University of California Press, 2005.

Cohn, Naftali. "Domestic Women: Constructing and Deconstructing a Gender Stereotype in the Mishnah." In *From Antiquity to the Postmodern World: Jewish Studies in Canada*, edited by Daniel Maoz and Andrea Gondos, 38–61. Cambridge: Cambridge Scholars Publishing, 2011.

Cohn, Naftali S. *The Memory of the Temple and the Making of the Rabbis*. Philadelphia: University of Pennsylvania Press, 2013.

Cohn, Yehudah. *Tangled up in Text: Tefillin and the Ancient World*. Providence, RI: Society of Biblical Literature, 2008.

Collins, Patricia Hill. *Black Feminist Thought: Knowledge, Consciousness, and the Politics of Empowerment*. Rev. 10th anniversary ed. New York: Routledge, 2000.

———. "Shifting the Center: Race, Class, and Feminist Theorizing About Motherhood." In *Representations of Motherhood*, edited by Donna Bassin, Margaret Honey and Meryle Mahrer Kaplan, 56–74. New Haven, CT: Yale University Press, 1994.

Cover, Robert. "Nomos and Narrative." *Harvard Law Review* 97, no. 4 (November 1983): 4–68.

———. "Obligation: A Jewish Jurisprudence of the Social Order." *Journal of Law and Religion* 5, no. 1 (1987): 65–74.

Daly, Mary. *Beyond God the Father: Toward a Philosophy of Women's Liberation*. Boston: Beacon Press, 1973.

Derrida, Jacques. *Adieu to Emmanuel Levinas*. Stanford, CA: Stanford University Press, 1999.

Dever, William G. *The Lives of Ordinary People in Ancient Israel: Where Archaeology and the Bible Intersect*. Grand Rapids, MI: W.B. Eerdmans, 2012.

Dewey, John. *The Later Works, 1925–1953*. Vol. 7. Carbondale: Southern Illinois University Press, 1981.

Diamond, Eliezer. *Holy Men and Hunger Artists: Fasting and Asceticism in Rabbinic Culture*. New York: Oxford University Press, 2004.

Dietz, Mary G. "Citizenship with a Feminist Face: The Problem with Maternal Thinking." *Political Theory* 13, no. 1 (February 1985): 19–37.

———. *Turning Operations: Feminism, Arendt, Politics*. New York: Routledge, 2002.

Dinnerstein, Dorothy. *The Mermaid and the Minotaur: Sexual Arrangements and Human Malaise*. New York: Harper & Row, 1976.

Douglas, Mary. *Leviticus as Literature*. New York: Oxford University Press, 1999.

Dreyfus, Hubert L., and Paul Rabinow, eds. *Michel Foucault: Beyond Structuralism and Hermeneutics*. 2nd ed. Chicago: University of Chicago Press, 1983.

Dubow, Sara. *Ourselves Unborn: A History of the Fetus in Modern America*. Oxford: Oxford University Press, 2011.

Ebeling, Jennie R. *Women's Lives in Biblical Times*. New York: T. & T. Clark, 2010.

Eilberg-Schwartz. *God's Phallus: And Other Problems for Men and Monotheism*. Boston: Beacon Press, 1994.

Eisen, Arnold M. *Rethinking Modern Judaism: Ritual, Commandment, Community*. Chicago: University of Chicago Press, 1998.

Elshtain, Jean Bethke. *Public Man, Private Woman: Women in Social and Political Thought*. Princeton, NJ: Princeton University Press, 1981.

Falk, Marcia. *The Book of Blessings: New Jewish Prayers for Daily Life, the Sabbath, and the New Moon Festival*. San Francisco, CA: HarperSanFrancisco, 1996.

Feldstein, Ruth. *Motherhood in Black and White: Race and Sex in American Liberalism, 1930–1965*. Ithaca, NY: Cornell University Press, 2000.

Finkelstein, Eliezer. *Sifre 'Al Sefer Devarim*. New York: Jewish Theological Seminary, 2001.

Firestone, Shulamith. *The Dialectic of Sex: The Case for Feminist Revolution*. New York: Morrow, 1970.

Fishbane, Michael A. *Sacred Attunement: A Jewish Theology*. Chicago: University of Chicago Press, 2008.

Fonrobert, Charlotte Elisheva. "When the Rabbi Weeps: On Reading Gender in Talmudic Aggadah." *Nashim* 4 (Fall 2001): 56–83.

Forster, Brenda. "The Biblical 'Omen and Evidence for the Nurturance of Children by Hebrew Males." *Judaism* 42, no. 3 (Summer 1993): 321–331.

Foucault, *The Birth of the Clinic: An Archaeology of Medical Perception*. Translated by Alan Sheridan. New York: Pantheon Books, 1973.

———. *Discipline and Punish: The Birth of the Prison*. Translated by Alan Sheridan. New York: Vintage Books, 1995.

Fraade, Steven D. *From Tradition to Commentary: Torah and Its Interpretation in the Midrash Sifre to Deuteronomy.* Albany: State University of New York Press, 1991.
———. "Ascetical Aspects of Ancient Judaism." In *Jewish Spirituality,* edited by Arthur Green, 253–288. New York: Crossroad, 1986.
———. "Rabbinic Views on the Practice of Targum, and Multilingualism in the Jewish Galilee of the Third-Sixth Centuries." In *The Galilee in Late Antiquity,* edited by Lee I. Levine. New York: Jewish Theological Seminary of America, 1992.
Freeze, ChaeRan Y. "Lilith's Midwives: Jewish Newborn Child Murder in Nineteenth-Century Vilna." *Jewish Social Studies, n.s.* 16, no. 2 (Winter 2010): 1–27.
French, Marilyn. *The Women's Room.* New York: Summit Books, 1977.
Fretheim, Terence. "The Repentance of God: A Key to Evaluating Old Testament God-Talk." *Horizons in Biblical Theology* 10, no. 1 (July 1988): 47–70.
Freud, Sigmund, and James Strachey. *The Future of an Illusion.* New York: Norton, 1975.
Friedan, Betty. *The Feminine Mystique.* New York: Norton, 1963.
Frymer-Kensky, Tikva Simone. *In the Wake of the Goddesses: Women, Culture, and the Biblical Transformation of Pagan Myth.* New York: Free Press, 1992.
Furey, C. M. "Body, Society, and Subjectivity in Religious Studies." *Journal of the American Academy of Religion* 80, no. 1 (March 2012): 7–33.
Galli, Barbara E. *Franz Rosenzweig and Jehuda Halevi: Translating, Translations, and Translators.* Montreal: McGill-Queen's University Press, 1995.
Gandolfo, Elizabeth O'Donnell. *The Power and Vulnerability of Love: A Theological Anthropology.* Minneapolis, MN: Fortress Press, 2015.
Gay, Peter. *Freud: A Life for Our Time.* New York: W.W. Norton, 1988.
Geertz, Clifford. "Religion as a Cultural System." In *Interpretation of Cultures: Selected Essays,* 87–125. New York: Basic Books, 1973.
Gillies, Val. *Marginalised Mothers: Exploring Working-Class Experiences of Parenting.* New York: Routledge, 2007.
Gilligan, Carol. *In a Different Voice: Psychological Theory and Women's Development.* Cambridge: Harvard University Press, 1982.
Glenn, Evelyn Nakano. "Social Constructions of Mothering: A Thematic Overview." In *Mothering: Ideology, Experience, and Agency,* edited by Evelyn Nakano Glenn, Grace Chang and Linda Rennie Forcey, 1–29. New York: Routledge, 1994.
Goldstein, Valerie Saiving. "The Human Situation: A Feminine View." *The Journal of Religion* 40, no. 2 (1960): 100–112.
Green, Arthur. *Radical Judaism: Rethinking God and Tradition.* New Haven, CT: Yale University Press, 2010.
———. "Shekhinah, the Virgin Mary, and the Song of Songs: Reflections on a Kabbalistic Symbol in Its Historical Context." *AJS Review* 26, no. 1 (April 2002): 1–52.
Greenberg, Moshe. "Some Postulates of Biblical Criminal Law." In *Essential Papers on Israel and the Ancient Near East,* edited by Frederick E. Greenspahn, 333–352. New York: New York University Press, 1991.
Griffith, R. Marie. *God's Daughters: Evangelical Women and the Power of Submission.* Berkeley: University of California Press, 1997.
Gruber, Mayer I. "Breast-Feeding Practices in Biblical Israel and in Old Babylonian Mesopotamia." *Journal of the Ancient Near Eastern Society* 19 (1989): 61–83.
———. *The Motherhood of God and Other Studies.* Vol. 57, Atlanta: Scholars Press 1992.

Gudorf, Christine E. "Parenting, Mutual Love, and Sacrifice." In *Women's Consciousness and Women's Conscience: A Reader in Feminist Ethics,* edited by Barbara Hilkert Andolsen, Christine E. Gudorf, and Mary D. Pellauer, 175–191. San Francisco: Harper & Row, 1985.

Harnack, Adolf von. *Marcion: The Gospel of the Alien God* [Marcion: Das Evangelium vom fremden Gott, eine Monographie zur Geschichte der Grundlegung der katholischen Kirche]. Durham, NC: Labyrinth Press, 1990.

Harrison, Beverly Wildung. "The Power of Anger in the Work of Love: Christian Ethics for Women and Other Strangers." *Union Seminary Quarterly Review* 36 (April 1985): 41–57.

Haskell, Ellen Davina. *Suckling at My Mother's Breasts: The Image of a Nursing God in Jewish Mysticism.* Albany: State University of New York Press, 2012.

Hauptman, Judith. *Rereading the Rabbis: A Woman's Voice.* Boulder, CO: Westview Press, 1998.

Hayes, Christine. *Between the Babylonian and Palestinian Talmuds: Accounting for Halakhic Differences in Selected Sugyot from Tractate Avodah Zarah.* New York: Oxford University Press, 1997.

Hayes, Diana L. *Hagar's Daughters: Womanist Ways of Being in the World.* Madeleva Lecture in Spirituality. New York: Paulist Press, 1995.

Held, Shai. *Abraham Joshua Heschel: The Call of Transcendence.* Bloomington: Indiana University Press, 2013.

Held, Virginia. *Feminist Morality: Transforming Culture, Society, and Politics.* Women in Culture and Society. Chicago: University of Chicago Press, 1993.

———. "The Obligations of Mothers and Fathers." In *Mothering: Essays in Feminist Theory,* edited by Joyce Trebilcot, 7–20. Totowa, NJ: Rowman & Allanheld, 1984.

Heschel, Abraham Joshua. *Heavenly Torah: As Refracted through the Generations.* Translated by Gordon Tucker. New York: Continuum, 2005.

———. *The Prophets.* New York: Perennial, 2001.

Hezser, Catherine. *The Social Structure of the Rabbinic Movement in Roman Palestine.* Tübingen: Mohr Siebeck, 1997.

Hoffman, Lawrence A. *Covenant of Blood: Circumcision and Gender in Rabbinic Judaism.* Chicago: University of Chicago Press, 1996.

Hollander, Dana. "Is the Other My Neighbor? Reading Levinas Alongside Hermann Cohen." In *The Exorbitant: Emmanuel Levinas between Jews and Christians,* edited by Kevin Hart and Michael Alan Signer, 90–107. New York: Fordham University Press, 2010.

Horwitz, Rivka. *Buber's Way to "I and Thou:" The Development of Martin Buber's Thought and His "Religion as Presence" Lectures.* New York: Jewish Publication Society, 1988.

Hrdy, Sarah Blaffer. *Mother Nature: A History of Mothers, Infants, and Natural Selection.* New York: Pantheon Books, 1999.

Hyman, Paula. *Gender and Assimilation in Modern Jewish History: The Roles and Representation of Women.* Seattle: University of Washington Press, 1995.

Idel, Moshe. *Ben: Sonship and Jewish Mysticism.* New York: Continuum, 2007.

Jaffee, Martin. "A Rabbinic Ontology of the Written and Spoken Word: On Discipleship, Transformative Knowledge, and the Living Texts of Oral Torah." *Journal of the American Academy of Religion* 65, no. 3 (Autumn 1997): 525–549.

Jaggar, Allison M. "Love and Knowledge: Emotion in Feminist Epistemology." *Inquiry* 32, no. 2 (1989): 151–176.

Jeon, Deborah A., Dina Baskt, Lenora Lapidus, Steven Shapiro, and Ariela M. Migdal. *Amicus Curiae Brief of the American Civil Liberties Union and a Better Balance, Et Al., in Support of Petitioner,* 2014.

Jonas, Hans. "The Concept of God after Auschwitz: A Jewish Voice." *The Journal of Religion* 67, no. 1 (January 1987): 1–13.

Kant, Immanuel. *Religion within the Bounds of Bare Reason.* Indianapolis, IN: Hackett, 2009.

Kant, Immanuel, Allen W. Wood, and J. B. Schneewind. *Groundwork for the Metaphysics of Morals.* Rethinking the Western Tradition. New Haven, CT: Yale University Press, 2002.

Kaplan, Lawrence. "Israel under the Mountain: Emmanuel Levinas on Freedom and Constraint in the Revelation of the Torah." *Modern Judaism* 18, no. 1 (Feb 1998): 35–46.

Kattan Gribetz, Sarit. "Conceptions of Time and Rhythms of Daily Life in Rabbinic Literature, 200–600 C.E." Princeton, NJ: Princeton University, 2013.

———. "Metaphors of Childbirth: Revisiting Women's Experience in Feminist Scholarship." Lecture given at the Society for Biblical Literature, Atlanta, 2015.

Katz, Jack. *How Emotions Work.* Chicago: University of Chicago Press, 2001.

Kavka, Martin. "Annulling Theocentrism." *Bamidbar* 4, no. 2. Special edition: Gender and Jewish Philosophy, edited by Susan Shapiro (forthcoming).

Kellenbach, Katharina von. *Anti-Judaism in Feminist Religious Writings.* Atlanta: Scholars Press, 1994.

Keller, Catherine. *The Face of the Deep: A Theology of Becoming.* New York: Routledge, 2003.

———. *From a Broken Web: Separation, Sexism, and Self.* Boston: Beacon Press, 1986.

Keller, Catherine, and Laurel C. Schneider. *Polydoxy: Theology of Multiplicity and Relation.* New York: Routledge, 2011.

Keller, Mary. *The Hammer and the Flute: Women, Power, and Spirit Possession.* Baltimore, MD: Johns Hopkins University Press, 2002.

Kessler, Gwynn. *Conceiving Israel: The Fetus in Rabbinic Narratives.* Philadelphia: University of Pennsylvania Press, 2009.

Kimelman, Reuven. "The Shema' Liturgy: From Covenant Ceremony to Coronation." *Kenishta: Studies of the Synagogue World* 1 (2001): 9–105.

Kittay, Eva Feder. *Love's Labor: Essays on Women, Equality, and Dependency.* New York: Routledge, 1999.

Klein, Ernest, and Baruch Sarel. *A Comprehensive Etymological Dictionary of the Hebrew Language for Readers of English.* New York: Macmillan, 1987.

Köhler, Ludwig, and Walter Baumgartner. *The Hebrew and Aramaic Lexicon of the Old Testament.* Translated by M. E. J. Richardson and Johann Jakob Stamm. Study ed. 2 vols. Boston: Brill, 2001.

Kueny, Kathryn. *Conceiving Identities: Maternity in Medieval Muslim Discourse and Practice.* Albany: State University of New York Press, 2013.

———. "Marking the Body: Resemblance and Medieval Muslim Constructions of Paternity." *Journal of Feminist Studies in Religion* 30, no. 1 (Spring 2014): 65–84.

Labovitz, Gail. "'These Are the Labors': Constructions of the Woman Nursing Her Child in the Mishnah and Tosefta." *Nashim: A Journal of Jewish Women's Studies & Gender Issues*, no. 3 (2000): 15–42.

Lancy, David F. *The Anthropology of Childhood: Cherubs, Chattel, Changelings.* 2nd ed. New York: Cambridge University Press, 2014.

Lareau, Annette. *Unequal Childhoods: Class, Race, and Family Life.* 2nd ed. Berkeley: University of California, 2011.

Lesnik-Oberstein, Karín. *On Having an Own Child: Reproductive Technologies and the Cultural Construction of Childhood.* London: Karnac Books, 2007.

Levenson, Jon D. *Inheriting Abraham: The Legacy of the Patriarch in Judaism, Christianity, and Islam.* Princeton, NJ: Princeton University Press, 2012.

——. *The Love of God: Divine Gift, Human Gratitude, and Mutual Faithfulness in Judaism.* Princeton, NJ: Princeton University Press, 2015.

——. *Sinai and Zion: An Entry into the Jewish Bible.* Minneapolis, MN: Winston Press, 1985.

Levinas, Emmanuel. *Nine Talmudic Readings.* Bloomington: Indiana University Press, 1994.

——. *Totality and Infinity: An Essay on Exteriority.* Translated by Alphonso Lingis. Pittsburgh, PA: Duquesne University Press, 1969.

Lewis, Thomas, Fari Amini, and Richard Lannon. *A General Theory of Love.* New York: Random House, 2000.

Lofton, Kathryn. "Religion and the Authority in American Parenting." *Journal of the American Academy of Religion* 84, no. 1 (March 2016): 1–36.

Lorberbaum, Yair. *Disempowered King: Monarchy in Classical Jewish Literature.* New York: Continuum, 2010.

——. *In God's Image: Myth, Theology, and Law in Classical Judaism.* New York: Cambridge University Press, 2015.

Lorde, Audre. "Uses of the Erotic: The Erotic as Power." In *Sister Outsider: Essays and Speeches.* Trumansburg, NY: Crossing Press, 1984.

Macdonald, Cameron Lynne. *Shadow Mothers: Nannies, Au Pairs, and the Micropolitics of Mothering.* Berkeley: University of California Press, 2010.

Madsen, Catherine. "Notes on God's Violence." *Cross Currents* 51, no. 2 (Summer 2001): 229–256.

Mahmood, Saba. *Politics of Piety: The Islamic Revival and the Feminist Subject.* Princeton, NJ: Princeton University Press, 2005.

Maimonides, Moses. *The Commandments: Sefer Ha-Mitzvoth of Maimonides.* 2 vols. New York: Soncino, 1967.

Malamat, Abraham. "You Shall Love Your Neighbor as Yourself: A Case of Misinterpretation." In *Die hebräische Bibel und ihre zweifache Nachgeschichte: Festschrift Für Rolf Rendtorff zum 65. Geburtstag,* edited by Erhard Blum, Chrsitian Macholz and Ekkehard Stegemann. Neukirchen-Vluyn: Neukirchener, 1990.

Marcus, Ivan G. *Rituals of Childhood: Jewish Culture and Accultaration in the Middle Ages.* New Haven, CT: Yale University Press, 1996.

Margalit, Natan. "Priestly Men and Invisible Women: Male Appropriation of the Feminine and the Exemption of Women from Positive Time-Bound Commandments." *AJS Review* 28, no. 2 (2004): 297–316.

May, Elaine Tyler. *America and the Pill: A History of Promise, Peril, and Liberation.* New York: Basic Books, 2010.

———. *Barren in the Promised Land: Childless Americans and the Pursuit of Happiness.* New York: Basic Books, 1995.

Mendelssohn, Moses. *Jerusalem, or, on Religious Power and Judaism.* Translated by Allan Arkush. Hanover: University Press of New England, 1983.

Mendes-Flohr, Paul. *Love, Accusative and Dative: Reflections on Leviticus 19:18.* Syracuse, NY: Syracuse University Press, 2007.

Milgrom, Jacob. *Leviticus 17–22: A New Translation with Introduction and Commentary.* The Anchor Bible. New York: Doubleday, 2000.

Miller-McLemore, Bonnie J. *Also a Mother: Work and Family as Theological Dilemma.* Nashville, TN: Abingdon Press, 1994.

———. "Feminism, Children, and Mothering: Three Books and Three Children Later." *Journal of Childhood and Religion* 2, no. 1 (January 2011): 1–32.

Mintz, Steven. *Huck's Raft: A History of American Childhood.* Cambridge, MA: Belknap Press, 2004.

Moran, William. "Ancient Near Eastern Background of the Love of God in Deuteronomy." *Catholic Biblical Quarterly* 25, no. 1 (January 1963): 77–87.

Moyn, Samuel. *Origins of the Other: Emmanuel Levinas between Revelation and Ethics.* Ithaca, NY: Cornell University Press, 2005.

Muffs, Yochanan. *Love and Joy: Law, Language, and Religion in Ancient Israel.* New York: Jewish Theological Seminary of America, 1992.

Munn, Penny. "Mothering More Than One Child." In *Motherhood: Meanings, Practices, and Ideologies,* edited by Ann Phoenix, Anne Woollett, and Eva Lloyd, 162–177. London: Sage Publications, 1991.

Murdoch, Iris. *The Sovereignty of Good.* New York: Schocken Books, 1971.

Niebuhr, Reinhold. *The Nature and Destiny of Man: A Christian Interpretation.* 2 vols. New York: Charles Scribner's Sons, 1946.

Noddings, Nel. *The Maternal Factor: Two Paths to Morality.* Berkeley: University of California Press, 2010.

Novick, Tzvi. *What Is Good, and What God Demands: Normative Structures in Tannaitic Literature.* Boston: Brill, 2010.

Nygren, Anders. *Agape and Eros.* Translated by Philip Watson. Philadelphia, PA: Westminster Press, 1953. 1930.

Oh, Irene. "Motherhood in Christianity and Islam: Critiques, Realities, and Possibilities." *Journal of Religious Ethics* 38, no. 4 (December 2010): 638–653.

Okin, Susan Moller. *Justice, Gender, and the Family.* New York: Basic Books, 1989.

———. *Women in Western Political Thought.* Princeton, NJ: Princeton University Press, 1979.

Orleck, Annelise. *Storming Caesars Palace: How Black Mothers Fought Their Own War on Poverty.* Boston: Beacon Press, 2005.

Oxenhandler, Noelle. *The Eros of Parenthood: Explorations in Light and Dark.* New York: St. Martin's Press, 2001.

Paley, Grace. "Midrash on Happiness." In *A Grace Paley Reader: Stories, Essays, and Poetry,* edited by Kevin Bowen and Nora Paley, 313–316. New York: Farrar, Straus and Giroux, 2017.

Pardes, Ilana. *The Biography of Ancient Israel: National Narratives in the Bible.* Berkeley: University of California Press, 2000.

———. *Countertraditions in the Bible: A Feminist Approach.* Cambridge: Harvard University Press, 1992.

Parens, Erik, and Adrienne Asch. *Prenatal Testing and Disability Rights.* Hastings Center Studies in Ethics. Washington, DC: Georgetown University Press, 2000.

Parsons, Susan Frank. *Feminism and Christian Ethics.* New Studies in Christian Ethics. Cambridge, MA: Cambridge University Press, 1996.

Penniman, John. *Lacte Christiano Educatus: The Symbolic Power of Nourishment in Early Christianity.* Bronx, NY: Fordham University, 2015.

Perdue, Leo G. *Families in Ancient Israel.* Louisville, KY: Westminster John Knox Press, 1997.

Peskowitz, Miriam. *Spinning Fantasies: Rabbis, Gender, and History.* Berkeley: University of California Press, 1997.

Plaskow, Judith. *Standing Again at Sinai: Judaism from a Feminist Perspective.* San Francisco: HarperCollins, 1991.

———. "Wrestling with God and Evil." In *Chapters of the Heart: Jewish Women Sharing the Torah of Our Lives,* edited by Sue Elwell and Nancy Fuchs Kreimer, 85–94. Eugene, OR: Wipf and Stock Publishers, 2013.

Plaskow, Judith, and Carol Christ. *Goddess and God in the World: Conversations in Embodied Theology.* Minneapolis, MN: Augsburg Fortress, 2016.

Purvis, Sally. "Mothers, Neighbors, and Strangers: Another Look at Agape." *Journal of Feminist Studies in Religion* 7 (Spring 1991): 19–34.

Rajak, Tessa. *Translation and Survival: The Greek Bible of the Ancient Jewish Diaspora.* New York: Oxford University Press, 2009.

Rashkover, Randi. *Revelation and Theopolitics: Barth, Rosenzweig, and the Politics of Praise.* London, New York: T&T Clark, 2005.

Raveh, Inbar. *Feminist Rereadings of Rabbinic Literature.* Translated by Kaeren Fish. Waltham, MA: Brandeis University Press, 2014.

Rich, Adrienne. *Of Woman Born: Motherhood as Experience and Institution.* 10th anniversary ed. New York: Norton, 1986 [1976].

Romero, Mary. *Maid in the U.S.A.* New York: Routledge, 1992.

———. *The Maid's Daughter: Living inside and Outside the American Dream.* New York: New York University Press, 2011.

———. "Who Takes Care of the Maid's Children: Exploring the Costs of Domestic Service." In *Feminism and Families,* edited by Hilde Lindemann Nelson, 151–169: London: Psychology Press, 1997.

Rosen-Zvi, Ishay. *Demonic Desires: Yetzer Hara and the Problem of Evil in Late Antiquity.* Philadelphia: University of Pennsylvania Press, 2011.

Rosenblum, Jordan. "'Blessings of the Breasts:' Breastfeeding in Rabbinic Literature." *Hebrew Union College Annual* 87 (2017): 147–179.

———. *Food and Identity in Early Rabbinic Judaism.* New York: Cambridge University Press, 2010.

Rosenzweig, Franz. "The Builders." Translated by N. N. Glatzer. In *On Jewish Learning,* edited by Nahum Glatzer, 72–92. New York: Schocken Books, 1965.

———. *The Star of Redemption.* Translated by Barbara E. Galli. Madison: University of Wisconsin Press, 2005.

Roth, Martha T. "Deborah, Rebekah's Nurse." *Eretz-Israel: Archaeological, Historical and Geographical Studies* 27 (2003): 203–207.

Rothman, Barbara Katz. *Recreating Motherhood: Ideology and Technology in a Patriarchal Society*. Revised ed. New York: Rutgers University Press, 2000.

Rousseau, Jean-Jacques. *Emile: Or, on Education*. Translated by Allan Bloom. New York: Basic Books, 1979.

Rubenstein, Jeffrey L. *Talmudic Stories: Narrative Art, Composition, and Culture*. Bloomington: Indiana University Press, 1999.

Ruddick, Sara. *Maternal Thinking: Toward a Politics of Peace*. Boston: Beacon Press, 1989.

Sands, Kathleen M. "Tragedy, Theology, and Feminism in the Time after Time." *New Literary History* 35, no. 1 (Winter 2004): 41–61.

———. "Uses of the Thea(o)Logian: Sex and Theodicy in Religious Feminism." *Journal of Feminist Studies in Religion* 8, no. 1 (Spring 1992): 7–33.

Satlow, Michael L. "'And on the Earth You Shall Sleep': *Talmud Torah* and Rabbinic Asceticism." *Journal of Religion* 83, no. 2 (April 2003): 204–205.

Schäfer, Peter. *Mirror of His Beauty: Feminine Images of God from the Bible to the Early Kabbala*. Princeton, NJ: Princeton University Press, 2002.

Scheper-Hughes, Nancy. *Death without Weeping: The Violence of Everyday Life in Brazil*. Berkeley: University of California Press, 1992.

Schneider, Laurel C. *Beyond Monotheism: A Theology of Multiplicity*. New York: Routledge, 2008.

Schofer, Jonathan Wyn. *Confronting Vulnerability: The Body and the Divine in Rabbinic Ethics*. Chicago: University of Chicago Press, 2010.

———. *The Making of a Sage: A Study in Rabbinic Ethics*. Madison: University of Wisconsin Press, 2004.

———. "Self, Subject, and Chosen Subjection: Rabbinic Ethics and Comparative Possibilities." *Journal of Religious Ethics* 33, no. 2 (June 2005): 255–291.

Schwartz, Seth. *Imperialism and Jewish Society, 200 B.C.E. To 640 C.E*. Princeton, NJ: Princeton University Press, 2001.

Seidman, Naomi. *The Marriage Plot: Or, How Jews Fell in Love with Love, and with Literature*. Stanford: Stanford University Press, 2016.

Seligman, Adam, Robert Weller, Michael Puett, and Bennett Simon. *Ritual and Its Consequences: An Essay on the Limits of Sincerity*. New York: Oxford University Press, 2008.

Senior, Jennifer. *All Joy and No Fun: The Paradox of Modern Parenthood*. New York: Harper Collins, 2014.

Sered, Susan Starr. *Women as Ritual Experts: The Religious Lives of Elderly Jewish Women in Jerusalem*. New York: Oxford University Press, 1992.

Shinan, Avigdor. "Live Translation: On the Nature of the Aramaic Targums to the Pentateuch." *Prooftexts* 3, no. 1 (January 1983): 41–49.

Simon-Shoshan, Moshe. "'People Talking without Speaking': The Semiotics of the Rabbinic Legal Exemplum as Reflected in Bavli Berakhot 11a." *Law & Literature* 25, no. 3 (2013): 446–465.

Sivertsev, Alexei. *Households, Sects, and the Origins of Rabbinic Judaism*. Boston: Brill, 2005.

Solomon, Andrew. *Far from the Tree: Parents, Children and the Search for Identity*. New York: Scribner, 2012.

Sommer, Benjamin D. *The Bodies of God and the World of Ancient Israel*. New York: Cambridge University Press, 2009.

Sommerville, C. John. *The Rise and Fall of Childhood*. Beverly Hills, CA: Sage Publications, 1982.

Soskice, Janet Martin. *The Kindness of God: Metaphor, Gender, and Religious Language*. New York: Oxford University Press, 2007.

Spinoza, Benedictus de. *Theological-Political Treatise*. Translated by Samuel Shirley. 2nd ed. Indianapolis, IN: Hackett, 2001.

Stack, Carol B., and Linda M. Burton. "Kinscripts: Reflections on Family, Generation, and Culture." In *Mothering: Ideology, Experience, Agency*, edited by Evelyn Nakano Glenn, Grace Chang, and Linda Rennie Forcey, 33–44. New York: Routledge, 1994.

Steinberg, Naomi A. *Kinship and Marriage in Genesis: A Household Economics Perspective*. Minneapolis, MN: Fortress Press, 1993.

Stern, David. *Midrash and Theory: Ancient Jewish Exegesis and Contemporary Literary Studies*. Evanston, IL: Northwestern University Press, 1996.

Stern, Sacha. *Jewish Identity in Early Rabbinic Writings*. Leiden: Brill, 1994.

Stiegman, E. "Rabbinic Anthropology." In *Aufstieg und Niedergang der römischen Welt*, edited by Wonfgang Haase, 487–579. Berlin: Walter de Gruyter, 1979.

Suleiman, Susan R. "Writing and Motherhood." In *Mother Reader: Essential Writings on Motherhood*, edited by Moyra Davey, 113–137. New York: Seven Stories Press, 1985.

Taylor, Janelle S. "A Fetish Is Born: Sonographers and the Making of the Public Fetus." In *Consuming Motherhood*, edited by Janelle S. Taylor, Linda L. Layne and Danielle F. Wozniak, 187–210. New Brunswick: Rutgers University Press, 2004.

Traina, Cristina L. H. *Erotic Attunement: Parenthood and the Ethics of Sensuality between Unequals*. Chicago: University of Chicago Press, 2011.

Trible, Phyllis. "Ominous Beginnings for a Promise of Blessings." In *Hagar, Sarah, and Their Children: Jewish, Christian, and Muslim Perspectives*, edited by Phyllis Trible and Letty M. Russell, 33–69. Louisville, KY: Westminster John Knox Press, 2006.

———. *Texts of Terror: Literary-Feminist Readings of Biblical Narratives*. Philadelphia, PA: Fortress Press, 1984.

Tronto, Joan C. "The Nanny Question in Feminism." *Hypatia* 17, no. 2 (2002): 34–61.

———. "'The Servant Problem' and Justice in Households." *Iris: European Journal of Philosophy and Public Debate* 2, no. 2 (April 3, 2010): 67–85.

Tropper, Amram. "A Tale of Two Sinais: On the Reception of the Torah According to Bavli Shabbat 88a." In *From There to Here (מהתם להכא): Rabbinic Traditions between Palestine and Babylonia*, edited by R. Nikolsky and Tal Ilan, 147–157. Leiden: Brill, 2014.

Urbach, Efraim Elimelech. *The Sages, Their Concepts and Beliefs*. Jerusalem: Magnes Press, Hebrew University, 1975.

Vermès, Géza. "'He Is the Bread': Targum Neofiti Exodus 16:15." In *Post-Biblical Jewish Studies*, 139–146. Leiden: Brill, 1975.

Walfish, Miriam-Simma. "Upending the Curse of Eve: A Reframing of Maternal Breastfeeding in BT *Ketubot*." In *Motherhood in the Jewish Cultural Imagination*, edited by Marjorie Lehman, Jane L. Kanarek, and Simon J. Broner, 307–325. Liverpool: Littman, 2017.

Wall, John. "Animals and Innocents: Theological Reflections on the Meaning and Purpose of Child-Rearing." *Theology Today* 59, no. 4 (January 2003): 559–582.

———. *Ethics in Light of Childhood*. Washington, DC: Georgetown University Press, 2010.

Wallace-Sanders, Kimberly. *Mammy: A Century of Race, Gender, and Southern Memory*. Ann Arbor: University of Michigan Press, 2008.

Weaver, Darlene Fozard. *Self Love and Christian Ethics*. New York: Cambridge University Press, 2002.

Weber, Max. *Economy and Society: An Outline of Interpretive Sociology*. 2 vols. Berkeley: University of California Press, 1978.

Weems, Renita J. *Just a Sister Away: A Womanist Vision of Women's Relationships in the Bible*. San Diego, CA: LuraMedia, 1988.

Wegner, Judith Romney. *Chattel or Person? The Status of Women in the Mishnah*. New York: Oxford University Press, 1988.

Wiesel, Elie. *Souls on Fire: Portraits and Legends of Hasidic Masters*. Translated by Marion Wiesel. New York: Random House, 1972.

Williams, Delores S. "Hagar in African American Biblical Appropriation." In *Hagar, Sarah, and Their Children: Jewish, Christian, and Muslim Perspectives*, edited by Phyllis Trible and Letty M. Russell, 171–184. Louisville, KY: Westminster John Knox Press, 2006.

———. *Sisters in the Wilderness: The Challenge of Womanist God-Talk*. Maryknoll, NY: Orbis Books, 1993.

Wolfson, Elliot R. *Through a Speculum That Shines: Vision and Imagination in Medieval Jewish Mysticism*. Princeton, NJ: Princeton University Press, 1994.

Wyschogrod, Michael. *The Body of Faith: Judaism as Corporeal Election*. New York: Seabury Press, 1983.

Young, Iris Marion. *Justice and the Politics of Difference*. Princeton, NJ: Princeton University Press, 1990.

Zank, Michael. *The Idea of Atonement in the Philosophy of Hermann Cohen*. Providence, RI: Brown Judaic Studies, 2000.

Zelizer, Viviana A. *Pricing the Priceless Child: The Changing Social Value of Children*. Princeton, NJ: Princeton University Press, 1994.

Zoloth, Laurie. "Into the Woods: Killer Mothers, Feminist Ethics, and the Problem of Evil." In *Women and Gender in Jewish Philosophy*, edited by Hava Tirosh-Samuelson, 204–233. Bloomington: Indiana University Press, 2004.

———. "Traveling with Children: Mothering and the Ethics of the Ordinary World." *Tikkun*, July–August 1995.

Zoloth, Laurie, and Alyssa A. Henning. "Hagar's Child: Theology, Ethics, and the Third Party in Emerging Reproductive Technology." In *Third-Party Reproduction: A Comprehensive Guide*, edited by James M. Goldfarb, 207–222. New York: Springer, 2013.

Zornberg, Avivah Gottlieb. *The Particulars of Rapture: Reflections on Exodus*. New York: Doubleday, 2001.

Index

bondage, 24–26
"bonded," as possible meaning of "commandment", 21–22n49
bonds, of obligation, 24
born Jews, xix
Boswell, John, 29
boundedness, xiv, xvi, 3, 5, 8, 15, 16. *See also* obligation
Bowlby, Rachel, 10, 19n25, 21n44, 72n10
Boyarin, Daniel, 62, 69, 75n40
breastfeeding, 74n31, 100–104, 109–10n34, 109n27, 109n31, 110n38, 110n39, 110n40
breastmilk, 65–66, 67, 110n40
breasts, 65, 67, 74n31
Brock, Rita Nakashima, 31
brotherhood, 116
Buber, Martin, xv, 21n39, 80, 121, 123
Budig, Michelle, 19n26
Burggraeve, Roger, 14–15, 90–91n18
Burton, Linda M., 19–20n28

Cain, 116
Caputo, John, 17n5
caregivers, 4; caregiving kin, xvii, 19–20n28; as employees, 94–95; God as caregiver, xxii; men as, xvii; nonparental adults as, 93–111; women as, xvii
caregiving, 64–65, 94–95; embodied practice of, 70; as love, 26–32; maternal love and, 28; repetitive cycle of, 28; as teaching, 69–70
caretakers, rabbinic, 68–69
celestial time, xxi
childbearing, cultural expectation of, xvii
childbirth, 64
childcare: feminist revolution and, 94. *See also* child-rearing
child-rearing, xiv, xv, xx–xxi; as analogous to Israel's journey from slavery through wilderness to Promised Land, 64; asymmetrical power relations and, 37–40, 43–44, 53, 56n23; attention and, 70–71; as being held hostage, 91n19; burdens of, 11; constraint and, 51–52; cultural expectation of, xvii; cyclic nature of, 91n24; disability and, 56n30; gender and, xvii–xviii, 107n10; intimacy and, 88–89; liberalism and, 14; lived reality, xiv; mystery and, 88–89; nuclear families and, 11; obligation and, xix; power and, 37–40; public sphere and, 115–26, 126n2; responsibility for, 107n10; restraint and, 53; as self-conscious practice of cultivation, 10; social ethics and, 113–14;

social interaction and, xvii, 113–28; successful parenting as self-effacing, 46–47; as teaching, 71n5; the Third and, 93–111; as translating, 119; two modes of becoming a parent, xviii–xix
children, 28, 62; agency of, xvi, 37–58; development of, 82–83; existential power and, 47–49; as extensions of parents, 30–31; formation of, 82–83; as independent beings, 120; needs of, 80–81; otherness of, 79, 80–81, 84–85; parents' obligation to, 129–31; particular needs of, 14; power exerted by, 42; power of, xvi, 37–58; power over, 44–45; recognition and, 48, 103, 104; responsibility and, 82–83, 129–31; sameness of, 81–82; separateness of, 80–81; spiritual, 62; strangeness of, 80; vulnerability of, 47–49
choice: hegemony of, xx; liberal model of, 14–15, 21n44; obligation and, 9–10; rational, 21n44; recognition of, 9–10, 14–15
Christ, *kenosis* of, 49
Christian theology, feminist, 32, 44
Christology, 57n38
circumcision, 6, 19n17, 19n18
civil society, 14, 115, 123–24
Cline, Erin, 93–94
Coakley, Sarah, 49
Coates, Ta-Nehisi, 40–41
coercion, 43; maternal power and, 44–45
Cohen, Hermann, xv, 12, 21n38, 80, 121, 128n21
collaboration, 42–47, 86
commandments, 129; in modern Jewish thought, xvi, 3–22; motherwork as commanded action, 28; otherness and, 86–87, 88; performance of, 27–28
compassion, 50, 121
"concerted cultivation," 60, 90n9
conditionality, maternity and, 16
confirmation ceremonies, xx
conflict, maternal power and, 44–45
Confucianism, 61, 72n14
connection. *See* interconnectivity
consciousness, power to shape, 47–49
constraint: parenting and, 51–52; recognition of, 14–15
covenant: love and, 23; obligation and, xix
"covenantal obligations," paternal obligations and, 63–64
Cover, Robert, 15, 16–17n2, 21n47
cultural authority, 69

daily life, xv, xvi, 60–61
Daly, Mary, 43

MARA H. BENJAMIN

is Irene Kaplan Leiwant Associate
Professor of Jewish Studies at Mount
Holyoke College. She is author of
*Rosenzweig's Bible: Reinventing
Scripture for Jewish Modernity.*

Printed and bound by CPI Group (UK) Ltd, Croydon, CR0 4YY

09/06/2025

14685940-0002